Irish London

Irish London

A Cultural History 1850–1916

Richard Kirkland

BLOOMSBURY ACADEMIC
LONDON • NEW YORK • OXFORD • NEW DELHI • SYDNEY

BLOOMSBURY ACADEMIC
Bloomsbury Publishing Plc
50 Bedford Square, London, WC1B 3DP, UK
1385 Broadway, New York, NY 10018, USA
29 Earlsfort Terrace, Dublin 2, Ireland

BLOOMSBURY, BLOOMSBURY ACADEMIC and the Diana logo are trademarks of Bloomsbury
Publishing Plc

First published in Great Britain 2022
Paperback edition published in 2023

Cover design: Terry Woodley
Cover image: The Old Bedford, Walter Richard Sickert (c. 1895) (Photo by: Picturenow/Universal
Images Group via Getty Images).

A catalogue record for this book is available from the British Library.

Library of Congress Cataloging-in-Publication Data
Names: Kirkland, Richard, author.
Title: Irish London : a cultural history, 1850–1916 / Richard Kirkland.
Description: London ; New York : Bloomsbury Academic, 2021. | Includes bibliographical
references and index. |
Identifiers: LCCN 2021006741 (print) | LCCN 2021006742 (ebook) | ISBN 9781350133181 (HB) |
ISBN 9781350133198 (ePDF) | ISBN 9781350133204 (eBook)
Subjects: LCSH: Irish–England–London–History–19th century. | Irish–England–London–History–
20th century. | Irish–England–London–Social conditions–19th century. | Irish–England–London–
Social conditions–20th century. | Rural-urban migration–England–London–History. | London
(England)–History–1800–1950.
Classification: LCC DA676.9.I75 K57 2021 (print) | LCC DA676.9.I75 (ebook) |
DDC 942.1/0049162009034–dc23
LC record available at https://lccn.loc.gov/2021006741
LC ebook record available at https://lccn.loc.gov/2021006742

ISBN: HB: 978-1-3501-3318-1
    PB: 978-1-3502-3005-7
    ePDF: 978-1-3501-3319-8
    eBook: 978-1-3501-3320-4

Typeset by Integra Software Services Pvt. Ltd.

To find out more about our authors and books visit www.bloomsbury.com
and sign up for our newsletters.

Contents

Illustrations

Acknowledgements

I have been working on this book for some time and I suspect it would never have been completed without the advice, encouragement and friendship of many people over the years. It is a privilege to have this opportunity to express my gratitude to them. Following a four-year period as Head of the Department of English, King's College London granted me an extended period of research time. I am grateful to King's for this and for the institution's overarching commitment to research in the humanities. Of equal importance was the award of a twelve-month Leverhulme Research Fellowship in 2019. I would like to place on record my sincere thanks to the Leverhulme Trust for enabling this work. I would also like to thank the journals *New Hibernia Review*, *The London Journal* and *Nordic Irish Studies*, where parts of this research have previously appeared. The image *Bad News in Troubled Times: 'An Important Arrest Has Been Made, That of a Young Man Named'* by Margaret Allen is reproduced courtesy of Ireland's Great Hunger Museum, Quinnipiac University, Hamden, CT.

The academic community at King's is remarkable in its collegiality and it has always been a great source of support and kindness. I especially would like to thank Rebecca Dean, Janet Floyd, Paul Gilroy, Russell Goulbourne, David Green, Eleanor Jubb, Clare Lees, Jo Malt, Alan Marshall, Josephine McDonagh, Darren Munn, Lucy Munro, Dorothy Pearce, Clare Pettitt, Alan Read, John Stokes, Mark Turner, Neil Vickers and Patrick Wright. I have supervised a number of very gifted PhD students during my time at King's and, in the context of the research in this project, I would particularly like to acknowledge the work of Niamh Campbell, George Legg, Melanie McMahon, Camilla Mount and Helen Saunders. I have learned much from their brilliant research.

I am hugely grateful to the Irish Studies community in Great Britain, Ireland and the United States, especially Shane Alcobia-Murphy, Matthew Campbell, Joe Cleary, Claire Connolly, Jeffrey Dudgeon, Brian Gilmore, Declan Long, Caroline Magennis, Brighid Mhic Sheáin, Catherine Morris and James Rogers. Colin Graham has always been a generous and wise friend and provided very astute feedback on a troublesome aspect of this work at an early stage. Members of staff at the British Library have been endlessly helpful, and I would particularly like to acknowledge their efforts in sustaining academic research during the Covid-19 restrictions. Although I do not know them all personally, I would also like to thank the many scholars in this field whose work has been a source of inspiration (and frequently intimidation), especially Frances Flanagan, Roy Foster, Sheridan Gilley, Reginald Hall, John Hutchinson, Mo Moulton, Ian Sheehy and Roger Swift.

Tim Bricheno, Conor Hanna, Emmett Hanna, Matthew Kirkland, Paul Morris, Vincent Newland and Helen Stoddart have been resolute in their kindness and generosity of spirit, while my many friends at the Pineapple pub in Kentish Town have been a constant source of encouragement, even while finding humour in the seemingly ludicrous nature of my preoccupations. My parents, Brian and Shelagh Kirkland, understand the scale of the debt I owe them, as does Emily Nadira Jones, who has been steadfast in her love and support.

Finally I would like to thank my daughters, Esme and Amity. Despite the fact that this project is older than they are, they have always expressed forthright opinions about its intellectual direction and, indeed, my ability to bring it to a proper conclusion. This book is dedicated to them with all my love and affection.

Introduction: 'That great and terrible city'

London again! That great and terrible city that forever stretches its tentacles out towards people who are hundreds, thousands, of miles away, and draws them inexorably towards her, in spite of themselves, and remakes them in her own image, to swallow them up, to recreate them.[1]

Pádraic Ó Conaire's Irish-language novel *Deoraíocht* (Exile) from 1910 describes the terrible experiences of an Irish exile cast adrift in London. Looking for work in the city, Micheál Ó Maoláin from Galway is hit by a car and badly maimed, losing an arm and a leg and suffering severe injuries to his face. Facing life as a 'poor cripple, at only twenty-seven years of age', he soon exhausts the £250 he receives in compensation for the accident and accepts an offer of work as a circus freak.[2] This takes him on tour around the country, to Ireland, and even back to Galway, where he encounters figures from his adolescence including his cousin, Máire Ní Laoi, whom he had once hoped to marry. In what is a rambling and discursive tale, it is at this point that the ostensible climax of the story takes place as Micheál, initially unrecognized because of his injuries and grotesque costume, finally loses his self-control and, in his 'madness, rage and hatred', denounces the entire freak show spectacle, crying out in Irish to his startled and angry audience.[3] A riot ensues and he takes his chance to escape back to London. After a further series of misadventures, he dies penniless and starving in a park on a 'beautiful spring morning on the nineteenth day of April in the year nineteen hundred and seven'.[4] Through this odyssey of misery Micheál's comforts are few, but while in London he forms a friendship with 'Big Maggie', also a Galway native, who recognizes his language and empathizes with his plight, providing, as he reflects forlornly, 'the kind of pity my mother would have for me if she could see me now'.[5]

Deoraíocht was a significant cultural achievement. The winner of a Gaelic League *Oireachtas na Gaeilge* literary award on its publication and described by Angela Bourke as 'the earliest example of modernist fiction in Irish', it describes the collision of Irish-speaking Ireland with English-speaking (or, to be more precise, polyglot) London

---

[1] Pádraic Ó Conaire, *Exile* [*Deoraíocht*], trans. Gearailt Mac Eoin (Indreabhán: Cló Iar-Chonnachta, 1994), 71.

[2] Ibid., 9.

[3] Ibid., 46.

[4] Ibid., 150.

[5] Ibid., 33.

and thus 'articulate[s] radical ideas about belonging and stigma among migrant speakers of a minority language'.[6] In this context the physical mutilation that Micheál suffers can be interpreted, as Pádraigín Riggs argues, 'as a metaphorical account of the trauma suffered by Irish-speaking Ireland following the seismic language shift that occurred in the country in the nineteenth century'.[7] As such, the book's two primary locations, London and Galway, are, as she continues, 'internal states', with 'each place […] defined as the obverse of the other'.[8] As a result *Deoraíocht* presents the reader with nothing less than the clash of two incompatible realities as a Gaelic culture deeply rooted in the life of its people is forced to negotiate a modern and essentially transitory urban space – the oppressive and threatening 'city of darkness'.[9] The function of Máire in the narrative is crucial to this reading. Married and pregnant when Micheál re-encounters her, she represents the union of land, family, faith and sexual fulfilment that he might have attained had he not embarked on his disastrous London adventure. Instead he is obliged to exist, 'depressed and unhappy', among the strays and foundlings of London, a city where 'the great gloomy houses would knock him down – would fall on him – crush him, if they could be bothered with a creature so insignificant'.[10]

Reading *Deoraíocht* in this way enables it to appear typically of its time – a text of the early twentieth-century Irish cultural revival marked by its preference for what was termed an 'Irish-Ireland' cultural vision and by a concomitant assumption that London is little more than a place of temptation and moral degradation for those young Irish foolish enough to make the crossing. Indeed, in its review of the novel the Gaelic League's newspaper *An Claidheamh Soluis* noted that 'the exile life of those of our race who go under has never before been pictured as it is pictured here, never before in Irish, and never so well in English. The picture is not a pleasant one. It could not be pleasant, but the book adds a new reason for the study of Irish and for its revival'.[11] In these terms Micheál's catastrophic maiming that begins the narrative is nothing other than a physical manifestation of the emotional and cultural violence the city has repeatedly enacted on its Irish inhabitants. However, there are aspects of the novel that challenge this vision and instead articulate something that might be regarded as closer to a distinctly London-Irish sensibility. For while the London of *Deoraíocht* is usually depicted as debilitating and bleak, it is also (sporadically at least) exciting, restless, and a place where the pleasures of modernity can be found and indulged. Even in the midst of his misery Micheál notices that the pub he is in is 'bright and glittering under the little electric bulbs which were of every colour in the rainbow', and he takes pleasure in its 'music machine', which displays a 'variety of pictures' including 'the lovely waterfall, the swift flowing river, the great forest with the moon shining above the trees, the

---

[6]   Angela Bourke, 'Legless in London: Pádraic Ó Conaire and Éamon A Búrc', *Éire-Ireland*, 38:3/4 (Fall/Winter 2003), 54–67, 54, 56.
[7]   Pádraigín Riggs, 'Pádraic Ó Conaire's London – A Real or an Imaginary Place?', in *Irish Writing London: Volume 1: Revival to the Second World War*, ed. Tom Herron (London: Bloomsbury, 2013), 94.
[8]   Riggs, 'Pádraic Ó Conaire's London', 92.
[9]   Ó Conaire, *Exile*, 23.
[10]   Ibid., 17, 88.
[11]   *An Claidheamh Soluis* (30 July 1910), 8.

sea and a sinking ship'.[12] Such images verge on the hallucinatory – *Deoraíocht*'s vision of the city is frequently distorted and even phantasmagorical as it is filtered through Micheál's language and cultural experience – but they offer a sensory stimulation that he could not find in Galway. Moreover, despite the novel's insistence on the essential loneliness of exile, it is also careful to present London's Irish community as a significant presence and certainly not one cast adrift from its cultural hinterland. In 'Little Ireland', the area of the city where Micheál lives, the people had 'inherited the traditions of bards and poets', 'all the neighbours knew each other', and they had 'social gatherings in the evenings, where you would find fiddlers and pipers and flute-players'. The novel adds further detail about the extent of this community:

> There would be a man there who could relate the contents of Keating's History of Ireland, as well as a man who knew nothing about it. And if somebody were to disagree with anything the savant said, he would just go to the big trunk he had brought with him from Ireland and take out a parcel wrapped in linen. He would open the parcel and take out a large book in manuscript. And how careful he was of that book! He would then show you in black and white where you had been wrong. And when he closed the book to put it away he would look at you as if to say. 'Now what have you to say for yourself?' But he never said a word. And the daytime trade of this man who spent his evenings reading history and learning poetry was the trade of the pick and shovel.

> This small population of exiles in a foreign city kept up the manners and customs of the people of the ancient Irish nation. The Irish heritage of language, music and literature, which rich people at home had abandoned in their efforts to imitate the English, who would as soon have seen them at the bottom of the sea, was kept alive by these people. They understood in their own way that a race should guard the culture which had come down to them from their ancestors and they guarded it like a precious jewel.[13]

This portrayal is not without qualification – the passage goes on to observe that subsequent generations of London Irish are much more vulnerable to the threat of cultural amnesia – but, nevertheless, the thriving sociability, self-reliance and collective cultural memory that it celebrates is striking. Despite the conditions of exile, Ó Conaire depicts this world as a mode of Irishness unalloyed and it is one that, despite or because of the unpromising environment, performs its cultural duties more assiduously than many back in Ireland itself. It is in these ways that *Deoraíocht* reveals itself as a text deeply immersed in London and the lives of the Irish who have made it their home. More profoundly, and despite some of its exhortations about the value of cultural purity, the novel recognizes implicitly that the experience of London is so overwhelming there can be no future return to a state of pre-exile consciousness; the city distorts memories of the homeland and the life that was lived there to the point

[12] Ó Conaire, *Exile*, 28.
[13] Ibid., 104–5.

where it becomes difficult to assert with confidence quite what it is that has been lost. Considering Micheál's various emotional entanglements as he makes his unhappy progress, Riggs reads the book as in part being about 'thwarted love – a theme that is to be found throughout Ó Conaire's fiction'.[14] The observation is astute and can be extended, as 'thwarted love' also well describes Micheál's relationship with London and the manner in which it simultaneously offers and withholds the possibility of happiness.

Deoraíocht, then, is a foundational text for my study of Irish London for a number of reasons. Perhaps most resonantly, as *An Claidheamh Soluis* noted, in 'telling the story of the beaten, of the hopeless, of the forgotten children of our country' in such unsparing detail the novel insists on the importance of those countless Irish lives that passed through the city, unheralded and often abandoned.[15] There was – and remains – something comfortless in this anonymity. An element of it can be detected in W. B. Yeats's description of what he called 'this melancholy London' in a letter to his friend and fellow Irish poet Katharine Tynan from 1888. In his vision 'the souls of the lost are compelled to walk through its streets perpetually […] one feels them passing like a whiff of air' – an image that might also serve as a description of the hopeless lives that populate Ó Conaire's later novel.[16] And yet alongside these depictions of isolated suffering, the Irish remain a determined collective presence in the novel's overall vision of the city. This contradicts *Deoraíocht*'s usual assumption that the inevitable result of exile from Ireland is a despairing loneliness and depicts a social endurance and a willingness to mobilize, which, as this book will argue, can be understood as a signature element of Irish-London communities through this period. Indeed, even in the seeming contradictions of this stance, Ó Conaire's novel bears the hallmark of a typical London-Irish text; its habit of favourably comparing Irish-Ireland cultural attitudes to what it sees as the degraded reality of London society while simultaneously (and frequently unwittingly) revealing how life in the city can be both sustaining and stimulating is a frequently expressed sentiment among the London Irish and one we will encounter repeatedly. Ultimately, however, *Deoraíocht*'s major concern is not London or Ireland, but language itself and especially the manner in which the collision of Micheál's spoken Irish with his experience of life in the British capital creates peculiar reality effects that distort both the urban present and the memory of his early years back in Ireland. This too is a typical phenomenon of the Irish-London experience. It is a sentiment often found in its poetry, novels and political pamphlets, and one declaimed by many Irish performers from the stages of the city's music halls. For many exiles London life was irreducibly unreal and somehow in excess of lived experience, while the Ireland that had been left behind became an increasingly unstable referent, the subject of both yearning and disdain, or idealization and denigration.

Aside from his remarkable novel, Ó Conaire's life story illuminates other aspects of Irish life in the city. Born in 1882 in Galway, he was orphaned by the age of twelve and

[14] Riggs, 'Pádraic Ó Conaire's London', 94.
[15] *An Claidheamh Soluis* (30 July 1910), 8.
[16] W. B. Yeats, letter to Katharine Tynan (25 August 1888), *The Collected Letters of W. B. Yeats: Volume I: 1865–1895*, ed. John Kelly and Eric Domville (Oxford: Oxford University Press, 1986), 43.

subsequently lived with his grandparents, eventually studying at Blackrock College in Dublin alongside the future Taoiseach and President of Ireland Éamon de Valera. Like many others of his generation he moved to London in 1900 to work in the Civil Service and stayed until 1915, when he returned to Ireland. During his time in the city he moved within Irish-Ireland circles and was especially active as a teacher of Irish in the Gaelic League. As Bourke notes, he was also an enthusiastic socialist and was 'widely read in contemporary European and Russian literature'.[17] It is noticeable, then, that unlike the unfortunate hero of his novel, Ó Conaire was not a forlorn piece of the city's flotsam but was an energetic member of a well-organized community. Patrick Sarsfield (P. S.) O'Hegarty, the indefatigable Gaelic League organizer and Irish Republican Brotherhood (IRB) Supreme Council member, knew Ó Conaire well from their time in London and many years later wrote perceptively about someone he described as a 'complete loveable human being, and foremost worker':

> Since his death, a legend has been created about him, which does him less than justice. He is shown to us as a sort of inspired tramp, with a whiskey bottle in his hand and rags upon his back. It is true that in his later years, long endured privations and physical deterioration had impaired his natural manners. But I prefer to think of him as he was then, when he was in his young manhood, working night and day for Irish. He taught, not alone at St. Andrews Hall on Mondays, but at outlying classes on weekdays. Whenever a class wanted a teacher he would be found if he was free. The one thing he believed in was the Irish language. He was merry, talkative, loved to move about after class time and circulate around the fringe of the dancing, but his life was not a happy one, and he remarked to me once 'Only for the Gaelic League, I'd be dead long ago.' He was a great worker in the cause, a good teacher and a great writer. Let his faults be remembered but let not the good be interred with his bones.[18]

By all accounts O'Hegarty's attitude to Irish activists in London was often censorious – for instance he blocked a young Michael Collins's entry to the IRB on the basis that he was concerned about his overfondness for alcohol – so the warmth of this tribute is significant. While Ó Conaire was clearly a figure held in affection and respect by the London Irish, from the sparse records that exist (and as O'Hegarty's alludes) it appears that his life would be much more difficult following his return to Ireland. Continuing his work with the Gaelic League he travelled around the country promoting and teaching Irish, but his drinking became excessive and his life increasingly erratic. He died destitute in Dublin in October 1928.

In its (perhaps foolhardy) ambition to tell the story of the Irish in London during a time of extraordinary political turbulence, this study takes inspiration from such nuanced and discursive literary texts as *Deoraíocht*, not least its recognition that not only are there many different stories, there are also many different ways of telling them.

---

[17] Bourke, 'Legless in London', 55.
[18] P. S. O'Hegarty, BMH Witness Statement: 839 (17–31 December 1952).

The period of its focus extends from the mass immigration caused by the economic and social catastrophes of mid-nineteenth-century Ireland, through the establishment of numerous Irish enclaves across the city, to the cultural revival in Irish literature and art and the assertiveness of the Home Rule movement, and on to the emergence of militant Irish Republicanism in the years leading up to the Easter Rising of 1916. The book analyses a wide variety of Irish experience and modes of performance across this period – particularly those of Irish women – and explores continuities and dialogues between such phenomena as Irish and Cockney performers in the music halls, Irish trade fairs and exhibitions, mass political protests, the Fenian Dynamite war of the 1880s, St Patrick's Day events and the tireless cultural agitation of revivalists such as Yeats and Tynan. In short, it seeks to map something of the range of Irish cultural activity taking place in a city that was both welcoming and hostile, that was frequently attracted to the cause of Ireland, while often fearful of what was assumed to be that cause's violent potential.

Given the nature of this material it is difficult to assume a clear point of beginning with confidence; 'in the beginning were the Irish', Jerry White declares in his own work on London social history, and indeed the Irish have been the largest ethnic minority group in London for the past three centuries.[19] For this reason if no other it is almost impossible to imagine the city without an Irish presence of some sort. In a similar manner, it is worth noting that it is difficult to conceive of the story of Ireland, however vast that story can sometimes seem, without London; the two spaces have been – and remain – inextricably interwoven. However, for the purposes of this book, a resonant place to start is in the years following the Irish famines of 1845–49, when the number of Irish in London grew very dramatically to over 100,000 (something like 5 per cent of the overall population). This had a profound social impact on the city and created social attitudes that would long endure. As Gearóid Ó Tuathaigh has observed, this immigration caused the 'flooding of ghetto areas by impoverished and disease-ridden Irish, and the violence and social misery which was a by-product of such a brutalizing environment, together with a ready acceptance of the notion that Irish peasant society was inherently violent'.[20] Many of the most desperate arrivals lodged in the squalid and overcrowded 'Rookery' of St Giles until its clearance towards the end of the century. This enduring slum was, to an important extent, a self-governing Irish enclave, sealed to the outside world and predominantly Irish speaking. Because of its role in the unfolding trauma of the Famine as well as its own long-standing status as a site of Irish collective memory in the heart of the city it was a location of huge symbolic significance for subsequent generations of London Irish and thus was freighted with intense emotional heft. For this reason my first chapter attempts to decode some of its mysteries and account for the longevity of an identifiable form of 'Rookery mindset' in the years that followed its dispersal. Certainly for many London Irish it was through the enduring idea of the Rookery that the memory of the Famine as a form of collective

[19] Jerry White, *London in the Nineteenth Century: 'A Human Awful Wonder of God'* (London: Random House, 2016), 131.

[20] M. A. G. Ó Tuathaigh, 'The Irish in Nineteenth-Century Britain: Problems of Integration', *Transactions of the Royal Historical Society*, 31 (1981): 149–73, 162.

violence enacted upon the Irish people would remain a powerful (and often politically incendiary) trope in the years that followed.

As Lynn Hollen Lees identifies in her foundational study *Exiles of Erin: Irish Migrants in Victorian London*, Irish immigrants at this time fell into three broad categories: the middle class, artisans and rural workers.[21] Of these, the latter category was by far the largest and the group that had the most difficulty in adapting its skill base to the demands of an urban economy. It was these Irish that populated London's many urban slums, usually in shocking conditions. Indeed, as Sheridan Gilley and Roger Swift observed when discussing their collection of essays *The Irish in the Victorian City*, for the poorest of the Irish immigrants conditions could scarcely have been worse:

> Our collective view was that the great mass of the Famine influx especially was poor; that it was discouraged and was in a large majority without any of the skills which the British economy was willing to reward; that it was without the contact with urban employers possessed by the English poor; and that many of the immigrants had left a rich Gaelic language and culture for a setting in which this past inheritance had no meaning and no encouragement to survive. Large numbers – already weakened by disease, exposure and hunger – died in Britain of starvation and cholera, while the collapse of Young Ireland and the eclipse of Chartism, in which some of the immigrants had taken part, had left them without a political voice. Disliked for their religion, their politics and their race, they were in Britain as exiles in Babylon; and it must have seemed highly problematic how far this separate social identity would survive.[22]

Despite these dire circumstances, there are always traces of an Irish collective presence across the city during this period, but in many ways these traces reveal only just how disparate – and indeed vulnerable – the Irish population was. Moreover, alongside the plight of Irish immigrants we need to account for the considerable number of Londoners who were born in England but claimed Irish heritage. This group grew dramatically over the period so that of the 435,000 people who were either Irish or of Irish descent in London in 1900 those born outside of Ireland outnumbered the Irish-born by something like 3:1.[23] This group had its own unique concerns and preoccupations, which included a notably different attitude towards the London British. Indeed, there were Irish nationalists at the time who doubted the extent to which this group could be termed 'Irish' at all given their presumed susceptibility to the forces of British urban cultural assimilation. However, as I will discuss in Chapter 6,

[21] Lynn Hollen Lees, *Exiles of Erin: Irish Migrants in Victorian London* (Manchester: Manchester University Press, 1979), 53.

[22] *The Irish in Britain 1815–1939*, ed. Roger Swift and Sheridan Gilley (London: Pinter Publishers, 1989), 1–2. They are referring to their collection *The Irish in the Victorian City*, ed. Roger Swift and Sheridan Gilley (London: Croom Helm, 1985).

[23] Jonathan Schneer, *London 1900: The Imperial Metropolis* (London: Yale University Press, 1999), 171. John Hutchinson, 'Diaspora Dilemmas and Shifting Allegiances: The Irish in London between Nationalism, Catholicism and Labourism (1900–22)', *Studies in Ethnicity and Nationalism*, 10:1 (2010), 107–25, 108.

the fact that a significant number of second-generation London-Irish men and women played important roles in the revolutionary wars of 1916–23 challenges such flat denials and tells a compelling story about the persistence of personal loyalty to a collective national identity.[24] Among these were striking figures such as Joe Good, a 'streetwise Cockney youth' born in Soho in 1895, whose Irish heritage was (at best) debatable.[25] Nevertheless, through the teaching of such bodies as the London Gaelic League he 'learned to hate and despise British imperialism' and, with Michael Collins as his mentor, would play a notable role in the Easter Rising.[26]

Although the number of Irish in London during this time is significant and would make London into one of the cities of Ireland in its own right, one should not assume from this that they were necessarily highly visible in the life of the metropolis. Indeed there are good reasons to consider the London Irish as, in Alan O'Day's phrase, 'shrouded', echoing a perception voiced in *Blackwood's Edinburgh Magazine* in 1901 that, to outsiders at least, they were a 'secretive people in spite of their expansive manner'.[27] Perhaps this is to be expected: given the historical travails of the Irish across the nineteenth century the emergence of a habitual mistrust of outsiders and a belief in self-reliance among the very poorest sections of the population is understandable. Alongside this reservation it is also important to account for what Ó Tuathaigh calls 'very strong opposition from many elements in the host society in their efforts to gain acceptance, not to speak of integration'.[28] In fact, such was the ghettoization of working-class Irish experience in London and the atomization of the Irish middle class across the strata of the city's civic realm during this time that the overall Irish presence in the city often appears fleeting and chimerical. Lacking social mobilization and consistent political leadership, or even a newspaper to articulate its case and press its claims, Irish London rarely recognized itself as such and, as a result, frequently evades the historical gaze. Another crucial factor in this was the religious and racial prejudice that the Irish faced, a prejudice that usually took an insidious form of social and economic exclusion, but which was also realized through individual acts of violence, communal riots and forced relocations. However, while the gradations of class and geography led to an experience of Irish national identity that was usually too fragmented for any grand declaration of shared purpose, it still generated numerous constellations of identity politics, strategic alliances and statements of presence, which, even if they never quite ran together like beads of mercury, spoke of a highly distinctive overall endurance in the face of constant discouragement.

Of course, in many ways, interpreting the experience of the London Irish in this manner begs as many questions as it answers. What, for instance, does 'endurance' look like? To what extent might it have a distinctly Irish manifestation? And in observing

---

[24] For the sake of clarity, in this study 'first generation' refers to those who were (usually) born in Ireland and emigrated. 'Second generation' refers to their children.

[25] Joe Good, *Enchanted by Dreams: The Journal of a Revolutionary*, ed. Maurice Good (Dingle: Kerry, 1996), xii.

[26] Good, *Enchanted by Dreams*, 13.

[27] Hugh Heinrick, *A Survey of the Irish in England*, ed. Alan O'Day (London: Hambledon Press, 1990 [1872]), xx. 'The London Irish', *Blackwood's Edinburgh Magazine*, 170 (July 1901), 124–34, 125.

[28] Ó Tuathaigh, 'The Irish in Nineteenth-Century Britain', 159.

such endurance do we run the risk of celebrating what might also be viewed as merely an ongoing process of oppression? For these reasons this book aims to put the idea of Irish communal 'endurance' under some scrutiny, trace its distinctive contours and explore if the instances of cultural resilience it identifies constitute a meaningful way of narrating a continuous history of experience. Indeed, although a subject such as 'Irish London' might initially appear to speak of a clearly demarcated constituency and thus offers itself as a story to be told – in other words a self-contained narrative with clear boundaries – the reality is inevitably other than that; the Irish in London were never one thing, were never entirely aware of each other at any one time and were never organized around a single political or cultural issue (although the response to the executions of the leaders of the Easter Rising in 1916 came close). Indeed the naturally imprecise boundaries of this topic suggest why it is tempting to concentrate instead on singular institutions within this social formation such as the Gaelic League or the Irish Literary Society (ILS), as the discreet history of these organizations offers a coherent story that ebbs and wanes, flourishes and flounders. However, while these stories should be told – as they are here – their telling also demands a degree of circumspection as they cannot embody the full extent of Irish life in the city or act as a substitute for it. Alongside such narratives something of the untidiness and the essential open-endedness of the Irish story in London must also be allowed and I have tried to recognize this in my account. In this W. G. Sebald's anxiety that historical process can become little more than 'pre-formed images already imprinted on our brains, images at which we keep staring while the truth lies elsewhere, away from it all, somewhere as yet undiscovered' has been a constant provocation.[29] Cultural histories, more than many types of academic labour, are acts of creation insofar as they juxtapose different narratives and experiences with the hope that at some point an overall story will emerge that does justice to the individual lives encountered along the way. Certainly in this study we will meet figures with unique expectations and personal histories, individuals who held political positions that were often antagonistic to that which had come previously, and Irish organizations that were in open ideological conflict with each other. To paraphrase Yeats, not all of this material can be hammered into an overall unity.

However, even allowing for these qualifications it is still possible to identify a number of distinct groupings that, taken as a whole, constitute something close to the extent of Irish London through this period. Firstly there was what can be termed (not always satisfactorily) 'elite' Irish London, consisting of the political and aristocratic class. Typified by figures such as John and Ishbel Hamilton-Gordon (Lord and Lady Aberdeen) and William Gibson (the second Baron Ashbourne or Lord Ashbourne) and nearly always Protestant, this group was tiny in number but always influential, advancing its causes through direct patronage, charitable work, and extensive networks of clubs, salons and coteries. Its developing interest in Home Rule and sympathy for the cause of Ireland more generally was a distinctive element of the period and created a fashion for certain tightly sanctioned expressions of cultural Irishness in the city,

---

[29] W. G. Sebald, *Austerlitz* (London: Penguin, 2011), 72.

which would endure into the twentieth century. Allied to and interpenetrating this elite group were journalists, artists, cultural activists and members of the intelligentsia such as Thomas Power (T. P.) O'Connor, George Bernard Shaw, Yeats, Alice Stopford Green, Tynan and Dora Sigerson. As R. F. Foster has noted, this class 'colonised central areas of London metropolitan life in the Victorian period' and was especially vigorous in the London press where a generation of talented Irish journalists, including big Fleet Street beasts such as O'Connor and Justin McCarthy, were able to influence public opinion on Irish matters to a striking degree.[30] Similarly, this was a period of intense activity in Irish arts and crafts, especially in the areas of literature and visual arts. The movement that became known as the Irish literary revival is the most significant expression of this, although the overall range of Irish artistic work in London at this time goes well beyond what might be termed the 'revival rubric'. Thirdly there was the Catholic Church, which extended across the city and constituted an entire social structure in its own right, knitting together 'the social, cultural and, indeed, the political life of Irish migrant communities', as Mervyn Busteed puts it.[31] This included the routines of frequent worship, a network of schools, and many social and cultural organizations including temperance societies and missions. Partly because many priests in London parishes were originally from Ireland, the Church played an important (if not always positive) political role in shaping the views of its adherents and was one of the few reliable sources of welfare and social support for many of the Irish poor. The fourth group consisted of the clerical and aspirational bourgeois class who, while always present in the city in some form, arrived in increasing numbers from the 1890s onwards to meet the burgeoning needs of the British civil service at a time of imperial expansion. Typically educated in the Irish National School system, 'the first system of state-supported (and compulsory) education in the British Isles' as Janet Nolan notes, and interested in economic and cultural self-improvement, they moved frequently between Ireland and London and, indeed, would often return to Ireland permanently once they had done with the city or the city had done with them.[32] Finally there was the vast constituency of the Irish poor, who, paradoxically, were both little understood while also the constant object of scrutiny and suspicion. Because London lacked the heavy industry found in the industrial north of Britain, Irish men tended to gain employment in skilled and semi-skilled occupations including warehouse work, the building trade, and in the sprawling London docks.[33] Women typically worked as fruit and flower sellers, or were in domestic service, while entire families would undertake seasonal work such as hop picking in Kent. At the beginning of the period this class typically inhabited overcrowded areas of central London but as

---

[30] R. F. Foster, 'An Irish Power in London: Making It in the Victorian Metropolis', in '*Conquering England': Ireland in Victorian London*, ed. R. F. Foster and Fintan Cullen (London: National Portrait Gallery, 2005), 12–25, 12.

[31] Mervyn Busteed, *The Irish in Manchester c.1750–1921: Resistance, Adaptation and Identity* (Manchester: Manchester University Press, 2015), 1–2.

[32] Janet Nolan, 'Education and Women's Mobility in Ireland and Irish America, 1880–1920: A Preliminary Look', *New Hibernia Review/Iris Éireannach Nua*, 2:3 (Autumn 1998), 78–88, 79.

[33] Harrington W. Benjamin, *The London Irish: A Study in Political Activism, 1870–1910* (PhD thesis, Princeton University, 1976), 53.

living standards gradually improved towards the close of the nineteenth century they dispersed to other parts of the city and developed a variety of employment skills. This was also the group most prone to assimilation with other elements of London society, a tendency that would cause occasional outbursts of moral panic among nationalist organizations in London and back in Ireland.[34]

Even allowing for such broad brush strokes it is important to recognize that the internal coherency of these groupings was distorted by factors such as religious affiliation (sectarianism was as common among the London Irish as it was in Ireland itself and similarly was capable of seemingly infinite nuance), intergenerational conflict and regional rivalries based on where in Ireland exile communities derived (although Munster tended to predominate). The different constituent parts of Irish London also frequently exhibited an inability to recognize shared allegiances and commitments as Irish inhabitants of the same city, although the manner in which elite Irish London in the 1880s was energized by the cause of poverty relief back in Ireland but wilfully blind to the appalling Irish poverty in London itself can appear less like an oversight and more as a morally convenient example of telescopic philanthropy. Finally, the overall picture is also complicated by the constant struggle for hegemonic dominance within specific groups. Here the historian Ian Sheehy's interpretation of the political dynamics of this period is especially valuable. Sheehy describes what he calls the '"Home Rule" generation' settling in London from the 1860s onwards and gradually becoming dominant.[35] These were generally 'educated men from the Catholic middle classes' who had been born in Ireland in the 1830s and 1840s and included figures such as McCarthy, O'Connor and Richard Barry O'Brien. Eventually the dominance of this group was challenged by a 'Revival generation' who arrived in London from the 1880s and were typified by figures such as William Patrick (W. P.) Ryan and David Patrick (D. P.) Moran. Unlike the previous generation, this group was 'influenced by the Irish revival rather than British Liberalism, becoming heavily involved in the Southwark Club, the ILS and, later, the Gaelic League'.[36] As this suggests, it was frequently preoccupied by cultural rather than explicitly political issues, and, unlike the Home Rule generation, it came to despair of London as a place that was perceived to be essentially corrupt and spiritually inert. The great value of Sheehy's thesis is that it interprets much of the complex institutional infighting of this period of London-Irish history as a dispute between these two generations and their conflicting understandings of Irish identity. As a result, in the history of an organization such as the ILS and its various internal disputes can be glimpsed the churn of great ideological forces. Indeed to extend Sheehy's two-generation model beyond his period of focus, we can add a third contesting group – what may be termed, following Foster, the 'revolutionary generation'.[37] This grouping was roughly coterminous with the clerical class I have

---

[34] See, for instance Nora Degidon, 'The Lives of Emigrants', *United Irishman* (17 January 1903), 6.

[35] Ian Sheehy, *Irish Journalists and Litterateurs in Late Victorian London c.1870–1910* (DPhil. thesis, Hertford College, University of Oxford, 2003), 16.

[36] Ibid., 17.

[37] R. F. Foster, *Vivid Faces: The Revolutionary Generation in Ireland, 1890–1923* (London: Allen Lane, 2014).

previously identified and typically consisted of educated rural Catholics who arrived in London from Ireland (again usually from Munster) from around 1900 onwards to work in organizations such as the London Post Office and Civil Service. Represented by figures such as O'Hegarty and Collins, this group had much in common with its revivalist predecessor but was more politically militant, frequently Anglophobic, and certainly more likely to be sympathetic to the use of physical force to achieve the goal of an independent Ireland.

The final (and particularly inflammatory) issue of methodology that any account of the Irish in London must negotiate relates to what can be termed the 'assimilationist narrative', in other words the extent to which Irish assimilation with the host community is considered either as a desirable outcome of the experience of living in London or a possibility to be deeply regretted. In his introduction to the two-volume collection of essays *Irish Writing London*, Tom Herron took issue with Peter Ackroyd's monumental 'biography' of London from 2000 and the 'secret of successful assimilation' he claimed the city possessed. As Ackroyd noted with what Herron described as 'an almost giddy sense of optimism', 'you can only be happy in London if you begin to consider yourself as a Londoner'.[38] Herron's response to this was uncompromising:

> Set against all the stories, all the records and all the studies that remind us that life for so many migrants in London was marked by discrimination, hostility and poverty; and by a general harshness of existence allied to a yearning for a lost homeland that very often had betrayed their needs and aspirations, Ackroyd's account might seem at worst, insensitive, or at best, naïvely heroic.

By Herron's reading such celebratory accounts of London life underplay the extent to which the Irish – and other ethnic groups – frequently faced almost insurmountable difficulties in establishing a space for themselves in the city. Alongside this we should also note the degree to which those social histories that emphasize the desirability of a seamless assimilation into London life potentially erase the particularities of immigrant history and personal experience. In short, they risk denying the extent to which the 'matter' of Ireland remained a marker of difference and a constant point of contestation.

Overall Ackroyd's book was far richer and more nuanced than the terms of this specific criticism indicate and it remains a touchstone for subsequent research into the history of the city, but the limited terms in which it encountered assimilation as an essentially frictionless process suggest something of the concept's overall unsatisfactory nature as a tool for understanding immigrant histories. This is especially so in the context of London, where a considerable variety of ethnic groupings have constantly sought space for economic and cultural expression and 'assimilation' itself is as likely to be 'horizontal' as 'vertical' – an outcome which fundamentally recasts the power dynamics assumed to be at play in the assimilationist narrative. For these reasons it

---

[38] Herron, *Irish Writing London: Volume 1*, 1, responding to Peter Ackroyd, *London: The Biography* (London: Chatto and Windus, 2000), 701.

is tempting to abandon this model entirely and propose instead the less incendiary concept of social 'integration', a term which appears to allow for the continued existence of specific cultural traits and practices unique to the Irish while acknowledging the substance of other forms of economic and cultural exchange with the host community. This is the frame through which the history of the Irish in Britain was viewed in Ó Tuathaigh's highly influential essay of 1981, 'The Irish in Nineteenth-Century Britain: Problems of Integration'. As he identified them, these 'problems' were multiple and multifaceted:

> In the case of the Irish immigrant, there were strong currents running against the desire to integrate. These currents were in the first instance psychological. The very proximity to home, the disappointment of those whose original aspirations had centred on a passage to America, the high mobility of a section of the Irish labour force; all these factors combined to encourage among many immigrants an attitude of refusal to accept the permanency of their exile. Furthermore, the Irish immigrant communities had, deriving from their historical sense, an unusually ambivalent attitude towards their host society. While acknowledging that Britain was providing them with the means to live, and while always ready to acknowledge the better wages and hopes of improvement which prompted emigration in the first place, among the immigrant Irish the sense of obligation or of gratitude for these benefits was nullified, to a considerable extent, by their belief that it was Britain's misgovernment of Ireland which had caused them to be uprooted in the first instance. These attitudes contributed to a situation where the primary loyalty of the immigrant Irish was to their homeland or to the immigrant community itself, and only lastly, if at all, to their new society.[39]

Ó Tuathaigh's observations are highly apposite and indicate something of the specific political and emotional dilemmas that many Irish immigrants to London encountered. However, the essay's assumption that successful integration was, in itself, the ultimate goal of immigration – and the concomitant assumption that those Irish who had failed to do this had somehow been unsuccessful – risked simplifying much of the fine detail of Irish-lived experience of the city in a manner similar to the assimilationist narrative previously discussed. Of course, this is not to propose that integration did not occur or that there were not many examples of effective assimilation among the London Irish, but rather to emphasize instead the persistent existence of an attitude better described as a kind of 'rubbing along': a mode of survival in the city that was not without its urban comforts and successes but which also encountered the inevitable friction that the metaphor describes. Such a state is far from assimilation – indeed it might be considered its opposite – but rather describes a process of constant adaptation or accommodation which allows for questions of Irishness to remain fully acknowledged. Certainly, the persistence of such Irishness could be remarkable. In 1902 *An Claidheamh Soluis* reported on a Gaelic League meeting at Limehouse distinguished

---

[39] Ó Tuathaigh, 'The Irish in Nineteenth-Century Britain', 159.

by 'the number of veteran Gaels who came forward to sing and dance, some being more than half a century in the East End of London'. Despite this, it claimed that 'their knowledge of Glenflesk, Sraid-a-Mhuilinn and "Droichead na Banndain," and of the people living there, is as real as if they had left Ireland but yesterday'.[40] Indeed in the same issue was an article about James McAnally, 'one of the oldest, if not the very oldest, of living Irish speakers', who was living in the 'Home for the Aged Poor' in south Lambeth at the time.[41] He claimed he was born in Dunmore, Co. Galway, in 1797 and thus was over 105 years old.

The nature of integration and whether it should be acknowledged as a reasonable aspiration was a key point of contention in the discussions of Irish organizations and cultural societies across the city at the time, while the difficult situation of the London Irish was frequently a source of bemusement for those who had remained in Ireland or had made the more ambitious crossing to America. Caught between strikingly different and often competing models of Irish identity, for good reason does Ó Tuathaigh describe the Irish in Britain as a 'somewhat peculiar minority'.[42] Often underwriting this sense of the London Irish as particularly anomalous is an assumption that national difference is an irreducible cultural or political category. Such interpretations are persuasive and yet it should also be acknowledged that Irish migrants to London shared much of their experience of deracination with the newly urbanized agrarian poor from impoverished rural England. Alongside this, there was also what Reginald Hall has termed 'several hundred years of social intercourse between working people from both countries', which included 'Irish male and female migrant harvesters, horse dealers, cattle drovers, navvies and tinkers working in England, Englishmen and Irishmen rubbing shoulders in the army, at sea and in the colonies, and English farm lads posted with their regiments in Ireland'.[43] And while, as Karl Marx noted in 1870, capitalism divided the Irish and English working class 'into two hostile camps' on the basis that 'the ordinary English worker hates the Irish worker as a competitor who lowers his standard of life', nascent labour movements in London as elsewhere in Britain had some success in building bridges between the communities through emphasizing the many shared features of their oppression.[44]

Despite such qualifications, for some cultural and political commentators any contact at all with London rendered an exile's Irish identity suspect. One such was Daniel Corkery, who argued that literature produced by Irish writers in London had made no contribution whatsoever to what he termed a 'national literature'. 'A normal literature is written within the confines of the country which names it. It is not dependent on expatriates,' he insisted sternly in his canon-defining *Synge and Anglo-Irish Literature*.[45] This claim was remarkable not least because, as Sheehy observes, 'by

---

[40] *An Claidheamh Soluis* (1 March 1902), 861.

[41] Ibid., 860.

[42] Ó Tuathaigh, 'The Irish in Nineteenth-Century Britain', 150.

[43] Reginald Richard Hall, *Irish Music and Dance in London, 1890–1970: A Socio-Cultural History* (PhD thesis, University of Sussex, 1994), 45.

[44] Karl Marx and Friedrich Engels, *Selected Correspondence* (Moscow: Progress Publishers, 1975), n.p.

[45] Daniel Corkery, *Synge and Anglo-Irish Literature* (Cork: Cork University Press, 1931), 3.

the 1880s the number of Irish literary figures plying their trade in London rather than Ireland had [...] reached an almost unprecedented level'.[46] To put this differently, if the contribution of Irish writers in London is excluded, for long periods of literary history there would scarcely appear to have been any Irish literature at all. That said, many expatriates shared something of Corkery's anxiety and sought always to keep the city at an emotional distance. Indeed, a considerable number of Irish Londoners managed to spend lengthy stretches of their life in the city while apparently hating every moment. Yeats was of this type; although deeply integrated into the life of what he called 'abhorred London', he constantly disparaged the city in his correspondence.[47] Despite his enjoyment of London's libraries, museums and taverns, as well as the extensive social network he developed, he insisted that the city was irredeemably fallen and its inhabitants doomed to endless drudgery. The London poor he regarded as particularly forlorn, especially when compared to the mysterious inner nobility possessed by the destitute of Dublin:

> In London I saw nothing good and constantly remembered that Ruskin had said to some friend of my father's, 'As I go to my work at the British Museum I see the faces of the people become daily more corrupt.' I convinced myself for a time that on the same journey I saw but what he saw. Certain old women's faces filled me with horror, faces that are no longer there, or if they are pass before me unnoticed: the fat blotched faces, rising above double chins, of women who have drunk too much beer and eaten too much meat. In Dublin I had often seen old women walking with erect heads and gaunt bodies, talking to themselves with loud voices, mad with drink and poverty, but they were different, they belonged to romance. Da Vinci had drawn women who looked so, and so carried their bodies.[48]

Yeats was not unusual in holding such attitudes about the city. James Francis Xavier (J. F. X.) O'Brien, the veteran Fenian and Irish Parliamentary Party MP, endured living in London for an extended period while never wavering in his loathing of the place.[49] Nothing short of his death in Clapham in May 1905 would provide him any relief. Similarly, for Michael Collins London was 'a terrible place'. 'I'll never be happy until I'm out of it,' he despaired melodramatically in 1915.[50] Others were better able to negotiate between their political beliefs and the experience of urban life. As I will discuss in Chapter 4, Francis Fahy, the founder of the hugely important Southwark Irish Literary Club in 1883, balanced his enjoyment of London life and the rich cultural world it offered him with a lifelong belief in the dignity and ultimate self-sufficiency of Irish Ireland. The suspicion remains, though, that Fahy's equanimity was rarely found among his compatriots.

[46] Sheehy, *Irish Journalists and Litterateurs*, 13.
[47] W. B. Yeats, 'The Trembling of the Veil: Book I. Four Years: 1887–1891', in *Autobiographies* (London: Macmillan, 1956), 191.
[48] Ibid., 155.
[49] Schneer, *London 1900*, 177.
[50] Letter from Collins to Susan Killeen (19 October 1915), reproduced in Tim Pat Coogan, *Michael Collins* (London: Arrow Books, 1990), 21.

There were, then, limits to what the idea of 'accommodation' could encompass and nowhere was this more evident than in the reactions of the London Irish to the turbulent political events of this period. Irish politics, especially, was frequently quite overwhelming; from the emergence of the Home Rule movement in the 1870s, through the Land War of the 1880s and the rise of Parnellism, the London Irish were continually shaken by events taking place elsewhere and were rarely political agents in their own right. Of all this activity, perhaps the most disruptive were the bombing campaigns of 1881–85 by Jeremiah O'Donovan Rossa's Skirmishers and Clan na Gael. As I discuss in the book's second chapter, these included the detonation of explosives on the London underground railway system, at the Tower of London and on Parliament. Although those responsible for these attacks often moved among London Irish society, they were not integrated into it, and the recklessness of their violence appeared to disregard the possibility of violent repercussions for the Irish domiciled in the city. It is of little wonder, then, that the campaigns were regarded almost entirely negatively. As this suggests, Irish politics generally and London-Irish politics specifically were scarcely coterminous. For instance, while Charles Stewart Parnell emphasized the importance of addressing London-Irish political groups while building a pro-Home-Rule consensus, and established the first National League Club in Southwark in 1873, the overall extent of Parnellism's penetration into the networks of London Irish society remained uneven at best. In general the majority of London Irish were liberal or, later in the period under consideration, tended towards nascent labour politics, but the dominant position of the Catholic Church exerted a conservative and patriotic influence especially during times of national crisis. This is not to suggest that there were not political events which galvanized the London Irish – the Boer War of 1899–1902, for instance, polarized political opinion among London immigrants and the events of Easter 1916 proved similarly electrifying – but these did not lead to the creation of a sustained local political movement able to articulate Irish London's specific needs. This was not helped by the fact that (for reasons that remain opaque) during this period no strong political leadership emerged from within Irish London itself.

One crucial development for London's immigrant Irish, as Ó Tuathaigh identified, was the 'conversion' of the Liberal prime minister, William Ewart Gladstone, to the cause of Home Rule in 1886. This 'effectively legitimized their political aspirations and objectives' and made it possible to 'advocate moderate nationalist demands (anything short of separation) without incurring the charge of treason or subversion of the empire'.[51] As I discuss in Chapter 4, this process of legitimization enabled, both implicitly and explicitly, the open expression of cultural nationalism across the city and encouraged the growth of a considerable number of Irish educational and social organizations. The sheer diversity of these reflected the striking range of political opinions that existed across Irish London as a whole. From patriots of the old school such as Alfred Perceval Graves (who, in O'Hegarty's view, 'reeked with a most offensive brand of loyalty, which was both pathetic and irritating, loyalty not alone to England's dominant position in Ireland but a personal and fulsome loyalty to the King as well'),

---

[51] Ó Tuathaigh, 'The Irish in Nineteenth-Century Britain', 172.

to the radical politics of figures such as the nationalist mobilizers Alice Stopford Green or Mark Ryan, London exhibited the full spectrum of Irish political opinion.[52] Even Fenianism – defined at its broadest as an unconditional adherence to physical force Irish nationalism – had an uninterrupted presence in the city during this time, although it rarely declared itself openly unless it wished to make a statement of intent. One such moment occurred in January 1879, when Pierce Nagle, an informer who had provided incriminating evidence at the Fenian Brotherhood and *Irish People* trials of 1865, was found murdered under a railway viaduct on Great College Street in Camden Town. As the *Wexford People* reported, 'a large cheese knife, such as grocers use, had been run through his heart, and upon the point, which penetrated several inches beyond his back, was fixed a paper containing his name, and the information that his life had been taken as the penalty of the suffering his treachery and perjuries had caused'.[53] As I have already noted, Fenianism also announced its presence through the American-funded gunpowder and dynamite campaigns of the 1880s, although of greater long-term significance in shaping the politics of Irish London specifically was the activity of the IRB. Originally founded in Dublin in 1858, it maintained a constant presence in London throughout its existence. Although it usually had very few members based in the city, in and of itself it remained hugely influential.[54] As O'Hegarty put it, in London as in Ireland, 'it watched everything, it was in everything'.[55] In practice this meant deploying its cellular structure of organization to infiltrate areas of London commercial life that were strategically important such as the postal service and shipping companies, taking over and steering Irish cultural and political organizations in the city such as the Gaelic League and the Gaelic Athletic Association (GAA) – both of which were effectively IRB fronts throughout their London existence – and assuming senior roles in paramilitary organizations such as the Irish Volunteers in 1914. The IRB even maintained a discreet presence in some of London's more middle-class cultural organizations such as the London Young Ireland Society (which was chaired by Yeats and coordinated celebrations of the centenary of the 1798 rebellion) and the ILS. Indeed there are very few organizations within Irish London during this period about which it can be stated with confidence that there was certainly no IRB infiltration.

Partly as a result of the startling events of 1916 and the central roles many of them would play as revolutionary agents in their aftermath, significant historical attention has been paid to these more radical 'Irish Ireland' elements of London's Irish community. But it is important to recognize that they were always a comparatively tiny aspect of the social and political structures of Irish London as a whole. More typical (if less dramatic) features of Irish life in the city included seemingly endless rounds

---

[52] O'Hegarty, BMH Statement: 839.

[53] *Wexford People* (5 July 1879), 7.

[54] Even in the years leading up to 1916 when the IRB was increasingly vibrant there were only 117 members in the entirety of England. By comparison there were 1,660 members in Ireland at this time. See Leon Ó Broin, *Revolutionary Underground: The Story of the Irish Republican Brotherhood 1858–1924* (London: Gill and Macmillan, 1976), 155.

[55] P. S. O'Hegarty, *The Victory of Sinn Féin: How It Won It, and How It Used It* (Dublin: Talbot Press Ltd., 1924), 12.

of suburban confraternity evenings, United Irish League (UIL) meetings, temperance social nights and, for the more established middle class, the genteel concerts of the 'Irish Social Club' in concert rooms at High Holborn. At these events sentimental music such as 'The Green Isle of Erin' or 'Kathleen Mavourneen' was performed by what the *Irish News* described as 'highly-accomplished artistes [...] in the presence of a large and fashionable audience'.[56] The main influence in creating and reinforcing this broad veneer of respectability was the Catholic Church. For the less affluent the Church was also the major factor discouraging Irish-immigrant assimilation with (what were usually assumed to be) British Protestant neighbours. In return the Church offered a degree of social protection for the vulnerable Irish Catholic poor, a class that had been rural in Ireland and was now obliged to be urban in London. Indeed, as Hall argues, 'for the Catholic churchgoer, the parish could provide a completely London-Irish world'.[57] As he continues:

> Priests, Marist brothers and nuns, mostly born in Ireland, satisfied spiritual needs and went a long way towards satisfying secular and social needs as well. Catholic elementary schools were available within each parish, and for a small proportion of working-class girls there was secondary convent education. The Gaelic League found outlets for its education programmes and social events on parish premises with ready-made groups of consumers and supporters among the parishioners. Confraternities flourished and the season of Catholic outdoor processions from May to August was the highlight of the social calendar, rivalled only by Archbishop Amigo's annual visit to the Kent hop-fields to say Mass for the London-Irish hop-pickers.

Despite this it is important to note that in fact the Church was frequently troubled by the London Irish and the relationship between the two was often uneasy. While in 1901 *Blackwood's Edinburgh Magazine* observed that local priests in London 'exercise a remarkable control over their flocks' and that the Church's 'hold on the women is certainly stronger than on the men', it also noted that this held true only 'up to a certain point'. Although one priest wielded such disciplinary authority that he 'used to rule his parish literally with a rod, carrying a stout cane under his cassock, which he would lay about the back of a burly docker caught knocking his wife about', as the article also acknowledged, 'priests have sorrowfully admitted to us that they retain little real hold upon London Irishmen of the third generation, though they feel sure of the first and second'.[58] The seriousness of this 'leakage', as it was termed, was recognized at the time. Indeed, as Ó Tuathaigh has observed, 'by the third quarter of the century it was deemed to be considerable enough to cause great anxiety to the hierarchies of Britain and Ireland, and indeed in Rome itself'.[59]

---

[56] 'The Irish Social Club, London', *Irish News and Belfast Morning News* (27 June 1901), 6.
[57] Hall, *Irish Music and Dance in London*, 77.
[58] 'The London Irish', 132–3.
[59] Ó Tuathaigh, 'The Irish in Nineteenth-Century Britain', 166.

Alongside such 'leakage', there was a connected and persistent anxiety that London's Irish population was in danger of what the journalist and Irish social commentator John Denvir in 1892 termed 'undoubted moral deterioration – even among those of purely Irish descent' as a result of 'contact and intermixing with the English population'.[60] In 1902, the Rev. Stephen Eyre Jarvis, Rector of St Etheldreda's in Holborn, reflected more broadly on this threat and the limits of the Church's control over its Irish congregation. While recognizing that 'the great emigration of the Irish over here at the time of the famine in Ireland has been, to a very large extent, the instrument of Divine Providence for bringing about the revival of the faith in this land', the Church was seemingly powerless to prevent the drift of second- and third-generation London Irish away from its authority.[61] 'Indeed, it is no exaggeration to say, that already in the courts and alleys of our London slums there are thousands upon thousands of poor Irish, who, if they have not as yet entirely lost their faith, have at least become so hardened and indifferent, that they have altogether given up the practice of their religion,' he continued. Blaming alcohol, the deprivations of the urban environment and the attractions of mixed marriage for this decline, he concluded that ultimately the movement of the Irish to London had been little short of a disaster and so urged 'our brother priests across the channel to do their utmost to prevent any of their poor from emigrating to England'.[62] Eyre Jarvis was not the only member of the Church proposing this extreme solution. In 1903 Nora Degidon's 'The Lives of Emigrants', a sensationalist article for the nationalist *United Irishman*, described a tour of London Irish slums with a local Irish priest as a guide. Degidon was horrified by what she encountered:

> To my oft-repeated query, 'Not here, surely– my country men and women have not sunk to this,' as we came into a court or alley, the very odour of which made one faint, the answer was, 'Yes, here surely, and worse than this. Several families in one room, consorting with the scum of earth, the very dregs of humanity. Pure minds, fresh and untainted from the green hills, how long will they keep their freshness and purity here, think you? What chance have they? Look at these wretched tenements. Why there is defilement lurking in the very bricks and mortar.' 'Cannot they be induced to return?' 'How can they? Why you, yourself, have often told me what little welcome there is for the unsuccessful returned emigrant. They have sold up their homes, such as they were, in Ireland, and what little money they had is long since spent.'[63]

Degidon leaves us in no doubt that the 'defilement' she finds 'lurking in the very bricks and mortar' of the Irish slums was to be understood to its fullest possible extent and that it included the likelihood of sexual ruin for those 'unworldly' young Irish girls 'thrust into this Babylon of wickedness'. As her priest guide lamented, 'how many

---

[60] John Denvir, *The Irish in Britain from the Earliest Times to the Fall and Death of Parnell* (London: Kegan Paul, 1892), 393.

[61] Stephen Eyre Jarvis, 'The Irish in London', *The Tablet* (8 February 1902), 222–3, 222.

[62] Eyre Jarvis, 'The Irish in London', 223.

[63] Nora Degidon, 'The Lives of Emigrants', *United Irishman* (17 January 1903), 6.

a beautiful Irish girl have I seen brought to an early grave, who told me in her last confession that she never sinned except for bread'. As a result it is unsurprising that, as with Eyre Jarvis's earlier diagnosis, the article concluded by proposing that Irish emigration to London should be discouraged wherever possible. This was, of course, probably exactly what many of the readers of the *United Irishman* back in Ireland wanted to hear, but it was still comfortless advice for a community that frequently had good reason to consider itself abandoned.

In these ways the Catholic Church in London found itself preoccupied with its Irish parishioners and this, in turn, helped shape it as an 'Irish' institution to a degree that sometimes distressed its English members. It was partly in response to such anxieties that in 1908 Archbishop Bourne, the English Prelate, ended the (Gaelic-League inspired) tradition of celebrating St Patrick's Day with a service in Irish at Westminster Cathedral, despite it being considered 'one of most impressive, beautiful, reverent, and touching ceremonies imaginable'.[64] Undeterred, the League moved the service to Holy Trinity Church at Dockhead in Bermondsey, a location where the organization had deep roots. Alongside this prejudice, the Church played a key role in what Harrington W. Benjamin calls 'keeping the London Irish isolated for religious and political purposes'.[65] As he further comments, the 'Church was interested in Irish nationalism only to the extent that it could be harnessed and used for the Church's interests' and these interests tended to have a reactionary impulse'.[66] Buttressing the work of the Church were two important secondary institutions: the UIL and the *Catholic Herald* group of newspapers. The UIL, which by 1900 had absorbed the various pro- and anti-Parnellite factions in the Nationalist party after its bitter split ten years previously, was vigorous across London and, beyond its primary political function to inhibit the process of integration with the host community and preserve a distinctive Irish identity, provided a wide range of social and cultural events for the London Irish including tea dances, lectures, concerts of Irish music and fund-raising events for children's charities back in Ireland. There were also many other organizations allied to the Church including the South London Catholic League; the League of the Cross, a devout organization with a minor interest in the dissemination of Irish culture; the 'Catholic Five Hundred of South London', a temperance organization which lobbied for better educational and social provision for (predominantly Irish) London Catholics; the Catholic Democratic League, which sought to increase the number of Catholics involved in British political life; and the Catholic Labour League, which functioned as a labour agency in the East End and sought to combat the habitual anti-Irish labour practices endemic in the area. This sense of an enclosed Irish Catholic world was illustrated vividly by the 'London Gleanings' section on the front page of the weekly *Catholic Herald*. This carried detailed reports of the minutiae of Irish-London society, although this was usually an Irish London characterized by its core religious identity, rather than anything resembling an 'Irish Ireland' or revivalist vision. Described by Michael

---

[64] 'Gaelic Service Forbidden at Westminster Cathedral', *Aberdeen Press and Journal* (18 March 1908), 5.
[65] Benjamin, *The London Irish*, Introduction, no page number.
[66] Ibid., 272.

P. Maguire as 'essentially [...] the voice of one man, Charles Diamond, an embittered former Nationalist MP and UIL leader', the Catholic Herald Group of newspapers had regional editions across the country but a central editorial policy based on Diamond's sometimes idiosyncratic political opinions.[67] During the early years of the twentieth century it tended increasingly towards a pro-assimilationist position until it reached a point in the 1920s when it was, to most intents and purposes, entirely Anglicized. As Maguire observes, 'its coverage of Irish Affairs, both in Britain and Ireland declined so substantially that by 1928 a reference to the "National Feastday" meant St George's Day and not St Patrick's Day as it would have earlier'.[68]

Although, as I have discussed, Irish London at this time can often appear to be socially and politically reticent, the literature produced by Irish people in the city through the same period is significantly more revealing and provides a detailed sense of the anxieties and motivations many discovered in London life. This is not to claim that this literature can be read as an articulation of collective experience. As Herron notes, beyond notable examples such as *Deoraíocht*, 'the literary production of Irish writers in London [...] is somewhat removed from the working class or subaltern groups who constituted the greatest numbers of Irish migrants in London' and with this 'there is little sense that those writers regarded themselves as spokespeople for some larger constituency of "London-Irish" people'.[69] That said, as he acknowledges, these writers still remained 'part of that constituency', and through their apprehension of the experience of being Irish in London – even if it was often the experience of individual isolation rather than social combination – we can glimpse a distinctive literary sensibility that expresses something more than mere geographical coincidence. For instance, a poem such as Tynan's 'At Euston Station' from 1910 precisely identifies a particular emotional dilemma typical of the London-Irish mindset.[70] A poem of transit between London and Ireland, it ultimately can apprehend neither place with clarity; Euston is 'blurred with rain' and indistinct while Ireland ('the belovèd place', as the poem describes it) has become spiritually unattainable with the passage of time. 'There is the train I used to take. / Be blest from shore to shore, / O land of love and of heart-break! / But I go home no more', it concludes sadly.

Perhaps the most famous London-Irish literary text of all – and a poem that established its own London-in-exile sub-genre – is 'The Lake Isle of Innisfree', written by a young Yeats in 1888 and first published in the *National Observer* in 1890.[71] Yeats's account of the poem's origin in his *Autobiographies* is compelling and, in itself, presents a deep apprehension of London life and the condition of exile:

---

[67] Michael P. Maguire, *A Community at War: The Irish in Britain and the War of Independence* (PhD thesis, University of Surrey, 1983), 150.

[68] Maguire, *A Community at War*, 835.

[69] Herron, *Irish Writing London: Volume 1*, 5.

[70] Katharine Tynan, 'At Euston Station', in *Collected Poems* (London: Macmillan, 1930), 23–4. First published in *McClure's Magazine* (March 1910), 492.

[71] W. B. Yeats, 'The Lake Isle of Innisfree', in *The Collected Poems of W. B. Yeats* (London: Macmillan, 1989), 39.

I had various women friends on whom I would call towards five o'clock mainly to discuss my thoughts that I could not bring to a man without meeting some competing thought, but partly because their tea and toast saved my pennies for the 'bus-ride home; but with women, apart from their intimate exchanges of thought, I was timid and abashed. I was sitting on a seat in front of the British Museum feeding pigeons when a couple of girls sat near and began enticing my pigeons away, laughing and whispering to one another, and I looked straight in front of me, very indignant, and presently went into the Museum without turning my head towards them. Since then I have often wondered if they were pretty or merely very young. Sometimes I told myself very adventurous love-stories with myself for hero, and at other times I planned out a life of lonely austerity, and at other times mixed the ideals and planned a life of lonely austerity mitigated by periodical lapses. I had still the ambition, formed in Sligo in my teens, of living in imitation of Thoreau on Innisfree, a little island in Lough Gill, and when walking through Fleet Street very homesick I heard a little tinkle of water and saw a fountain in a shop-window which balanced a little ball upon its jet, and began to remember lake water. From the sudden remembrance came my poem *Innisfree*, my first lyric with anything in its rhythm of my own music.[72]

Yeats's recollection of this moment describes a number of his personal preoccupations: his shy awkwardness, the awareness of a momentary sexual possibility and the subsequent mild humiliation it provokes, and, at this stage of his life, the constant financial hardship he negotiated. In the context of his greater poetic purpose all of this detail will prove to have a function. For instance, it is the embarrassment caused by his rival pigeon enticers that triggers the eventual poem, causing him to flee imaginatively to the emotional self-sufficiency represented by the 'little island in Lough Gill'. But the account also depicts mental states that seem to speak of the more universal condition of exile in London: an implicit loneliness, social discomfort in the face of local manners, hauntological glimpses of future lives that might yet be lived and, most importantly, the degree to which the interruptions of capitalist modernity constantly distort memories of an increasingly idealized pre-exile life. It is Yeats's deployment of this final apprehension that produces the explosive charge of the poem, as two competing modes of consciousness, Innisfree and London, clash and ultimately synthesize. Indeed such was the centrality of this moment for Yeats that he would revisit it on a number of different occasions, sometimes relocating the shop a few yards west to the Strand, as in his novel *John Sherman* from 1891, and sometimes adding other detail so that the fountain/ball arrangement becomes more precisely what he calls 'an advertisement I think for cooling drink'.[73] Given the scale of the epiphany it is unsurprising that he

---

[72] Yeats, *Autobiographies*, 152–3.

[73] 1. W. B. Yeats, *John Sherman and Dhoya* (London: T. Fisher Unwin, 1892), 124: 'Delayed by a crush in the Strand, he heard a faint trickling of water nearby; it came from a shop window where a little water-jet balanced a wooden ball upon its point. The sound suggested a cataract with a long Gaelic name that leaped crying into the Gate of the Winds at Ballah.' 2. W. B. Yeats, *The Collected Works of W. B. Yeats, Volume X: Later Articles and Reviews*, ed. Colton Johnson (New York: Scribner, 2000), 224.

considered the subsequent poem to be 'my first lyric with anything in its rhythm of my own music':

> I will arise and go now, and go to Innisfree,
> And a small cabin build there, of clay and wattles made:
> Nine bean-rows will I have there, a hive for the honey-bee,
> And live alone in the bee-loud glade.
>
> And I shall have some peace there, for peace comes dropping slow,
> Dropping from the veils of the morning to where the cricket sings;
> There midnight's all a glimmer, and noon a purple glow,
> And evening full of the linnet's wings.
>
> I will arise and go now, for always night and day
> I hear lake water lapping with low sounds by the shore;
> While I stand on the roadway, or on the pavements grey,
> I hear it in the deep heart's core.

Like many canonical poems 'Innisfree''s familiarity is such that it can now appear a little shopworn, but, despite this, it still retains a capacity to shock. What Foster calls 'an astonishingly accomplished and original intervention for a poet of twenty-three', the poem takes flight effortlessly and in just twelve lines establishes its imaginative fiefdom through an act of pure poetic will.[74] At the same time – and despite its title – it can be argued that the poem never actually leaves Fleet Street. The poem's incantatory power summons Innisfree's presence, but what appears is a fantastical, distorted, vision – a hallucinatory reaction to the greyness of the city. In this way Innisfree and London are balanced materially and spiritually, with one a function of the other. As such, Innisfree's assault on the senses can be understood as a hyperreal anticipation of a self-sufficient Ireland filtered through the distorted longings and fragmented recollections of emigrant consciousness.

Read in this way, the poem tells us less about Innisfree than might be anticipated and more about the emotional privations of exile. It gains its power as a lament cried from the heart of London's theatreland although, as Adrian Paterson has discussed in impressive detail, it is a poem not just of the Strand and Fleet Street, but of the London suburbs, the Chiswick Eyot (a small island in the Thames that functioned in Yeats's imagination as a variation on Innisfree), and nearby Bedford Park, where the Yeats family were living at the time.[75] Yeats's sister Lily recalls spending a quiet evening there when suddenly:

---

[74] Foster, 'An Irish Power in London', 20.
[75] Adrian Paterson, "'On the Pavements Grey': The Suburban Paradises of W. B. Yeats and William Morris', Herron, *Irish Writing London: Volume 1*, 34–53.

Willy bursting in having just written, or not even written down but just having brought forth 'Innisfree', he repeated it with all the fire of creation & his youth – he was I suppose about 24, I felt a thrill all through me and saw Sligo beauty, heard lake water lapping […] None of us knew what a great moment it was.[76]

Lily's excitement was justified; in its absolute confidence in the integrity of its subject matter the poem acts as nothing less than a gateway into the Irish literary revival as a whole. Indeed such was its influence that Shaw joked privately to Mabel Fitzgerald that the revival movement 'is not Irish; it was invented in Bedford Park, London, W'.[77] Perhaps less enticingly, 'Innisfree' shares something of the revival's occasional habit of unconscious entitlement. In its ability to simply 'arise and go', the poem enacts in microcosm a certain Anglo-Irish attitude towards Irish Ireland as a place of temporary consolation within convenient reach. By comparison the vast majority of Yeats's fellow London Irish remained very much grounded in the reality of the city's grey pavements. In short, the revivalist's constant gaze to the distant west of Ireland meant that the Irish living in their close proximity were easily overlooked.

Startling though 'Innisfree' remains, the poem is misread if it is considered only as an example of what we can term 'Yeatsean exceptionalism'. In fact it took its place – albeit nearly at the head – as part of what was a flourishing genre of 'exile-in-London' revival poems in which the city was figured as the fallen and degraded site of yearning for an Ireland that was, by contrast, regarded as beautiful, distant and usually imperilled. Yeats was influenced in this by the poetry of William Allingham, a Donegal poet of a previous generation who had moved to London to edit *Fraser's Magazine* in 1874. The great success of 'Innisfree' popularized the genre further and variations on its basic theme would appear in many collections of revival verse over the next thirty years. However, such were the form's rigid rules of emotional engagement that this became a process of diminishing returns and in the hands of poets less talented than Yeats it would soon become hackneyed. For instance, Tynan's 'The Foggy Dew', published in 1898, revisited the Innisfree template but expressed its yearnings in a manner that veered close to doggerel:

A splendid place is London, with golden store,
For them that have the heart and hope and youth galore;
But mournful are its streets to me, I tell you true,
For I'm longing sore for Ireland in the foggy dew.[78]

Something of a serial offender in this regard, Tynan returned to the form in 1907 with the poem 'The Grey Streets of London', although arguably the outcome was even less satisfactory:

[76] R. F. Foster, *W. B. Yeats: A Life, Vol. 1: The Apprentice Mage 1865–1914* (Oxford: Oxford University Press, 1997), 79.
[77] Foster, *Vivid Faces*, 18.
[78] Katharine Tynan, *The Wind in the Trees: A Book of Country Verse* (London: Grant Richards, 1898), 71.

The grey streets of London are greyer than the stone,
The grey streets of London where I must walk my lone,
The stony city pavements are hard to tread, alas!
My heart and feet are aching for the Irish grass.[79]

In poems such as this the desire for Ireland is typically so overwhelming that it capsizes the comparison, reducing London to a few synecdochal traces – usually a mix of greyness, endless pavements, excessive heat and dirty smog. For this reason the proponents of the form required no particular experience of the specifics of London life beyond an apprehension that it was probably unpleasant, so Irish poets such as Cathal O'Byrne and Richard Rowley – both firmly rooted in Ulster but willing to turn their hand to anything associated with the revival – felt able to explore its possibilities. As with Tynan's poems, O'Byrne's 'The White Road to Ireland', from his 1917 collection *The Grey Feet of the Wind*, presented London as little more than a jumble of disagreeable sensory experiences – an ordeal that could be relieved only by anticipation of a return from exile:

Och, the weary's on you, London,
With your hot street's all ablaze,
In a rain o'yellow sunshine,
And the drought o' summer days,
Sure I mind me well a white road
That goes westward to the sea,
And the white road to Ireland
Is the right road for me.[80]

More overheated again is Rowley's 'In London', which describes a dream of Ireland viewed through 'tear-brimming eyes' by a speaker trapped 'midst London bricks, / And black 'midst London smoke'.[81] The ecstasy of the vision does not endure. Woken by 'rattling traffic', our protagonist is returned to 'London's fog and smoke' and 'the constant pain that gnaws my heart'. O'Byrne's and Rowley's contributions to the genre appeared in 1917, twenty-seven years after 'Innisfree', and a point when the aesthetic resources of such Celticism were quite exhausted. In 1913 the London Gaelic League's newspaper, *The Irishman*, anticipated this and gently satirized the form as the typical hobby of homesick Irish civil servants who lament: 'With pen and ink in office pent, / I'm sick of Cockney clather, / I want my blackthorn stick again, / My brogues of Irish leather'.[82]

The call-and-response nature of this subgenre suggests that it was something of an imaginative cul-de-sac and, typically, James Joyce was especially alert to the ironies it generated. His story 'A Little Cloud', written in 1906 and included as part of the

---

[79] Katharine Tynan, *Innocencies: A Book of Verse* (Dublin: Maunsell, 1905), 55.
[80] Cathal O'Byrne, *The Grey Feet of the Wind* (Dublin: Talbot Press, 1917), 30–1.
[81] Richard Rowley, *The City of Refuge and Other Poems* (Dublin: Maunsell and Co., 1917), 47–8.
[82] *The Irishman* (July 1913), 7.

'Maturity' section of *Dubliners* in 1914, cast a particularly wry eye on the revivalists' endless positioning of Ireland and London and detected in the cultural banality of the opposition a hypocrisy that was essentially self-serving. In the story 'Little Chandler', a law clerk living in Dublin with frustrated ambitions to be a poet of the 'Celtic school', meets his old acquaintance Gallaher, now (seemingly) 'a brilliant figure on the London Press', for what proves to be a drink-fuelled evening riven by petty jealousy and barely concealed mutual distaste.[83] Trapped in the stultifying morality of Dublin's lower middle class, Chandler dreams of 'the great city London', an imagined location which represents everything his 'own sober inartistic life' cannot accommodate.[84] Joyce's scrutiny of Chandler's delusions is merciless: in his artistically and morally impoverished world view London represents commercial success, 'bustle and competition', and a sexual licentiousness which he finds both titillating and offensive.[85] Most telling, however, is Chandler's untroubled awareness that the cultural gatekeepers of the 'Celtic School' which he so yearns to join are in fact 'English critics' vested with the authority to discern the authenticity or otherwise of what they deem the 'Celtic note' (a phrase already in circulation among radical nationalists such as Moran as a sarcastic means of dismissing seemingly obsequious revivalist gestures).[86] In this manner Joyce recognized that while the Celtic Twilight genre sought to disparage London and its amorality at every opportunity, it was validated and underwritten commercially by critics and publishers based in the city. As such the hierarchies of cultural and spiritual value that the genre promoted constituted a flat reversal of its actual economic subservience. Given this it was appropriate that the Innisfree template would have a lengthy and peculiar afterlife, as its sentiment of yearning mutated into the pathological cheeriness of music hall standards such as 'It's a Long Way to Tipperary' by Harry Williams and Jack Judge from 1912, which announced: 'Goodbye, Piccadilly, / Farewell, Leicester Square! / It's a long long way to Tipperary, / But my heart's right there'. In this song what was once the pain of the romantic exile desperate to escape the urban present through the memory of an idealized rural Irish past would be transformed into a kind of melancholy if indefatigable joviality. The amorphous quality of this sentiment could be redeployed and it is appropriate that it gained phenomenal success when revived as a marching song by Florrie Forde in 1914. It was in this form that it accompanied many Irish and British soldiers – most famously the Connaught Rangers – to their deaths in the First World War. As this book will describe, the history of Irish London contains many such bitter ironies.

This account of the London Irish ends in 1916 with the Easter Rising in Dublin in April and the subsequent executions of sixteen of its leaders, including that of Roger Casement in Pentonville Prison in north London. In some ways concluding the narrative at this point may appear slightly perverse as it marks the beginning of a period

---

[83] James Joyce, *Dubliners: Text, Criticism and Notes*, ed. Robert Scholes and A. Walton Litz (London: Penguin, 1996), 71, 74.

[84] Ibid., 73.

[85] Ibid., 77.

[86] Ibid., 74. D. P. Moran, 'English Literature and Irish Humbug', *An Claidheamh Soluis* (29 April 1899), 105.

when Irish political life would be lived with an unusual intensity, not least in London itself. However, 1916 also marks the conclusive end of a number of modes of belief, cultural possibilities and assumptions about emigrant life in the city that had sustained waves of London Irish experience during the previous forty years. In short, while the events of the Easter Rising created the possibility for a new kind of Irish revolutionary political subject, it also rendered other versions of Irish identity quite obsolete. In this what Foster describes as the effect of the Rising in Ireland was equally true for the Irish in London: 'What happened in 1916 drew attention to a change of mentality, a change in hearts and minds, whereby within two or three years Irish opinion would shift dramatically away from the old, constitutionalist Home Rule idea, and towards a more radical form of republican separatism, achieved if necessary by force of arms.'[87] For those who struggled to adapt to this new reality, such as Tynan and Dora Sigerson, this sense of an ending was imagined in starkly personal and emotionally devastating terms, but for others it was nothing less than emancipatory. Certainly one of the less appreciated but still highly significant elements of the fight for, and the achievement of, national independence was the sense that it acted, as Ó Tuathaigh has argued, 'as a kind of liberation, a collective rise in self-esteem for the expatriates' which 'signalled the end of an era in Irish immigrant history'.[88] This is not to say that life in London suddenly became easier for the Irish or that the degree of everyday prejudice they faced was lessened, but it did mean that there were now ways of understanding the constant emigration of people from Ireland to London as something other than the ongoing expression of a historical trauma and a national humiliation. In these terms 1916 was nothing less than a psychological leavening.

In his path-clearing thesis of 1976 Benjamin concludes his analysis by arguing that 'the Irish London community [of 1870–1910] was not an inert, apathetic mass, reacting to forces over which it had little control' but was instead 'a dynamic, responsive community'. 'The overall assessment must be one of positive accomplishment, visible maturity, and growth in political awareness, all of which marked a beginning in civic responsibility,' he summarizes.[89] The argument was perhaps slightly overstated, but it remains welcome as a corrective to those narratives of London Irish experience that find only the melancholy of a bondaged people trapped in the house of its oppressor. Similarly inspirational was the work of Lees from the same period, whose history of the Irish in Victorian London encountered Irish culture not as a troublesome hindrance preventing assimilation but rather as an inheritance 'that helped migrants to survive in an alien, sometimes hostile environment'.[90] With it, 'the Irish produced a remarkably resilient, tenacious subculture that not only sheltered but bound its members'. The research I have conducted for this study builds upon these awarenesses and argues that Irish culture itself was a hugely important resource which the London Irish would deploy in striking and unexpected ways to press for political and social justice. This could occur via the paths of revivalism, the relentless belief in self-improvement

---

[87] Foster, *Vivid Faces*, xviii.
[88] Ó Tuathaigh, 'The Irish in Nineteenth-Century Britain', 173.
[89] Benjamin, *The London Irish*, 345.
[90] Lees, *Exiles of Erin*, 250.

offered by the Gaelic League, or even, as I discuss in Chapter 5, in the Irish/cockney music hall songs performed by Bessie Bellwood in venues such as the Jolly Tanners in Southwark. It is at such moments that any sense of the London Irish as 'shrouded' dissipates and, in turn, an understanding of Irish culture as a constantly evolving and adapting set of lived practices comes into sharp focus. To put this more directly, it is in its cultural responses to the dangers and opportunities of London life that the Irish found solace, sustenance and forms of resistance.

1

'Nature intended Paddy for a rural existence': The St Giles Rookery and its afterlives

The Editur of the Times Paper

Sur, – May we beg and beseech your proteckshion and power. We are Sur, as it may be, livin in a Wilderniss, so far as the rest of London knows anything of us, or as the rich and great people care about. We live in muck and filth. We aint got no priviz, no dust bins, no drains, no water-splies, and no drain or suer in the hole place. The Suer Company, in Greek St., Soho Square, all great, rich and powerfool men, take no notice watsomedever of our cumplaints. The Stenche of a Gully-hole is disgustin. We all of us suffur, and numbers are ill, and if the Colera comes Lord help us.

Some gentlemans comed yesterday, and we thought they was comishioners from the Suer Company, but they was complaining of the noosance and stenche our lanes and corts was to them in New Oxforde Street. They was much surprized to see the seller in No. 12, Carrier St., in our lane, where a child was dyin from fever, and would not beleave that Sixty persons sleep in it every night. This here seller you couldent swing a cat in, and the rent is five shillings a week; but theare are greate many sich deare sellars. Sur, we hope you will let us have our cumplaints put into your hinfluenshall paper, and make these landlords of our houses and these comishioners (the friends we spose of the landlords) make our houses decent for Christions to live in. Preaye Sir com and see us, for we are living like piggs, and it aint faire we shoulde be so ill treted.

We are your respeckfull servents in Church Lane, Carrier St., and the other corts. Teusday, Juley 3, 1849.

John Scott, Emen Scott, Joseph Crosbie, Hanna Crosbie [and fifty others].[1]

Located at the southern edge of St Giles in the Fields at the northwest end of Drury Lane, the St Giles 'Rookery' was the first and most notorious Irish district in nineteenth-century London. About eight acres in extent, the Rookery was a perpetually decaying slum seemingly always on the verge of social and economic collapse; Lynn Hollen Lees in her influential history of the Irish in Victorian London, *Exiles of*

---

[1] John Scott, et al., 'A Sanitary Remonstrance', *The Times* (5 July 1849), 5.

Erin, described it simply as 'one of the foulest places in London'.[2] At the heart of this sprawling settlement was a tangled mass of alleys and walkways, which became known during the eighteenth century as the 'Irish Rookery', the 'Holy Land' or 'Little Dublin'. Here the residents were almost entirely of Irish extraction and the district often served as the first accommodation for those newly arrived in the city. This was in part because, as Roger Swift notes, 'it had a reputation in Ireland for being generous in poor relief', although – in Swift's account, at least – this generosity had the side effect of attracting 'the least desirable Irish who quickly became demoralized and absorbed into a rookery of thieves and beggars'.[3] Even by the standards of the time, living conditions at St Giles were appalling. A survey of 7 Church Lane, a typical property in the Rookery, from 1849 reported that:

> the privy had been taken away and the cesspool covered with boards and earth. The soil underneath oozed up through the boards, saturating the earth with foetid matter. In one of the back rooms several Irish families lived. [...] The room opposite was occupied by only three families in the day, but as many as could be got into it at night.[4]

It was out of sheer desperation, then, that in the same year fifty-four inhabitants of St Giles wrote a letter of complaint to the *Times*, which it published under the headline 'A Sanitary Remonstrance'. At this point, the already terrible conditions had been worsened by overcrowding as a result of the Famine in Ireland and the piecemeal demolition of other parts of the Rookery. It is mildly surprising that the *Times* published the letter at all, although its condescension in leaving unaltered its many spelling errors – an editorial practice it did not follow for its other correspondents – is more predictable and was possibly intended to evoke a mode of Dickensian pathos. Despite this, there is reason to be grateful for the decision, as 'A Sanitary Remonstrance' constitutes one of the few examples we have of testimony by, as opposed to about, actual Rookery inhabitants. Certainly its depiction of their suffering and the force of their appeal for relief remain vivid. As Thomas Beames noted in 1852, 'Rookeries are bad, but what are they to Irish Rookeries?'[5]

As with several other sites of urban deprivation in London, the Rookery was established on the site of an old leper colony and was organized around a series of interlinked galleried courts that were essentially medieval in origin. It was this confusion of alleys that suggested to the curious observer the image of the labyrinth, dark and impenetrable. Charles Knight's extensive report of 1842 describes the Rookery as 'one great maze of narrow crooked paths crossing and intersecting in labyrinthine

[2] Lynn Hollen Lees, *Exiles of Erin: Irish Migrants in Victorian London* (Manchester: Manchester University Press, 1977), 66.

[3] Roger Swift, 'Heroes or Villains?: The Irish, Crime, and Disorder in Victorian England', *Albion: A Quarterly Journal Concerned with British Studies* 29:3 (Autumn 1997), 399–421, 408.

[4] David Green, *People of the Rookery: A Pauper Community in Victorian London*, Occasional paper 26, *Kings College Department of Geography* (London: King's College London, 1986), 10.

[5] Thomas Beames, *The Rookeries of London* (London: Frank Cass, 1972 [1852]), 38.

convolutions'.[6] Similarly, John Timbs's retrospective account from 1855 recalled that the district was:

> one dense mass of houses, through which curved narrow tortuous lanes, from which again diverged close courts – one great mass, as if the houses had originally been one block of stone, eaten by slugs into numberless small chambers and connecting passages. The lanes were thronged with loiterers; and stagnant gutters, and piles of garbage and filth infested the air. In the windows, wisps of straw, old hats, and lumps of bed-tick or brown paper, alternated with shivered pains of broken glass; the walls were the colour of bleached soot, and doors fell from their hinges and worm-eaten posts.[7]

As Timbs's horrified description indicates, the Rookery was a disorientating place that for many years defied the attempts of London's developers to impose order and rationality on its seeming chaos. To enter its environs was to wilfully surrender one's status under the law and to place oneself in the jurisdiction of quite different social economies. To express this differently, what happened in the Rookery had a regulation of its own; there were frequent stories of people unwittingly straying into the maze of alley ways and never emerging. It was, as the *Morning Chronicle* put it as early as 1834, a 'place known as a receptacle for persons of the lowest description', a base for predatory 'barefooted gangs' of young Irish men who 'in the most discordant strains bawl out sea songs to the annoyance of peaceable inhabitants'.[8] It was also what passed for home for hundreds of the city's beggars. Friedrich Engels would be still more vivid, reporting with horror that:

> here live the poorest of the poor, the worst paid workers with thieves and the victims of prostitution indiscriminately huddled together, the majority Irish, or of Irish extraction, and those who have not yet sunk in the whirlpool of moral ruin which surrounds them, sinking daily deeper, losing daily more and more of their power to resist the demoralizing influence of want, filth, and evil surroundings.[9]

The worst of the Rookery was yet to come, however. Following the Famine of the mid-1840s, a new wave of Irish migrants swelled the already overcrowded settlement to the point where it reached near breaking point. This created conditions of almost unimaginable squalor culminating in a serious cholera outbreak in 1848. As this indicates, the Rookery's final years, before its prolonged demolition from the early 1850s onwards, were also its most traumatic and it became a resonant symbol for urban poverty at its most extreme. As Edward Walford's *Old and New London* of 1897 noted: 'The parish of St Giles, with its nests of close and narrow alleys and courts

6 Charles Knight, *London*, vol. III (London: Charles Knight & Co., 1842), 267.
7 John Timbs, *Curiosities of London* (London: Virtue & Co., 1867), 379.
8 *The Morning Chronicle* (14 January 1834), 4.
9 Friedrich Engels, *The Condition of the Working-Class in England in 1844* (London: Allen & Unwin, 1943 [1887]), 27.

inhabited by the lowest class of Irish costermongers, has passed into a by-word as the synonym of filth and squalor.'[10] As this chapter will discuss, there were other activities going on in the Rookery that challenge this vision of the Rookery as little more than a breaking yard for the human spirit. Nonetheless, there was nothing unusual in the sad fate of George Masters, an elderly beggar, who was reported to have starved to death in the Rookery in 1837.[11]

As such accounts constitute the predominant way in which the life of the Rookery has been understood, the need to speak with greater historical acuity about Walford's 'lowest class of Irish costermongers' remains vivid. Certainly such lives deserve better than to be remembered only through the often abusive clichés of the evangelists and philanthropists who frequently attempted to penetrate the Rookery's mysteries and who recorded their activity with zealous detail. More broadly, a reorientation of the history of Irish experience in London that locates the St Giles Rookery as a point of beginning and that speaks meaningfully about those that lived there is important, not because the Rookery was home to a particularly large number of Irish people (its population was significant but not as a proportion of the overall Irish population in the city, which by 1851 was something like 109,000 or 5 per cent of the city as a whole) but rather because of the way in which the intensity of Rookery life, its proximity to sites of economic and high cultural value, its fostering of the Irish language, and the lessons it can teach us about the experience of Irish emigration under capitalism enable new stories to be told and familiar accounts of the experience of the Irish diaspora to be recast.[12] For many, the Rookery symbolized social desperation, the ruin of the Famine, cultural amnesia and economic deprivation. Yet it also spoke of self-reliance and an acknowledgement of the social contract implicit to the idea of hospitality; as David Green has observed of Rookery life, those newly arrived could expect to benefit by gaining the means for basic survival but 'the participants in exchange had to be accountable and subject to communal sanctions'.[13] As such, it was recognized that it was only through social combination that ultimately any form of long-term individual existence could be countenanced.

Understood in these terms, the Rookery was an ethnic ghetto where the impossibility of assimilation was imposed both from above – by the urban economies of a city that placed the migrant Irish somewhere near the bottom (if not quite the actual bottom) of subaltern Victorian London – and from below, in that the Rookery itself exercised communal sanctions and protected its borders. It resisted the rule of law both figuratively and literally, organizing itself against the police raids that increased in frequency during the 1840s.[14] Ultimately, the will of the Rookery was only to be broken

[10] Edward Walford, *Old and New London: A Narrative of Its History, Its People, and Its Places*, vol. III (London: Cassell, Petter and Galpin, 1897), 206.

[11] *The Ipswich Journal* (14 January 1837), 5.

[12] As Francis Sheppard, among others, has noted, this figure is itself misleading as it does not include the children born in London of Irish parents. If these are also counted as part of the Irish population, then the overall total in 1851 is closer to 156,000. See *London 1808–1870: The Infernal Wen* (London: Secker and Warburg, 1971), 6.

[13] Green, *People of the Rookery*, 30.

[14] Kellow Chesney's *The Victorian Underworld* (London: Penguin, 1972, 127–8) vividly describes a police raid on a coiner's workshop in the Rookery in November 1840 and the manner in which the raid was resisted.

by its demolition. Traces of it remained, however, in the memory and experience of those who were dispersed from its narrow alleys and scattered across the rest of the city. With this, the Rookery became a state of mind and a powerful metaphor for Irish social and cultural survival in London through the following decades of the nineteenth century and later. Alongside this figuration as a marker of Ireland, the Rookery also played an important role in the story of London itself – usually serving as a symbol of the residual, the decaying and the uselessly medieval. The district was notorious for obstructing new commercial developments, which, in Engels's phrase, first 'penetrated' the Rookery in 1844.[15] Such accounts present the Rookery's habitual condition as permanently decaying, always anachronistic and perpetually on the verge of being swept away by the twin forces of rising land prices in the fashionable west end of the city and the insistent calls of social reformers. Yet despite this teetering existence, its demise was seemingly always deferred. The Rookery clung on, in ever-diminishing forms, for the next three decades until its final, longed-for, eradication.

This endurance indicates why the Rookery played a significant role in enabling London's dreams of modernity. It stood in a stubborn and antithetical relationship to the bright symbols of capitalism that surrounded it. And alongside the revulsion it provoked, there was also a seemingly endless fascination. The Rookery was a key stopping point for those chroniclers of London engaged in 'poverty tourism', and its iconic status repeatedly demanded their attention. In this, it was both a beneficiary and a victim of what Seth Koven has referred to as the 'vast and growing machinery of private benevolence in London' during this period.[16] The central location of the Rookery meant that it was, as Sian Anthony has observed, 'one of the first slums to be investigated by social and sanitary reformers' and it became a place of experimentation for those driven by the relentless desire to implement social improvement, however that often unhappy concept might be interpreted.[17] Posterity might look less than generously on these interventions, but, as Koven notes, in truth the efforts at improvement usually worked with a messy 'mingling of good intentions and blinkered prejudices that informed their vision of the poor and themselves'.[18] Either way, such is the weight of textual evidence describing the conditions of life in St Giles that it is hard to escape the conclusion that it was the subject of an overwhelming and near constant scrutiny by what Gearóid Ó Tuathaigh has described as 'an army of social investigators, philanthropists, clergymen, royal commissions and parliamentary committees'.[19] Despite being conveniently situated in the centre of London the Rookery was a place where impoverishment could be observed in its purist form. Typically such enquiries were motivated by the pursuit of more ambitious cultural narratives. As well as standing synecdochally for Ireland and its ongoing suffering, as Pamela K. Gilbert has observed,

---

[15] Engels, *The Condition of the Working-Class in England*, 27.

[16] Seth Koven, *Slumming: Sexual and Social Politics in Victorian London* (Princeton: Princeton University Press, 2004), 57–8.

[17] Sian Anthony, Medieval Settlement to 18th-/19th-century Rookery: Excavations at Central St Giles, London Borough of Camden, 2006–8 (London: Museum of London Archaeology, 2011), 56.

[18] Koven, *Slumming*, 3.

[19] M. A. G. Ó Tuathaigh, 'The Irish in Nineteenth-Century Britain: Problems of Integration', *Transactions of the Royal Historical Society*, 31 (1981), 149–73, 149.

'the filth of the slum was associated with a barbaric past, out of which the nation must progress; St Giles became a byword for this embarrassing barbarism to be eliminated'.[20] It is of little surprise, then, that reports of its complex internal dynamics and habitats are frequently distorted by extraordinarily convoluted modes of representation.

As this suggests, any attempt at a modern understanding of Rookery life has to contend both with the deliberate act of eradication that sought to wipe all trace of the settlement from the centre of the city and with the inevitable disruption of the historical gaze provoked by the degree to which we are forced to attend to the 'spectacle' of poverty around which the chroniclers of London's poor insistently shaped the material under consideration. Indeed, it is useful to position much writing about the Rookery as a kind of unwitting and extended meditation on the spectacle of observation itself, or, to put this differently, an act of self-conscious performance. Certainly, despite the best efforts of their authors, it is striking how often the ostensible subject of these accounts – the Rookery itself – remained slightly beyond, or in excess of, the powers of description. Indeed, in Knight's 1842 report what he termed 'the dull prosaic accounts given by policemen and constables' proved 'more appalling than anything a mere imaginative writer could conceive'. This realization led, in turn, to what he perceived as a peculiar dissociation:

> Imagination falls short of reality on one hand (Bill Sparkes could patter flash ten times faster and funnier than that cove, said an eleve of the flash-house, tossing aside contemptuously one of those novels which attempts to be striking by imitating the language of thieves); and, on the other, there is a liveliness excited by the effort of describing incompatible with the representation of the utter apathy and moral deadness sometimes to be found in men.[21]

The incompatibility that Knight identifies here is found in many attempts to read the Rookery as a social totality. It was as if the despairing ennui such accounts encountered not only refused accommodation in a suitably sentimental prose style, but would also eventually exhaust the very nature of the task of description itself. As a result, such texts often become little more than caricatures of an obdurate reality – a reality that remained annoyingly elusive. Even the very name 'Rookery' was problematic in that it indicated both a fearful containment and a determined insularity. It also suggested a distinct demarcation of boundaries that, in reality, was by no means clearly evident.

One crucial element of the Rookery's symbolic significance, and much of its appeal for these observers, is what can be termed its 'positionality', and, specifically, its unsettling proximity to fast-developing major centres of commerce. For social historians and improvers, the fear, notoriety and fascination provoked by the Rookery were intensified by its immediacy to the expansive world of London commerce at its most energetic as represented by Oxford Street and its environs. It was as if the

---

[20] Pamela K. Gilbert, *Mapping the Victorian Social Body* (Albany: State University of New York, 2004), 86.

[21] Knight, *London*, 268.

Rookery's very presence served as a constant reminder of the fragility of the rapid economic development that surrounded it. This troubling juxtaposition preoccupied many contemporary accounts. Engels noted with some wonder that the Rookery 'is in the midst of the most populous part of the town, surrounded by broad, splendid avenues in which the gay world of London idles about, in the immediate neighbourhood of Oxford Street, Regent Street, of Trafalgar Square and the Strand'.[22] Indeed, as Knight observed, the Rookery did not even offer the convenience of being clearly demarcated. Instead, and troublingly, 'its limits are not very precisely defined, its squalor fades into the cleanness of the more civilized districts in its vicinity, by insensible degrees, like the hues of the rainbow'.[23] The threat of the Rookery, then, was always that it might prove to be infectious to those areas forced by the insistent demands of modernity to nuzzle close to its unprepossessing facades. As Knight marvelled, 'One step conveys us from a land of affluence and comfort to a land of hopelessness and squalid want'.[24] A vivid symptom of this unease was the persistent fear of miasmic infection, a concern that noxious, disease-bearing, fumes of decay would drift from the Rookery into increasingly genteel areas such as nearby Bloomsbury.

Thomas Beames, curate of St James in Piccadilly, captured the effects of this often disturbing juxtaposition in his *Rookeries of London* in 1852:

> You seem for a time to leave the day, and life, and habits of your fellow-creatures behind you – just to step out of the din and bustle of a crowded thoroughfare – to turn aside from streets whose shops teem with every luxury – where Art has brought together its most beautiful varieties, – and you have scarce gone a hundred yards when you are in *The Rookery*. The change is marvellous: squalid children, haggard men, with long uncombed hair, in rags, most of them smoking, many speaking Irish; women without shoes or stockings – a babe perhaps at the breast, with a single garment, confined to the waist by a bit of string; wolfish looking dogs; decayed vegetables strewing the pavement; low public houses; linen hanging across the street to dry; the population stagnant in the midst of activity; lounging about in remnants of shooting jackets, leaning on the window frames, blocking up the courts and alleys; with young boys gathered round them, looking exhausted as though they had not been to bed. Never was there so little connection between masses of living beings and their means of livelihood.[25]

Beames's account is particularly powerful because it perceives the poverty of the Rookery not simply as a function of its deprivation, but rather as a mode of anti-capital, responding dialectically to the structures and preoccupations of the new London that encircles it. If the new London was one of movement and haste, so the Rookery spoke only of stasis and stagnation; if the advancing energies of retail capitalism presented a seemingly infinite variety, then the Rookery reflected back plain uniformity, the

---

[22] Engels, *The Condition of the Working-Class in England*, 27.
[23] Knight, *London*, 267.
[24] Ibid., 271.
[25] Beames, *The Rookeries of London*, 30.

regularity of a poverty that had forced people into identical templates of suffering. Eventually the remorseless nature of this endless positioning revealed only the vanity of the capitalist project, exposing its inherent lack of substance and its status as mere veneer. As Knight observed astutely, 'men are beginning to suspect that spacious lines of streets, with rows of stately fronts of houses on each side, in which the decorations of Grecian temples are superinduced upon shops of all kinds, are of little avail, so long as close and noisome lanes and courts are allowed to remain in their rottenness behind'.[26] It was as if in response to the energy of modernity, the Rookery could offer only exhaustion and ennui; so many accounts of Rookery life during this time emphasize its languor, stasis and, what Henry Mayhew, the social reformer and journalist, called 'painful silence'.[27] As a result, it was, in Kellow Chesney's phrase, 'an oddly devitalized little piece of London'.[28] Thomas Miller's account of the St Giles Rookery in 1852 was typically florid but keenly observant of detail:

> Many of the door-posts are worn smooth and bright, through the idle loungers, who have rubbed and rested against them while smoking and looking out into the streets, hour after hour, and day after day, – men who seem to have no business upon earth, having to smoke and sleep, and when they awake, to smoke and lean against the self-same doorways until it is time to sleep again. On the steps, and on the edges of the pavement, or at the entrance of those unexplored courts, withered old women sit with folded arms scowling at you as you pass, and proclaiming by their looks that you are an intruder.[29]

The rubbed-smooth doorpost that Miller notices here is a detail that others too would focus on – for instance Knight's account is revolted by the 'door-posts worm-eaten and greasily polished from being long the supports of the shoulders of ragged loungers' – and it served as a convenient metonym for depicting Rookery idleness as fetishistic.[30] In Miller's account this is intensified by the fact that it is observed from the perspective of a gaze that appears to perceive such languid gestures as mildly erotic. There was, of course, always a fundamental mobility about the Rookery in that its meanings and significations were constantly shifting, but at the level of its declared symbolic function – the face it presented to the world – it chose an abject fixity. It was, as Knight noted with horror, 'a land of utter idleness'.[31] As such, in its refusal to display a meaningful connection between the process of life and Beames's 'means of livelihood', the Rookery was a potent example of, to use David Harvey's term, a 'potential blockage point to capital accumulation'.[32] And, as Harvey explains, it is in capitalism's very nature to

[26] Knight, *London*, 271.
[27] Henry Mayhew, *London Labour and the London Poor*, Vol. 4 (London: Dover Publications, 1968 [1861]), 237.
[28] Chesney, *The Victorian Underworld*, 108.
[29] Thomas Miller, *Picturesque Sketches of London Past and Present* (London: Office of the National Illustrated Library, 1852), 236.
[30] Knight, *London*, 267.
[31] Ibid.
[32] David Harvey, *The Enigma of Capital: And the Crises of Capitalism* (London: Profile, 2010), 105.

strive to circumvent such obstructions. For this reason alone, the Rookery would always give offence.

If these elements of Rookery life were, in themselves, unpleasant to contemplate for a city eager to turn its back on all that was regressive and archaic, the fact that much of the Rookery's discontent was articulated in Irish, the language of impoverishment, exclusion and, ultimately, of denial, only compounded the offence. Indeed the prolonged existence of the Irish language in the Rookery was one of its more remarkable characteristics, and another crucial way in which it maintained a degree of cultural and economic autonomy despite its location. One example of this in practice came in 1851, as a result of official attempts at regulating common lodging houses in order to limit the number of people that could be accommodated in individual rooms and to impose a degree of sexual segregation. Given the Rookery's labyrinthine nature, the enforcement of these regulations was, in their early years, almost impossible but the attempts that were made reveal something of the extraordinary microcultures that existed within it. On 5 April 1852, the *Times* reported that seven defendants were prosecuted at Bow Street Magistrate's Court 'for having infringed the regulations of the act for the Improvement of Common Lodge Houses, passed last session'. The article provided further details:

> The defendants were the occupants of the eight rooms of a small house in Church-lane, St. Giles, long known as one of the most filthy remnants of the old 'Rookery'. The rooms in each house are let separately to different tenants, pay about 3s. per week. And by them underlet, nightly or weekly, to the hordes of low Irish who infest the neighbourhood, and who are crammed into each apartment, without reference to number, age, sex or disease, to sleep in groups upon the floor; 36 persons having been sometimes found thus heaped together in a room, which had been registered under the new act as capable only of accommodating seven.[33]

The first case before the magistrate was that of Michael Sullivan, the occupant of one of the upper rooms, which the inspectors found to 'contain 22 women, and children without bedsteads or partitions'. Under cross-examination, it soon became apparent that Sullivan could speak only Irish and thus had 'not the slightest notion of what was going on'. Because of this the magistrate decided that the case must begin again and that an interpreter should be found. After some searching, a 'widow woman' – who, bizarrely, was one of the defendant's lodgers – 'was intrusted, by Mr Bodkin, with the office of interpreter'. Unfortunately 'she talked so continuously, both in English and Irish that the Court was obliged to dispense with her assistance and try another case'. As it transpired that the next defendant could not speak English either, the magistrate decided to have all the accused placed in the dock together. The court then heard evidence from Charles Reeve, the surveyor, who had inspected the whole of the house on the night of 8 March. He had found, in total, 107 people sleeping in the one property. His evidence noted that:

[33] 'Police News', *The Times* (5 April 1852), 7.

there is only one privy to the whole house, and that inaccessible from the filth which has overflown and flooded the yard. The yard is used as a common privy, and it was impossible to walk in it without being soiled. The rooms all emitted a filthy stench, and it was difficult to breathe in some of them. There were no bedsteads in any of the rooms, nor any partitions or other means of keeping the families or sexes apart; and there was no water in the house.

Despite these horrific details, it was clear that because of the insurmountable language barrier the trial could not proceed and the defendants were eventually all discharged.

Cases such as this reveal the extent of overcrowding and exploitation in St Giles, but its complex resonances also illustrate the manner in which the Rookery collapsed spatial and temporal distance – in this instance bringing the material reality of the Great Famine directly into the heart of London and revealing the longevity of its effects. In these terms, for those recently escaped from the catastrophe in Ireland conditions in the Rookery were a vivid physical manifestation of the violence that Marx writes of in *Capital* 'when great masses of men are suddenly and forcibly torn from their means of subsistence, and hurled onto the labour-market as free, unprotected and rightless proletarians. The expropriation of the agricultural producer, of the peasant, from the soil is the basis of the whole process'.[34] Moreover, while these refugees were vulnerable to exploitation by wider London society, they were also the victims of prejudice and violence from within the Rookery itself as the newly arrived Irish poor were frequently a cause of resentment for those London Irish who were already established in the area.

The matter of Ireland was, then, needled through every element of the Rookery's existence. Indeed commentators were often keen to emphasize the uniquely Irish nature of life there, depicting its habits and customs as the natural manifestations of a national characteristic rather than the only mode of survival possible in the circumstances. 'Here, as in most Rookeries', observed Beames in *The Rookeries of London*, 'are colonies of Irish, who seem particularly given to courts in which the only egress is a narrow alley. Many a cul-de-sac is there in this district, which the sons of Erin have chosen as their own'.[35] In this way, Beames presents the spatial form of the Rookery as both entrapment and protection, a dual function that is directly responsible for creating the indolence he sees as typical of its average inhabitant. In his discussion of an Irish Rookery a little to the east of St Giles in Holborn Hill, Beames's extensive – if not always trustworthy – investigation provides rare evidence of the economic structure of a typical Rookery and its surroundings. At its heart, he suggested, is hopelessness and desperation, displayed in the intensively overcrowded lodging houses wherein gather the 'motley groups whose necessities, or whose evil deeds force them to take refuge here'.[36] Surrounding this despair are zones of more productive, if still transitory, economic activity, including 'street singers, dogs' meat men, crossing sweepers (in some cases a lucrative trade), pie-men, muffin-sellers, dealers in lucifer matches, watercresses, fruit, and sweet-meats, cabmen, dustmen'. As he notes, any 'who

---

[34] Karl Marx, 'Twenty-Six: The Secret of Primitive Accumulation', *Capital: Volume One*. Available online: http://www.marxists.org/archive/marx/works/1867-c1/ch26.htm (accessed 8 July 2018).

[35] Beames, *The Rookeries of London*, 54.

[36] Ibid.

prefer a desultory to a regular employment, settle in this quarter'.[37] Nonetheless, more substantial (albeit still underground) manufacturing activity also took place. A fire that broke out in the St Giles Rookery in 1842 revealed to the astonished firefighters what was described as an 'extensive illicit trade of glass blowers' located right at the heart of the labyrinth.[38] Similarly, the examination of remnants of crucibles found at the site of the Wild Court Rookery (an Irish settlement a little to the south of St Giles) in 2009 indicates that they had been used for the illicit refining and melting of gold alloys.[39] Shops and commerce, however, were markedly less common; Knight comments in detail on the meagre extent of the commercial transactions that actually took place:

> Half-way up Bainbridge Street is one in which a few withered vegetables are offered for sale; in George Street another, where any kind of rags, with all their dirt, are purchased; along Broad Street, St. Giles's, are some provision shops, one or two of those suspicious deposits of old rusty keys called marine stores, and opposite the church a gin-shop. Here a few miserable women may be seen attempting to help each other to arrange their faded shawls, when by any means they have procured liquor enough to stupefy themselves – exhilaration is out of the question.[40]

Clearly, the typical labour of the Rookery Irish was, at best, fitful. For the most straitened it was usually a mixture of begging, seasonal work, street selling and costermongering, although those who were more established could engage in economic activity of greater substance, including work on major construction projects such as the railway network or the water and sewerage system. Labour was distributed across all elements of the Rookery's community. Children would work from an early age busking and selling newspapers, and women would also undertake seasonal labour and sell flowers, nuts and oranges.

Alongside these more-or-less legal activities, the squalor of the Rookery also disguised a complex defence system designed to confuse and repel the forces of law and authority when they attempted to encroach its boundaries. In *Victorian Underworld*, Chesney notes that at St Giles:

> Over the years the whole mass of yards and tenements had become threaded by an elaborate complex of runways, traps and bolt-holes. In places cellar had been connected with cellar so that a fugitive could pass under a series of houses and emerge in another part of the Rookery. In others, long established escape routes ran from the maze of inner courts and over the huddled roofs: high on the back wall was a double row of iron spikes, 'one row to hold by, and another for the feet to rest on', connecting the windows of adjacent buildings.[41]

---

[37] Beames, *The Rookeries of London*, 54–5.
[38] *The Standard* (13 September 1842), 1.
[39] David Dungworth, *Wild Court Rookery, City of London Scientific Examination of Early 19th-century Crucibles* (London: English Heritage Technology Report, 2010).
[40] Knight, *London*, 267.
[41] Chesney, *The Victorian Underworld*, 110.

It was because of such innovations (which were detailed breathlessly in the 'Police pages' of British and Irish provincial papers) that the Rookery became notorious. Reports of life in the Rookery at night, when a quite different set of fears, superstitions and mythologies came into play, were more sensational again. As an account from 1842 described:

> Not until after night-fall does the vitality of the Rookery spring into full action. Many of its inhabitants, who live perpetually in dark cellars, are distressed, like bats and owls, with the day-light, many more dare not face it. It is then that a few wretched females, shoeless and unbonneted – their matted hair twisted carelessly round their heads, and a coarse dirty shawl hugged over their shoulders – emerge into the nearest thoroughfare, in the hope of gaining a half-quartern from some idle frequenter of the gin-shops. Squalid children also creep out in search of what they may purloin – children who never knew what childhood was, but who grew up at once from the baby to the adult, cunning and precocious.[42]

Half-asleep during the day, nightfall in the Rookery awakened a host of the living dead, anxious to scavenge an existence on the fringes of a liminal, crepuscular, world. It was in this nocturnal economy that what little 'vitality' there was in the Rookery resided, a space one step up from death itself. For Peter Ackroyd the St Giles Rookery 'embodied the worst living conditions in all of London's history; this was the lowest point which human beings could reach before death took hold of them, and to the Irish it seemed that the city and its inhabitants were already given over to the devil'.[43]

The Rookery, then, was both an enclosed system – a world of its own possessing particular codes, rules and shibboleths – and a place that engaged economically with the wider city. As such, it was a complex site of flux and permanence, order and dissonance, the kind of location that Harvey, in his discussion of the relationship of slums and capitalism, describes as a 'dynamic ecological space'.[44] Many of its inhabitants were destined to remain only briefly – those Irish migrants that appeared 'to come in and go out with the flies and the fruit', as Beames put it – but others would spend their lives there, rarely straying beyond its narrow limits.[45] Indeed, according to Green, even among the pauper population of the Rookery 'long term residence was the norm rather than the exception'.[46] It was as if the Rookery possessed a centripetal force pulling people into, and then holding them within, its vortex. This, in itself, is not surprising; as Ackroyd notes, one distinctive feature of urban overcrowding is a reluctance on the part of individuals to stray far from their immediate habitat.[47] Despite itself, the rapidly expanding and protean shape of nineteenth-century London could also create lives of the most extraordinarily restricted geographical range. Thomas Miller's sentimental account of the earliest clearances of the Rookery in 1852 noted that 'many

[42] *The Penny Satirist* (25 June 1842), 13.
[43] Peter Ackroyd, *London: The Biography* (London: Chatto and Windus, 2000), 138.
[44] Harvey, *The Enigma of Capital*, 152.
[45] Beames, *The Rookeries of London*, 26.
[46] Green, *People of the Rookery*, 31.
[47] Ackroyd, *London: The Biography*, 139.

of the inhabitants who were then old were born in those tumble-down houses, then doomed to stand no longer. There they had tended the sick couch, and through those dilapidated doorways carried out their dead; smiles and tears had brightened and fallen in those apartments, which to them bore the endearing name of home'.[48]

The redevelopment of the Rookery area was slow and executed in a piecemeal fashion. Even so, by 1846 the demolition and clearances were so well advanced that only a part of what had originally been considered the Rookery proper, the tight network of alleys and passages at its heart, remained. In 1847 the construction of New Oxford Street, linking Holborn with Oxford Street, was finished, sweeping away much of what lingered. Despite the ambition of the project it would prove to be an incomplete solution as much of the Irish immigrant population simply moved slightly further south to the Seven Dials and Endell Street areas. As Miller noted in his familiar style:

> True, the wedge has been driven into the rotten heart of the old Rookery of St. Giles's, and New Oxford-street has sprung up from the corruption; but what has become of the inhabitants who battened on the core of the decayed tree? Like a nest of ants, they are turned loose to overrun other neighbourhoods. The new houses and splendid streets which have risen above the old sites of sorrow, misery, and wretchedness, have but driven them from their ancient haunts, and compelled them to seek shelter in other quarters, where the poverty-stricken populace.[49]

In fact, the commercial redevelopment of the area proved to be financially disastrous for its investors. The enduring proximity of ghettoized poverty made the new retail outlets an unattractive prospect and the grandest part of the development, the 'Royal Bazaar', was declared bankrupt in 1854.[50] This was not the only unforeseen problem caused by the population relocation. For instance, in 1855 an appeal was made to the Marylebone Vestry to provide more police on the streets as a 'large number of lazy idle boys, belonging to families who came from the St Giles rookery' had 'infested Portland-town'.[51] Similarly pathological images were deployed by the *Morning Post*, which referred to the presence of Irish people from 'the old broken-up establishment of Saint Giles' in the normally pleasant aspect of Kensington High Street as a 'sore' and an 'infection'. 'The naked feet of the children and the ragged and dissolute looks of men and women present a painful contrast to the general decency', it continued.[52] Cast adrift from the Rookery, the inhabitants scattered to wherever they could find space elsewhere in the city, often settling in other predominantly Irish areas such as Bermondsey and in the process exacerbating what were already serious problems of overcrowding in their new neighbourhoods. As Engels noted in 1872, 'the breeding places of disease, the infamous holes and cellars in which the capitalist mode of production confines our workers night after night, are not abolished; they are merely

---

[48] Miller, *Picturesque Sketches of London Past and Present*, 236.
[49] Ibid., 229.
[50] Jerry White, *London in the Nineteenth Century: 'A Human Awful Wonder of God'* (London: Random House, 2016), 32.
[51] *The Morning Chronicle* (23 July 1855), 3.
[52] *The Morning Post* (5 September 1853), 3.

shifted elsewhere! The same economic necessity that produced them in the first place, produces them in the next place'.[53] Perhaps predictably, the demolition of the Rookery did not lead to the hoped-for transformation of the St Giles area itself. In 1863, the *Morning Post* reported on an 'atrocious murder' on the corner of Endell Street and noted the proximity of the crime to the area 'what was formerly known as the old St Giles's "Rookery"', which is inhabited by costermongers and the very poorest class of Irish'.[54] Church Lane itself, the heart of what had been the Rookery proper, also remained a benighted spot well in the 1870s. In 1874 Walter Thornbury noted that, 'of all the dark and dismal thoroughfares in the parish of St. Giles's, or, indeed, in the great wilderness of London', Church Lane remained exceptionally squalid. 'Its condition is a disgrace to the great city, and to the parish to which it belongs', he concluded.[55] Partly because of the need to keep Irish workers close to their major sources of employment, such as portering in Covent Garden market and scene-shifting in the theatres of the west end, there was protracted resistance to the redevelopment of the area. Even in the mid-1890s the *Graphic* referred to the 'disestablishment of rookeries' when outlining plans to clear the 'densely populated, squalid, and terribly insanitary area', east of Drury Lane in preparation for the building of Kingsway's grand boulevard.[56]

Other areas adjacent to the Irish rookery, around Seven Dials and Drury Lane, were also predominantly Irish, and likewise infamous for their economic deprivation. The area known as Wild Court, for instance, was, by any standard, a place of appalling living conditions (see Figure 1). In 1854 Lord Shaftesbury's 'Society for Improving the Condition of the Labouring Classes' inspected the area prior to a planned renovation and found 'thirteen rickety ten-room houses that together held more than a thousand people. The gutters, which flowed uncovered through garret rooms, were used as sewers; in the mornings backyards flowed six inches deep in filth'.[57] An 1852 lecture by the Reverend Samuel Garratt placed at least part of the blame for this overcrowding on the Irish tradition of hospitality. He observed that new arrivals from Ireland would never be turned away if a spare corner for them to lodge could be found, adding that:

> you must not suppose that this wretched way of living is felt by them to be uncomfortable. They have no taste for anything different. The misery of an Irish hovel is proverbial, and though I think that some of them do miss the hills and the valleys outside, yet the accommodation inside is not worse than they have been accustomed to. Their habits are set immeasurably lower, as far as comforts and decencies of life are concerned, than those of our English poor.[58]

[53] Harvey, *The Enigma of Capital*, 177.
[54] *The Morning Post* (13 April 1863), 6.
[55] Walter Thornbury, 'Chapter XXVI, St Giles-in-the-Fields', in *Old and New London*, Vol. 3 (London: Cassell, Petter and Galpin, 1878), 202.
[56] *The Graphic* (12 October 1895), 4.
[57] Lees, *Exiles of Erin*, 75.
[58] Samuel Garratt, 'The Irish in London. A Lecture. Delivered on Monday, 6 December 1852, at the Music Hall Store Street by the Rev Samuel Garratt, B.A. Minister of Trinity Church, Little Queen Street, Lincoln's-Inn-Fields' (London: Sampson Low and Son, 1853), 189–90.

Figure 1 Wild Court, off Great Wild Street, Drury Lane, 1855.

Despite Garratt's supercilious tone, his account provides us with another glimpse of that immediate post-Famine generation of Irish migrants, anxious to flee an island that had dealt them catastrophe, but with no material resource to help them negotiate their changed reality. The commitment to hospitality notwithstanding, this wave of migration also caused social tension within these Irish communities. As he wrote:

An Irish man on his first arrival in London is called in the language of the courts 'a Greek'. When he has eaten his first Christmas dinner he goes by the name of Irishman, but his children born in this metropolis are termed 'Cockneys'. Between the Irish and 'Cockneys' there exists a most decided animosity, even greater than that subsisting between either of these two classes and the English.[59]

Garratt had been appointed minister at Trinity Church in St Giles-in-the-Fields in 1850 and held the position for sixteen years. His ambition in the church was notable and would not go unrewarded; he would eventually leave St Giles for a parish in Ipswich and in 1895 became the canon of Norwich. Garratt's first parish, however, was adjacent to notorious slums on Little Queen Street, an area which was swept away in the redevelopment that culminated in the construction of Kingsway in the early 1900s. Such was Garratt's zeal that it was the very deprivation of St Giles that excited him about his slum posting. 'It was just what I wanted', he recorded, 'a church in one of the worst parts of London, with a district of 15,000 souls. It was just what, if I had sought for a sphere, I should have desired, and it came direct from God'.[60] Garratt, then, exemplifies the type of philanthropist and charity worker of the period who was, in Koven's arresting definition, 'deeply invested in the titillating squalor of the slums, which they used as stages upon which they enacted emancipatory experiments in reimagining themselves'.[61] Certainly his talent for self-promotion burned as brightly as his evangelism. He made the conversion of slum-dwelling Irish Catholics in his parish one of his most urgent tasks. As numerous entries in his diary record, these expeditions frequently did not go to plan:

> July 23 1856 – I have been preaching in the open in Great Wild Street ... A great crowd assembled ... began to throw stones, some of which hit my face, but did not hurt me. Threw dust at me. At last I was obliged to move away ... went slowly up Wild Court after making ineffectual attempts to quiet them. A little boy went with me and said, 'Please Mr Garratt tell me some more'. ... Two young men came up to me and said I had acted very unwisely in going down Wild Court as the whole mob was coming after me. ... By the time I reached Great Queen Street I was surrounded by them. At last I went into Gregory's shop and a Police Inspector dispersed them.[62]

Garratt's daughter, Evelyn, records that it was common 'to see my father arrive home with his hat battered in and his coat torn. But the work was not in vain'.[63]

---

[59] Garratt, 'The Irish in London. A Lecture', 188.
[60] Evelyn R. Garratt, *Life and Personal Recollections of Samuel Garratt* (London: James Nisbet and Co., 1908), 37.
[61] Koven, *Slumming*, 5.
[62] Garratt, *Life and Personal Recollections of Samuel Garratt*, 39–40.
[63] Ibid., 40. In fact Koven notes that during this time evangelists in London were often attacked while attempting to disseminate their message and that it was a danger they frequently liked to emphasize in accounts of their activities (Koven, *Slumming*, 111).

Ultimately any understanding of the complexity of the Rookery as a site of Irish settlement is travestied if it is considered only in terms of its mute resentments, or simply as a suitable case for social and religious reform. Indeed, alongside those accounts of Rookery life that saw only its desolation and the necessity of immediate demolition, there were counter-narratives which indicate that other attitudes and sensibilities were at work. Social rites such as weddings, christenings and funerals were especially significant in establishing cohesion and a sense of the Rookery's communal identity. According to a report from 1874, Rookery funerals 'were attended by hundreds and thousands of people, already inflamed with the spirits consumed in "waking" the corpse, and they were followed by faction fights on such a large scale that the soldiers had occasionally to be sent for to restore order'.[64] Of equal importance was the celebration of Ireland's national day; an extraordinary story from the *Era* in 1841 reported that on St Patrick's Day:

> Precisely as St Giles's Church struck twelve o'clock, a motley group of men, women, and boys, with their hats decorated with shamrock, issued forth from the Rookery, St Giles, preceded by a band of music, proceeded up Oxford-street and Regent-street into Piccadilly, and on to Hyde Park-corner, where they met, according to annual custom, their devoted saint, and returned in the same order to St. Giles's where they welcomed St. Patrick with whiskey of real Irish production.[65]

This performance of an identity position is notable, not least because it represents an early manifestation of what would become a significant tradition of Irish parading in London. But it also constituted a rare moment when the Rookery, which, inward-looking by habit and preference, chose to face outwards to the rest of the city. As such it acts as a powerful riposte to the vision of the St Giles Rookery as a place of mere isolation and brutality, the 'crowd of foul existence that crawls in and out of gaps in walls and boards; and coils itself to sleep in maggot numbers', fictionalized by Charles Dickens (who had toured the Rookery with a police escort in 1850) as 'Tom-All-Alone's' in *Bleak House* in 1853.[66]

It is because of such moments that we can argue that if the historical experience of the Irish in London can be said to have a spiritual and political *omphalos* then it resides in the St Giles Rookery. In its structure and preoccupations the Rookery was both a symptom of the dizzying imperial expansion of the city during the period and also, to some degree, an antidote to the brutalities of those forces in that it offered a degree of self-protection and self-organization for a vulnerable people. In these terms, those Irish that found themselves in St Giles were in important ways the agents of change, but also the deracinated victims of change. What happened to them following the protracted demolition of the Rookery and similar sites across central London is difficult to chart with precision. For some the experience of the Rookery would be

[64] 'The Irish in London', *The Graphic* (21 March 1874), 266–7, 266.
[65] *Era* (21 March 1841), 3.
[66] Charles Dickens, *Bleak House* (London: Bantam, 1983 [1853]), 204.

fleeting. They would return to Ireland when economic conditions slightly improved; some would disperse to other parts of Britain; and there were a considerable number whose time in the Rookery was little more than a stopover as part of a more ambitious odyssey to other parts of the world. Many, however, would stay close to the site of the Rookery itself. Some of those displaced early in its clearance ended up in Agar Town, a forlorn pop-up slum located between King's Cross and Euston stations in north London. Begun in 1841 and demolished in 1866 to make way for the Midland Railway's expansion into St Pancras, the properties were built of the cheapest materials on twenty-one year leases and, according to Steven Denford, 'were little more than huts made from bricks and rubbish'.[67] Agar Town had no drains, sewers or street lighting, and, hemmed in by a nearby canal, railway and gas works, it was disease-ridden and filthy. The area was inhabited by the displaced Irish as well as those newly arrived to the city and was, as an article by T. M. Thomas (aka William Moy Thomas) about the settlement published in Charles Dickens's magazine *Household Words* in 1851 titled it, a 'Suburban Connemara'. Describing it as 'a disgrace to the metropolis', the article concluded by observing that 'in Agar Town we have, within a short walk of the City – not a gas-light panorama of Irish misery, "almost as good as being there," but a perfect reproduction of one of the worst towns in Ireland'.[68] Like the St Giles Rookery, which it seemed to parody in distorted ways, Agar Town had its own distinct codes of behaviour and micro-economies such as turf cutters and caged-bird sellers. However such has been the eagerness to present the settlement as little more than an embodiment of Hibernian indolence and what Thomas terms 'a genuine Irish apathy' these have been little considered.[69] As such, its disappearance from the map was little mourned. Its inhabitants were poorly recompensed for the loss of their homes and were forced to move, with many of them settling in Somers Town, an adjacent neighbourhood which was almost as deprived as Agar Town itself. Such relocation was invariably difficult not least because attitudes towards new Irish settlement in London at this time were usually hostile. Following an influx of Irish settlers to Bell Street off the Edgware Road John Hollingshead remarked in 1861 that 'the whole place looks like a flourishing branch of some great central bank of costermongers, dingy brokers' shops, and Irish labourers. The Irish have a marvellous power of lowering the standard of comfort and cleanliness in any court, street, or colony in which they appear'.[70]

Unfortunately, in the absence of other sources, our knowledge of the dispersal of the Rookery Irish across the city is more reliant on prejudiced accounts such as Hollingshead's than is ideal. Indeed our ignorance about their lives is part of a greater historical narrative that has wrapped the poorest London Irish from this period in either cold disdain or (worse) silence. More positively, John Denvir's *The Irish in*

---

[67] Steven L. J. Denford, *Agar Town: The Life and Death of a Victorian 'Slum'* (London: Occasional Paper of the Camden History Society, 1995), 10.

[68] William Moy Thomas, 'A Suburban Connemara', *Household Words* (8 March 1851), 562–5, 565.

[69] Thomas, 'A Suburban Connemara', 564. Denford's *Agar Town: The Life and Death of a Victorian 'Slum'* and Steven P. Swensen's *Mapping Poverty in Agar Town: Economic Conditions Prior to the Development of St. Pancras Station in 1866* (London: London School of Economics Working Papers on the Nature of Evidence, 2006) are welcome corrections to this tendency.

[70] John Hollingshead, *Ragged London in 1861* (London: Smith, Elder and Co., 1861), 147.

Britain from the Earliest Times to the Fall and Death of Parnell from 1892, while scarcely more exact in its methods, was more enlightened in its perspective and provides a useful snapshot of the extensive range of Irish settlement across London at the end of the nineteenth century:

> The Irish are numerous in Clerkenwell, where, until recently, when the jail was pulled down, you could see by the new brickwork in the wall where the gap was made by the terrible explosion of 1867. In St Luke's parish, East Finsbury, you also find them in considerable numbers. In these two districts they are mostly of the class to be found in the Holborn division of Finsbury, already referred to. South Hackney, Bethnal Green, and Haggerston are noted centres of the boot and shoemaking trade, which gives employment to a portion of the Irish population in these districts. In Marylebone, North Kensington, Chelsea, Fulham, and Westminster, there are districts where the Irish and their descendants are largely in evidence. […] On the south side of the Thames you find small colonies of our people in Camberwell, Peckham, and other centres. In fact they are everywhere – even in places where you never dream of finding them, as any priest will tell you who has ever opened a new mission in London. […] Perhaps the densest mass of Irish is to be found among the river-side population stretching for miles eastward of London Bridge, on both sides of the Thames. On the north side you meet them in large numbers in Whitechapel, Wapping, Shadwell, Limehouse, Poplar, Millwall, Barking Road, and Silvertown, their chief employment being in connection with shipping. […] On the south side of the Thames the Irish population is largest in Southwark, Bermondsey, Rotherhithe, and Deptford, and mostly employed at the docks and the river-side. In and about Bermondsey you find a number of them connected with the various branches of the leather trade, for which the district is noted, both as employers and work people.[71]

Although Denvir's approach is impressionistic, his account of Irish settlement in the city still registers some significant tendencies. Most notably, the scattering of inner city rookeries was clearly a process of integration and accommodation with other communities, as the Irish adapted to new labour patterns and gained skills beyond the possibilities offered by ghetto life. The end of these settlements also marked the end of Irish as a language of currency among the London Irish and, concomitantly, the Catholic Church gained in importance as an identifying marker of political loyalty and cultural identity. Contemporary accounts indicate that there was a palpable energy about this movement. As Denvir observes, second-generation immigrants were 'increasing and multiplying in the huge city; not sitting down, as the children of Israel did of old, to weep by the waters of the Assyrian Babylon, but […] fighting successfully the battle of life'.[72] In short, if the experience of London for many Irish in the 1850s

---

[71] John Denvir, *The Irish in Britain from the Earliest Times to the Fall and Death of Parnell* (London: Kegan Paul, 1892), 392–4.
[72] Ibid., 389.

was that of an ethnic ghetto – the kind of cultural and imaginative restriction given material form by St Giles's foetid alleyways and windowless rooms – the increasing confidence of the Irish from this point onwards was matched by their urban mobility. An anonymous article in *Blackwood's Edinburgh Magazine* in July 1901 detailed the range of this new economic activity.[73] Alongside traditional Irish activities such as costermongering and flower selling – both of which remained popular – the Irish were increasingly employed as navvies on landmark projects such as the construction of Tower Bridge between 1886 and 1894 (although, according to our source, 'they soon fell off by scores, and were replaced by steadier men from the north of England'), as railway workers, and, less securely, as casual porters in markets and delivery workers.[74] These tasks were poorly paid and so income was frequently supplemented by seasonal work such as hop picking in Kent in the late summer. More stable employment was found in the docks on both banks of the Thames. There had been Irish settlements along the river for generations and many were engaged in skilled and relatively well-paid professions such as stevedoring. Alongside working-class labour, the article also describes the distinctive activity of what it calls the 'Irish "lower middles"', noting, for instance, the significant number of London Irish working as bespoke tailors and shoemakers in Soho.[75] Finally, it acknowledges the relatively tiny element of Irish London engaged in law, politics and journalism, although the cultural and political disconnection of this group from the main body of Irish London and its concerns is seemingly so stark as to not warrant further mention.

As these accounts indicate, while there was a notable decline in the Ireland-born population in London during this period – in 1851 it was something like 109,000, in 1871 it was 91,000 and by 1901 a total closer to 60,000 – those that remained were, in fact, increasingly visible through a combination of cultural influence and economic mobility. Moreover, there were also many more second- and third-generation Irish people living across the city. This group continued to have close links to Ireland through family, friendship, political affiliation and religion but was also alive to non-Irish allegiances and influences. These 'Irish cockneys' as they were often dubbed shifted the cultural compass of Irish London in significant ways and, as I will discuss in Chapter 5, were a vivid presence in the realms of popular entertainment and culture. They were also frequently considered to be a cause of serious social problems and were often scapegoated as 'habitual criminals', as Mayhew and John Binny's *The Criminal Prisons of London* labelled then in 1862.[76] Mayhew's explanation as to why this was the case was convoluted and cited, among other things, 'the extreme poverty of the parents on their coming over to this country, and the consequent neglect experienced by the class in their youth', 'the natural quickness of the Hibernian race for good or evil', and 'that extreme excitability of temperament which leads, under circumstances of want

[73] 'The London Irish', *Blackwood's Edinburgh Magazine*, 170 (July 1901), 124–34.
[74] Ibid., 126.
[75] Ibid., 124.
[76] Henry Mayhew and John Binny, *The Criminal Prisons of London and Scenes of Prison Life with Numerous Illustrations from Photographs* (Cambridge: Cambridge University Press, 2011 [1862]), 165.

and destitution, to savage outrages'. Perhaps more persuasively, he also recognized that poverty-level labour conditions prevented any form of adequate child care. As a result Irish children were 'virtually orphans in this country, left to gambol in the streets and courts, without parental control, from their very earliest years; the mothers, as well as the fathers, being generally engaged throughout the day in some of the ruder forms of labour or street trade'.[77]

As such anxieties indicate, the emergence of the 'Irish cockney' as a distinct social group with different habits and aspirations to the older Ireland-born generation was significant and it provoked something of a moral panic in London's popular imagination. 'Untrained to habits of daily work' and with no ability 'to control the desire to appropriate the articles which he either wants or likes, by a sense of the rights of property in others', the Irish cockney was deemed to be quite unlike his or her Irish parents (who, in turn, were increasingly regarded sentimentally rather than as a potentially dangerous enemy within).[78] Many of the problems caused by this group were attributed to what was diagnosed as their essential 'out-of-placeness', a sense that they were unsuited to modern urban life and were liable to be frequently overwhelmed by its intensity. As the *Graphic* noted in 1875:

> In London it is notorious that numbers of minor depredators belong to the class known as Irish Cockneys, and the experience of Irish immigration in the United States shows exactly the same result. The truth seems to be that Nature intended Paddy for a rural existence – in his own island (barring agrarian crimes) he is usually well behaved enough – but when he gets into places teeming with human life, high wages, and whisky shops at every corner, he is apt to lose his head. At the same time it does not speak well for the Roman Catholic religion that its efficiency as a controlling power should be limited by geographical conditions, and it should not be forgotten that the Protestants of the Northern Province, whether they emigrate to Liverpool, Australia, or America, are everywhere regarded as valuable acquisitions, on account of their general steadiness and good conduct.[79]

The casual sectarianism of this account was actually less common in the popular media at this time than might have been expected, possibly because the role of the Catholic Church in providing relief in Irish areas of London that other organizations neglected was well known and usually favourably regarded. Indeed the emergence of the Irish cockney was also a source of unease for those concerned with the welfare of the London Irish as well as those that wished to denigrate them, and this frequently took the form of anxiety about the possible effects of assimilation and inter-marriage. Denvir's patriotic survey of the Irish in London noted that 'thousands of the Irish have been gradually merged into the general population' and argued that 'this contact and intermixing with the English population has produced an undoubted moral deterioration – even among

---

[77] Mayhew, *The Criminal Prisons of London*, 403.
[78] Ibid.
[79] *The Graphic* (9 October 1875), 340.

those of purely Irish descent – during the past twenty years'.[80] As this suggests, any form of miscegenation was deemed to be potentially dangerous; alongside the threat it posed to the ideal of Irish moral decency, it was also thought to stunt physical vigour and cause a general deterioration in strength. As a report on the state of the London Irish from 1874 asserted, 'the first generation, fortified by the rural life of their youth, feel the ill effects with comparative lightness, though even they, unless very temperate, rarely attain old age but their children are far inferior in physique to their parents, while the children of the third generation, unless crossed with fresh country blood, can seldom be reared to maturity'.[81] Similarly *Blackwood's Edinburgh Magazine* noted that 'dock foremen make a broad distinction between native-born and Cockney Irish, to the disadvantage of the latter. A docker newly arrived from County Cork will discharge five tons against the one of the grandson of the immigrant of '46. The Thames air seems, somehow, to blight them between the critical ages of eighteen and two- or three- and twenty'.[82] This degeneracy was also a feature of the Irish cockney's leisure time which, the article asserted, consisted of little more than 'an occasional visit to the gallery of the Cambridge Music Hall, surreptitious games with greasy packs of cards in a derelict barge or a house condemned for demolition, and loafing up and down the street, cutty in mouth. [...] Cherishing a romantic regard for the green fields of Erin, they seldom visit Epping Forest, though it lies at their door'.[83]

It is not difficult to find evidence of Irish cockney activity that contradicts such hostile accounts. Indeed, far from the sordid cultural life described by *Blackwood's Edinburgh Magazine*, many of the second-generation London Irish were active social organizers and were energetic in pursuit of better living and working conditions. Irish areas were also distinguished by a strong sense of community and a commitment to mutual care. As Louise Raw notes, 'neighbours would commonly contribute money for funeral expenses, if the deceased's kin could not raise sufficient funds themselves. Neighbours loaned money and kitchen utensils, helped orphans to find jobs and lodging, and attended wakes and weddings. Newcomers were given a corner of a room in which to sleep, and were helped in their search for work'.[84] Typical of this collective instinct towards cooperation was the phenomenon of the 'public house concert', a fund-raising evening of entertainment intended to raise money for individuals and families who were in financial or legal distress.[85] More significantly again, in the summer of 1888 young London-Irish women – many from the notorious area known as the 'Fenian Barracks'[86] – were leading protagonists in what became

[80]   Denvir, *The Irish in Britain*, 392–93.
[81]   'The Irish in London', *The Graphic* (21 March 1874), 266–7, 266.
[82]   'The London Irish', 131.
[83]   Ibid., 132.
[84]   Louise Raw, *Striking a Light: The Bryant and May Matchwomen and Their Place in Labour History* (London: Continuum, 2011), 87.
[85]   'The London Irish', 128.
[86]   Charles Booth described the Fenian Barracks area: 'The worst streets in the District, worse than almost any in London. Three policemen wounded there last week. This block sends more policemen to hospital than any other in London. "They are not human, they are wild beasts". You take a man or a woman a rescue is always organised. They fling brick bats, iron, anything they can lay their hands on. All are Irish Cockneys. Not an Englishman or a Scotchman would live among them' (*The Booth Police Notebooks* B346, 30–3. Available online: https://booth.lse.ac.uk/notebooks/b346 (accessed 22 June 2019)).

known as the 'Match Girls' Strike' at the Bryant and May factory in Bow in the East End. Protesting at what were, by any measure, appalling working conditions (which included exposure to toxic phosphorous vapours, a punitive fine regime, twelve-hour working days and exploitative pay rates), 1,400 women joined the strike. The industrial action was galvanized by the support of Annie Besant, a radical journalist of Irish descent, who publicized their cause in numerous ways, most strikingly in an exposé about the women's working conditions published in *The Link* titled 'White Slavery in London'.[87] Despite her outrage (and indeed the manner in which history has credited her with a leading role in the management of the action), Besant was in fact sceptical about the likely success of the strike and favoured instead a boycott of Bryant and May's products. In fact, as Raw has described in detail, the strike was led by female workers at the factory, including such impressive figures as Mary Driscoll, who was of Irish descent and only fourteen years of age at the time the dispute commenced. The dispute lasted three weeks and became a *cause célèbre* in the popular press, casting in sharp relief some of the worst inequities of life in London's industrialized East End. Following a meeting of the strike committee with the Bryant and May directors on 16 July 1888, ultimately all the strikers' demands were met including an end to the fines and deductions system, an improvement in wages, the introduction of a grievance procedure and the provision of a canteen space so that food could be consumed away from the lethal phosphor.

The story of the Bryant and May strike is important in the context of British labour history as it led to the creation of the first women's trade union in Britain, provided a template for the successful conduct of later industrial disputes and showed 'that "unskilled" women workers could discipline themselves into an effective trade union'.[88] Alongside this, the strike is crucial to the history of Irish London as it provided a vivid example of what could be achieved through a combination of self-reliance and political mobilization. Indeed, during the closing decades of the century the London Irish were increasingly involved in labour organizations and progressive politics to the extent that Denvir could refer to them with little hyperbole as 'the backbone of [...] popular movements in London'.[89] Most significant among these was the prominent role of the London Irish in the successful London Dock Strike of 1889, a foundational event in the history of British labour. This instinct towards social combination would continue to be a distinctive element of London-Irish life into the new century. Indeed a productive way of understanding the importance of the Irish cultural revival as it swept across Irish areas of the city from the mid-1880s onwards is as a movement that sought to weaponize this deep-rooted instinct towards self-reliance by giving it a broadly political and national impetus. In short, the desperate necessity for hospitality that life in the St Giles Rookery demanded continued to resonate in the historical memory of the London Irish, emphasizing the centrality of endurance, resourcefulness and community.

[87] Annie Besant, 'White Slavery in London', *The Link*, 21 (23 June 1888), 2.
[88] Seth Koven, *The Match Girl and the Heiress* (Princeton: Princeton University Press, 2014), 78.
[89] Denvir, *The Irish in Britain*, 395.

2

'A secret, melodramatic sort of conspiracy': Fenian violence and the dynamite war

Our Irish skirmishers would be well-disguised. They would enter London unknown and unnoticed. When the night for action came; the night that the wind was blowing strong – this little band would deploy, each man setting about his own allotted task, and no man, save the captain of the band alone, knowing what any other man was to do, and *at the same instant strike with lightning the enemy of their land and race [...] In two hours from the word of command London would be in flames, shooting up to the heavens in fifty different places.* Whilst this would be going on, the men could be still at work. The blazing spectacle would attract all eyes, and leave the skirmishers to operate with impunity in the darkness.

'O'Donovan Rossa's Dynamiters', *The Irish World* (28 August 1880)[1]

On the evening of the 30 October 1883 there were two near-simultaneous bomb blasts on the London Underground. The first occurred between Praed Street (now Paddington) and Edgware Road stations and seriously damaged the windows and wooden frames of the heavily crowded last three carriages of a Metropolitan Railway train. Later inspection revealed that the bomb had also blown a small crater in the tunnel wall. Seventy-two passengers were injured, many of them seriously. Eleven minutes later there was a second explosion, two hundred yards into the tunnel between Charing Cross station and Westminster station. It is likely that the bomb had been thrown from the window of a moving train as it headed westwards. The device exploded on impact and, according to the *Pall Mall Gazette*, 'the walls of the tunnel were battered as if they had been struck by artillery'.[2] As there were no other trains passing at the time collateral damage was limited, but something of the force of the explosion was indicated by the fact that its shockwave passed along the tunnel in both directions causing damage and great alarm on the platforms of both stations. The windows in the platform staircases at Charing Cross were blown out and all the lights in the station and in a train that was waiting at the platform were extinguished. Westminster station, a quarter of a mile down the line, was less seriously affected, but the windowpanes of

[1] 'O'Donovan Rossa's Dynamiters', *The Irish World* (28 August 1880), from *Voices of Terror: Manifestos, Writings and Manuals of Al Qaeda, Hamas, and Other Terrorists from around the World and throughout the Ages*, ed. Walter Laqueur (New York: Reed Press, 2004), 117–18, 118.
[2] 'The Explosions on the Underground Railway', *Pall Mall Gazette* (31 October 1883), 3.

a signal box were shattered by the reverberations. Fortunately the explosion occurred underneath a vent through which much of the force of the blast escaped. If this had not been the case, it is likely that the damage would have been much more extensive.

Initial investigations of the Praed Street bomb indicated that it had been left on the track by the bombers just before the train arrived at the station. The train's guard reported that 'when the train left Praed-street station he looked out of the window as usual and saw a stream of sparks like the burning of a fuse under one of the carriages. Immediately afterwards he heard an explosion, and was knocked down insensible'.[3] Those injured in the attack were in the third-class carriages and were mostly artisans, shopkeepers and servants. One of the victims of the blast, John Hodnett, 'sustained severe injuries to the head and face' and recounted his experience to *The Standard*:

> Whilst laughing and talking with some of his friends he felt a dreadful crash, and was thrown violently towards the side of the train. The next moment the gas lamp was dislodged, and the glass as it fell cut his eyes and face. The window panels and the sides of the carriage fell in, and all was in darkness. The greatest consternation prevailed, and the passengers rose and commenced screaming. Had the train stopped a number of persons would have jumped out, and fatal consequences might have ensued. In the meantime the shrieks of the female passengers were heartrending. Many were bleeding and were terribly crushed, for the compartments were closely packed with people from the Fisheries Exhibition. On reaching Edgware-road Station the greatest confusion prevailed. The injured passengers were assisted out by the officials and others, and taken to the waiting rooms, but these places were already crowded. Surgeons dealt with the cases as rapidly as possible, and sent those who were the worst injured to St. Mary's Hospital, where he himself was eventually taken.[4]

George Patey, a carpenter, was also badly injured in the attack. He reported that after the explosion 'the lights of the carriages were extinguished, and total darkness prevailed, and he, together with a mass of living beings began struggling for life'. As he recalled, 'the suspense was awful, as no one could tell what else was likely to happen'. Another survivor in the same carriage, Elizabeth Lee, stated that during the aftermath, 'Suddenly a train passed on the opposite side and illuminated their carriages and a ghastly and sickening spectacle of men and women bleeding profusely from fearful gashes in the head and limbs was presented'.[5] Railway officials later discovered the worst affected of the compartments to be 'thickly splashed with blood, presenting a ghastly appearance'.[6] That night the centre of London was locked down. All available police were stationed on patrol around the two affected stations and at other major public buildings including the Houses of Parliament. The anticipation of further violence paralysed the city.

---

[3]   'The Explosions on the Underground Railway', *The Standard* (1 November 1883), 3.
[4]   Ibid.
[5]   Ibid.
[6]   'Terrible Explosions in London', *North-Eastern Daily Gazette* (31 October 1883), 3.

It was clear that the attacks had been carefully planned. A subsequent enquiry into the incident chaired by Colonel Vivien Majendie, a bomb disposal expert and the Government Inspector of Explosives, reported that the terrorist's intention was 'to produce explosions on the Inner Circle of the London Underground Railway, at points as nearly as possible opposite to one another and, as nearly as might be, the same time'.[7] Such careful synchronization alongside a willingness to deploy dynamite in a confined urban space indicated that the perpetrators were not only professional in their planning but ruthless in their intentions. The explosions took place along what was at this time the only underground railway in the world, and the choice of this target, combined with the technology contained in the improvised devices, spoke powerfully of the jarring juxtapositions of modernity. Certainly, the vivid descriptions of the fearful anxiety of the survivors of the Praed Street attack as they were trapped in their carriage awaiting rescue seem both universal and, indeed, uncannily reminiscent of the plight of those caught in the London Underground bombings of 7 July 2005, over 120 years later. As such, the symbolic logic of the bombings continues to resonate in a city that has subsequently endured many other terrorist attacks.

The attacks were part of the 'dynamite war', a campaign waged in Britain mostly by Irish-American Republicans organized under the banner of Clan na Gael and a splinter group, usually referred to as Jeremiah O'Donovan Rossa's Skirmishers. The war was (and, to a degree, remains) a contentious event in Irish history, principally because its instigators were willing to use extreme violence against civilian targets, and as such demonstrated a readiness to transgress established codes of martial honour that had previously been regarded by militant Irish nationalists as largely sacrosanct. Perhaps for this reason it has traditionally been afforded little significance in the history of Irish political self-determination, being considered (if at all) as aberrant or as little more than a slightly embarrassing episode in the greater liberation struggle. That said, compelling recent research has cast new light on the dynamite war and demonstrated that the technological and strategic innovation of the campaign and the manner in which this provided a template for subsequent urban terrorism across the globe makes it highly important as an archetype.[8] Moreover, while the war was limited in its scope, the terror that it provoked was real enough as the many references to it in the popular culture and literature of the time testify. The unpredictability of the attacks and the degree to which they appeared to disregard acceptable limits of ethical behaviour raised the temperature of Irish politics and strained relationships both between the

---

[7] Shane Kenna, 'The Philosophy of the Bomb: Dynamite and the Fear in Late Victorian Britain', *Postgraduate History Journal: A Collection of Essays Presented at the TCD-UCD Postgraduate History Conference*, 1 (2009), 89–100, 92. Available online: https://issuu.com/gearoid.orourke/docs/phcj_2009 (accessed 6 November 2018).

[8] For an excellent history of the campaign see Niall Whelehan, *The Dynamiters: Irish Nationalism and Political Violence in the Wider World, 1867-1900* (Cambridge: Cambridge University Press, 2012), for a discussion of its innovative nature see Lindsay Clutterbuck, 'Countering Irish Republican Terrorism in Britain: Its Origin as a Police Function', *Terrorism and Political Violence*, 18:1 (2006), 95–118, and for an analysis of the ways in which the campaign is represented in literature see Deaglán Ó'Donghaile, *Blasted Literature: Victorian Political Fiction and the Shock of Modernism* (Edinburgh: Edinburgh University Press, 2011).

Irish and the British and between different shades of opinion within Irish nationalism itself. These tensions were particularly marked for the London Irish who were in the unfortunate position of being victims of the violence while being regarded by many as potential collaborators in its creation. For this reason, and as this chapter will argue, the dynamite war would play a crucial, if intricate, role in defining the attitudes of Irish London towards the city as a whole.

The dynamite campaign was the result of a complex series of overdetermined events. In 1867 a Fenian uprising in Ireland planned by the Irish Republican Brotherhood (IRB) had proved to be a spectacular failure. Badly organized and compromised from the start by widespread informing, the insurrection revealed the limitations of the IRB's established military tactics and, for the more radical figures within the movement at least, indicated that a drastic change in strategy was required. Significantly this realization coincided with dramatic developments in the technology of explosives, timers and detonators. It would prove to be a potent mix. Dynamite itself, as Paul Avrich has noted, was 'cheap in price, easy to carry, not hard to obtain'. As such, it was regarded by many as nothing less than 'the poor man's natural weapon, a power provided by science against tyranny and oppression'.[9] Clearly the preconditions for further violence were securely in place. On 18 September 1867 two suspected leaders of the uprising, Thomas J. Kelly and Timothy Deasy, both Irish-American veterans of the Fenian struggle, were in transfer to Belle Vue Gaol in Manchester when the police van in which they were held was intercepted by a large group of men. Kelly and Deasy escaped but a Police Sergeant, Charles Brett, was shot dead during the attack. State retribution was uncompromising. Twenty-six suspects were soon apprehended and interrogated and, as a result, five were identified as 'principal offenders' and sentenced to death. Of these five Thomas Maguire was pardoned, and O'Meagher Condon's sentence was commuted, but the other three, William Allen, Michael Larkin and Michael O'Brien (the 'Manchester Martyrs' as they became known), were hanged from the walls of Salford Gaol on the morning of 23 November 1867. The injustice and cruelty of the executions – the hangings were botched by an incompetent executioner – galvanized the Fenian cause and revitalized the membership of both the IRB in Ireland and Britain and Clan na Gael in the United States. It also led to a number of sporadic individual protests in the years that followed including that of Arthur O'Connor, a seventeen-year-old Irish nationalist from London, who, in February 1872, scaled the fence of Buckingham Palace and waylaid Queen Victoria with a document demanding the release of Fenian prisoners. Armed only with a broken pistol he was quickly apprehended by John Brown, the Queen's personal servant.

The brutal fate of the Manchester Martyrs elicited considerable sympathy from the London Irish. A few days after their deaths a procession from Clerkenwell Green culminated in a mock funeral in Hyde Park at which up to 20,000 people were present. According to the *Illustrated Police News*, the crowd mostly consisted of 'the poorer class of Irish', but also present were 'English artisans', 'a large sprinkling of men whose cut of beard and hair, gold ear-rings, and peculiar bearing proclaimed them Irish-American',

---

[9]   Paul Avrich, *The Haymarket Tragedy* (Princeton: Princeton University Press, 1984), 166.

and 'a fair proportion of women'.[10] One of the event's organizers was James Finlen, a local Chartist activist and politician whose support for Fenianism through this period made him something of a hate figure for the London press. He was effectively hounded out of the city in 1869, but not before hosting a defiant 'Farewell to England' party at the Hall of Science on Old Street, at which he declared he would leave England 'without regret, because it was a country the capital of which was the home of the most infamous aristocratic mob that ever disgraced a nation'.[11]

Little more than two weeks after the Hyde Park protest, the Fenian campaign switched to London in spectacular fashion. On 20 November 1867 two notable Fenian operatives, Ricard O'Sullivan Burke and his accomplice Joseph Casey, were arrested in the city and placed on remand in Clerkenwell House of Detention to await trial. Such was their importance to the movement that a reckless plan of escape was devised. On 12 December a wheelbarrow containing a barrel of gunpowder was placed against the prison wall. The intention was to synchronize a large explosion with Burke's daily period of exercise in the prison yard and thus enable him to escape through the hole in the wall caused by the blast. Due to a faulty fuse, however, the improvised bomb malfunctioned. The Fenians tried again on the next day and this time successfully detonated the gunpowder. Unfortunately the explosion was far larger than anticipated. It caused a massive breach in the prison wall and destroyed a row of houses on Corporation Lane. Twelve people were killed (six of them instantaneously) and many more injured. The plan was an utter failure and, in fact, could never have succeeded as the authorities had been warned that an attack was imminent and so ensured Burke remained locked in his cell throughout.

The immediate effects of the Clerkenwell explosion for the Irish nationalist cause were highly negative. As Francis Fahy and D. J. O'Donoghue noted in their pioneering survey of 1899 *Ireland in London*:

> The explosion, occurring in the very heart of the metropolis, and so soon after the rescue of Kelly and Deasy at Manchester, created a sort of panic not alone in London but all over England. One thousand men were added to the London police, special constables were sworn in in large numbers throughout the country, and the provincial papers were filled with reports of wholesale arrests for Fenianism and of magisterial meetings to enrol defenders of law and order.[12]

The attack also lessened the sympathy that the British working class had for the cause of Irish independence – a development predicted by Karl Marx in the immediate aftermath of the explosion when he noted to Friedrich Engels that the attack had been 'a very stupid thing'. 'One cannot expect the London proletarians to allow themselves to be blown up in honour of Fenian emissaries. There is always a kind of fatality about such a secret, melodramatic sort of conspiracy', he continued.[13] Indeed, even the IRB

[10] *Illustrated Police News* (30 November 1867), 4.
[11] *Holborn Journal* (18 September 1869), 3.
[12] F. A. Fahy and D. J. O'Donoghue, *Ireland in London* (Dublin: Evening Telegraph, 1889), 50.
[13] Michael O'Riordan, 'Marx: The Irish Connection', *The Crane Bag*, 7:1 (1983), 164–6, 165.

itself would eventually condemn the failed rescue as a 'dreadful and deplorable event' in April 1868.[14] For these reasons, and despite the amount of consternation it caused, the Clerkenwell explosion gave the IRB a reputation for a certain degree of incompetence which, in the British popular press at least, fed off existing racial stereotypes. To some extent this interpretation of Irish terror as simultaneously both blundering and terrifying has remained within British culture since. That said, the significance of the Clerkenwell explosion on the subsequent course of Irish history should not be underestimated. Indeed, according to Lindsay Clutterbuck, 'its consequences continue[d] to resonate throughout the twentieth century'.[15] This is because it inadvertently provided a model for a new kind of political violence based not on the mobilization of traditional military tactics but rather on spectacular individual acts whose meaning was intended to be grasped (at least in part) symbolically. In short, it was noticed that while the Clerkenwell explosion had failed as a plot, its abrupt shattering violence had been successful in focusing influential minds on the matter of Ireland and its discontents.

For these reasons the strategy of the subsequent dynamite war was to generate spectacle and spread alarm through a series of carefully planned and interlinked explosions. As such, it was conducted with a strong sense of theatre, with the performative element implicit to the idea of an 'outrage' to the fore. The targets chosen were a mixture of the symbolic, the strategic and those locations where destruction could be maximized. This made the campaign, as Michael C. Frank has observed, 'the first of its kind in the history of terrorism'.[16] The war began on 14 January 1881 when the Skirmishers detonated an explosive in a ventilation shaft in the wall of Salford Barracks, Manchester. Attacking the site of the executions of the Manchester Martyrs carried an obvious significance and the outcome – the bomb killed a seven-year-old boy and injured three other civilians – indicated the ruthlessness of the new approach. Indeed, although both the Clan na Gael dynamiters and the gunpowder-using Skirmishers expressed a desire to attack property rather than individuals, given the nature of some of the targets chosen it is hard to believe that the possibility of loss of life was not at least weighed in the balance as an effect of the campaign. As such, and as Clutterbuck has noted perceptively, the activities of both groups crossed a 'conceptual Rubicon'.[17] Once such violence was deemed justifiable there could be no way back and it was only because of the unreliability of the explosive technology and a degree of amateurishness on the part of the Skirmishers that a greater loss of life did not occur.

The dynamite war came to London on the evening of 16 March 1881 with a failed attempt to blow up the Mansion House in the City. The explosion was planned to

[14]   James Lydon, *The Making of Ireland: From Ancient Times to the Present* (London: Routledge, 1998), 308.
[15]   Lindsay Clutterbuck, 'The Progenitors of Terrorism: Russian Revolutionaries or Extreme Irish Republicans?', *Terrorism and Political Violence*, 16:1 (2004), 154–81, 159.
[16]   Michael C. Frank, 'Plots on London: Terrorism in Turn-of-the-Century British Fiction', in *Literature and Terrorism: Comparative Perspectives*, ed. Michael C. Frank and Eva Grube (Amsterdam: Rodopi, 2012), 48.
[17]   Clutterbuck, 'Progenitors of Terrorism', 175.

coincide with a Lord Mayor's banquet, but the event had been cancelled at short notice because of heightened security fears following the assassination of Czar Alexander II. The bombers must have known of this cancellation as the building was deserted, but they proceeded with the operation anyway. The fuse was lit and the bomb was close to detonation when it was discovered by a policeman on patrol. His response was extraordinary. As K. R. M. Short notes, 'he hurriedly put out the burning wrapping paper and fuse only an inch from the powder, and carried the unexploded device off to Bow Lane police station'.[18] Despite the slightly half-hearted nature of this attack, it was soon clear that the intent of the campaign was determined, and for the next five years London would be targeted repeatedly. On 15 March 1883 there were explosions at the offices of *The Times* at Blackfriars (possibly in response to the newspaper's anti-Fenian editorializing) and Government offices in Whitehall, the latter causing very extensive damage in an area that was strategically highly sensitive. At this point the focus of the campaign switched to the transport network and dynamite, rather than gunpowder, became the preferred explosive. Following the attacks at Praed Street and Charing Cross in October 1883, on 25 February 1884 a clockwork-timed bomb, deploying a small revolver as a detonator, exploded at one o'clock in the morning in the cloakroom of Victoria Station. The damage was extensive, although no one was seriously injured (see Figure 2). The bomb had been disguised in a handbag, as were three other identical bombs subsequently discovered at Charing Cross, Paddington and Ludgate Hill stations. These failed to explode. As a report of the Charing Cross incident in *John Bull* revealed, the devices were ingeniously hidden in case the bags were opened prematurely. Finding his suspicions aroused by an unusually heavy 'shabby black American leather portmanteau', James Chamberlain, the clerk of the cloakroom, opened the case with a duplicate key and found 'in the right hand well, covered by some newspapers, a quantity of dirty white-looking cakes of an oily nature, 4in. by 2in., packed closely around a tin box in the centre, the box being about 4in. square, hermetically sealed with black sealing wax, pushed in between an old pair of trousers to fill up the space'.[19] The mechanism of the bomb itself was inventive if rather crude:

> The box, which was a small japanned tin box, contained a small ordinary clock of American manufacture such as is sold in the shops, and it had behind it a small pistol so arranged that by clockwork it should explode a cap. In proximity to this was placed a cake of a species of dynamite which is not known in this country, and not used or manufactured here. It is called 'Atlas powder'. In that cake of dynamite were six of the detonators for exploding dynamite, and loosely arranged about the box were forty of these cakes, amounting to 20lb. weight of dynamite. (Sensation.) It appeared that the clockwork had let off the pistol, but that the cap had missed fire in the midst of this dynamite.[20]

---

[18] K. R. M. Short, *The Dynamite War: Irish-American Bombers in Victorian Britain* (Dublin: Gill and Macmillan, 1979), 55.

[19] 'The Dynamite Outrages', *John Bull* (1 March 1884), 148.

[20] Ibid.

Figure 2 Drawing of a Fenian 'infernal machine', designed to explode in London Railway Stations (*The Graphic*, 8 March 1884).

William Lomasney, one of the bombers who had planned and executed this attack, was later 'blown to atoms' alongside two fellow bombers (including his brother) on 13 December of that year – the anniversary of the Clerkenwell explosion – when a bomb they were planting in a drain hole under London Bridge exploded prematurely (see Figure 3).[21] Although damage to the bridge was minimal, the huge blast was heard as far away as Highbury in north London.[22] The bodies of the bombers were never recovered although Clan na Gael paid a pension to Lomasney's widow. The loss of Lomasney was profoundly damaging to the campaign. Described by John Devoy, the Clan na Gael leader and a consistent opponent of the dynamite campaign, as 'a fanatic of the deepest dye' who 'never got heated or lost his temper', he had been a Fenian activist since the planned rising in Ireland of 1865 and was a figure of great authority and military experience.[23] Despite this setback, the ambition of the attacks became more pronounced. In the spring of 1884, Scotland Yard received an anonymous letter stating that on the 30 May Clan na Gael intended to dynamite a number of public buildings in London, including Scotland Yard. On that night there were explosions at the Junior Carlton Club and the London home of the Conservative MP Sir Watkin Williams-Wynn, both on St James Square. Damage to the buildings was significant and five people at the club were injured, but no one was killed. A short time later an explosion occurred underneath the headquarters of the Special Irish Branch at Scotland Yard in a public toilet. A hole twenty feet in diameter was blown into the side of the building and a nearby pub, 'The Rising Sun', was destroyed. Considering the extent of the damage, it was again remarkable that no one was killed or seriously

---

[21] John Devoy, *Recollections of an Irish Rebel* (Shannon: Irish University Press, 1969 [1929]), 212.

[22] Joseph McKenna, *The Irish-American Dynamite Campaign: A History, 1881–1896* (North Carolina: McFarland and Co., 2012), 96.

[23] Devoy, *Recollections of an Irish Rebel*, 212.

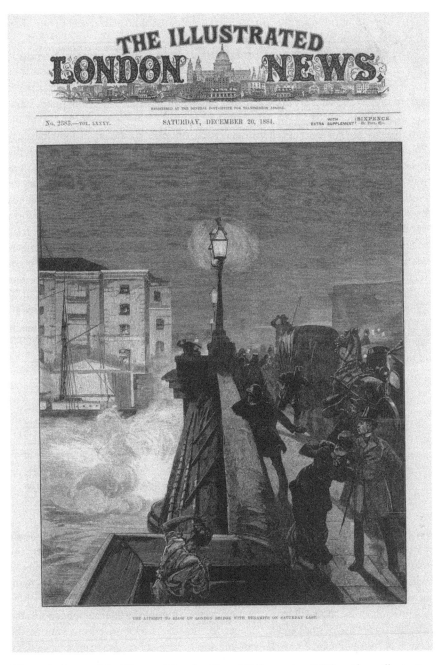

Figure 3 Cover of the *Illustrated London News* (20 December 1884), with an illustration depicting the attempt to blow up London Bridge with dynamite.

hurt. The next morning another unexploded bomb was found placed next to one of the monumental bronze lions in Trafalgar Square.

The final acts of the dynamite war came in 1885. On 2 January, in a repeat of previous attacks, a small percussion bomb was detonated on an underground train between Gower Street and King's Cross stations. The carriage was very badly damaged but no one was seriously hurt. Later that month on 24 January – a day that became known as 'Dynamite Saturday' – there was a bomb attack at the Tower of London and two explosions in Westminster Hall and the Commons Chamber in the Houses of Parliament. The terrorists posed as tourists (and in the case of the Parliament bombs, man and wife) and concealed explosives underneath heavy coats and skirts. In this way they were able to convey the bombs right to the heart of their intended targets. Again the meticulous planning of the event was to be let down by the unreliability of the explosives themselves. The bomb at the tower exploded prematurely and the bomber, James Gilbert Cunningham, an Irish American, was apprehended as he tried to flee the scene. Two women and two children were injured by the blast. The bombers of Parliament escaped in the general chaos of the explosions' aftermath, but the blasts themselves only caused slight injuries to two policemen.

The fear that this series of bombings caused was considerable and for a period, as Short notes, 'London was under siege'.[24] Clearly the security of the city could not be guaranteed, and it was gradually acknowledged in the popular media that the bombers were capable of striking at their targets almost at will. As the *Pall Mall Gazette* reflected in the wake of 'Dynamite Saturday', this made the police's task almost impossible:

> As if all the police in the world could prevent a dynamitard dressed as a woman carrying twice as much dynamite as was used on Saturday under his dress improver! Who is to detect that, we wonder? Unless we are to make a cast-iron rule that no persons wearing petticoats or dress improvers, or even a hunchback, shall enter any public building, it will be impossible to prevent the introduction of infernal machines into buildings under the very eyes of the police. An apparently *enceinte* matron could conceal under her apron enough dynamite to wreck the Abbey. How can police vigilance prevent that?[25]

Despite the vulnerable security situation that Dynamite Saturday exposed, the events of that day were also to mark a conclusion (of a sort) to the campaign in London. The reasons for this are unclear, although following the death of Lomasney – who had been skilled at importing dynamite into Britain from the United States – and the deployment of heightened security around the Channel ports, it became increasingly difficult to obtain explosives. Alongside this, Clan na Gael was ruptured by internal splits, while the security force's use of spies and informers became markedly more effective during the period of the campaign. As Mark Ryan, the one-time member of the Supreme Council of the IRB, noted in his memoirs, 'the vigilance of the authorities made recruiting for

[24] Short, *Dynamite War*, 208.
[25] 'Occasional notes', *Pall Mall Gazette* (26 January 1885), 3.

our organisation very difficult. Any person we approached would be "shadowed", and his private and business address noted. His employer would also be interviewed by detectives, and he might soon find himself in the ranks of the unemployed'.[26] However, despite these logistical difficulties, it is clear that the will to carry out further attacks remained. According to Sir Robert Anderson, Home Office expert on Fenianism and assistant commissioner of the Metropolitan Police at the turn of the century, more attacks were planned including further explosions at the House of Commons and at Westminster Abbey during Queen Victoria's Jubilee celebration of 1887.[27]

The dynamite war proved to be a debilitating campaign for the Fenians. Alongside the deaths of three operatives – including the exceptional Lomasney – twenty-five others were given long prison sentences, sixteen of which were life terms. Even by the usual standards of the Victorian penal system, conditions for these prisoners were exceptionally harsh, consisting of an unremitting regime of surveillance and harassment that threatened both the inmates' physical well-being and their sanity. This was described in painful detail in Thomas Clarke's *Glimpses of an Irish Prison Felon's Life*:

> This was a scientific system of perpetual and persistent harassing, which gave the officers in charge of us a free hand to persecute us just as they pleased [...] Harassing morning, noon, and night, and on through the night, harassing always and at all times, harassing with bread and water punishments, and other punishments, with 'no sleep' torture and other tortures.[28]

Clarke, an implacable nationalist and a future signatory to the Easter Rising, had been sent to London in 1883 by O'Donovan Rossa ostensibly to blow up London Bridge. The plan was compromised by informers and he was arrested in the city in April 1883 while in possession of a case of nitroglycerin. He was convicted of treason felony and sentenced to penal servitude for life. Clarke spent fifteen years in prison and was one of the last Fenians to be released in September 1898. His unwavering fortitude during this long incarceration demonstrated extraordinary resilience.

Aside from the human suffering caused by the campaign, the dynamite war caused significant tensions within Irish nationalism, between Clan na Gael and the IRB (which had always opposed the attacks) and between constitutional nationalists and those committed to the use of physical force. During this period the IRB was increasingly supportive of Charles Stewart Parnell's programme of parliamentary constitutionalism with the Irish Parliamentary Party, activity which the dynamiting of London with its subsequent effect on public opinion seriously compromised.[29] Other influential

---

[26]   Mark F. Ryan, *Fenian Memories* (Dublin: Gill and Son, 1945), 136.
[27]   Robert Anderson, *Sidelights on the Home Rule Movement* (New York: Dutton and Company, 1906), 126.
[28]   Thomas J. Clarke, *Glimpses of an Irish Felon's Prison Life* (Dublin: Maunsel and Roberts, 1922), 6–7.
[29]   Although the discovery of a huge IRB arms cache in May 1882 in a stable at 99 St John's Road, Clerkenwell suggests the organization was also prepared for violence on a large scale if necessary. The cache consisted of 70–80,000 rounds of ammunition, 400 rifles with stocks marked with the shamrock, bayonets and sixty revolvers (Short, *The Dynamite War*, 92–3).

voices within Irish Republicanism also spoke out against the war. John O'Leary, the veteran Fenian leader exiled in Paris, denounced the attacks in London on the basis of their 'inexpediency and criminal character', while for another great Fenian, James Stephens, the dynamite war was a flat contradiction of his ideal of armed revolution. As such, he claimed that it would lead to 'the certain death of revolutionary agitation during the present generation, and perhaps forever'.[30] For the one-time Fenian and Home Rule League MP John O'Connor Power, the war represented a failure of basic ethics. 'It was impossible to find language to express adequately the mingled feeling of shame and indignation, of humiliation and horror with which these atrocious crimes were regarded by all true Irishmen', he declaimed at a meeting in Vauxhall in south London in February 1885.[31] Those closer to the campaign also expressed doubts; Devoy opposed the dynamite strategy from the beginning and even operatives such as Lomasney would on occasion question its legitimacy. As this indicates, for the broad constituency of Irish nationalism as a whole, one of the outcomes of the war was to starkly demarcate where individual ethical boundaries lay. This, in turn, brought an ideological clarity to internal debates about strategy that was not always welcome.

The war also hardened political attitudes in Britain and encouraged the spread of anti-Irish sentiment in the media. As *The Standard* thundered on 26 January 1885: 'These are not the deeds in which an Emmett or a Fitzgerald would take pride. No Irish maiden would break her heart for the sneaking wretch who creeps about in woman's clothes to commit an outrage which kills the innocent, and runs away himself in safety.'[32] Satirical magazines were similarly brusque in their judgement. 'The Irish Terror in London', an article in London's *Funny Folks* from 1883, prophesized that the war would escalate to include such acts as 'the blowing up of the Nelson column', an attempt 'to shoot Mr. Gladstone with an airgun, during his walk across St James's Park', 'the burning of Madame Tussaud's, and the houghing of the Temple Bar Griffin'. As a result, it continued, newspapers 'preached a crusade against the Celtic inhabitants of London, and fearful scenes were enacted in the Irish quarters about Drury-lane and the Seven Dials. The tocsin pealed from the churches of St. Mary-le-Strand and St. Giles, and the hands of the metropolis were red with Hibernian gore'.[33] So barbed was the humour of the piece that it was ultimately difficult to tell whether *Funny Folks* would have objected to such genocide or not. Indeed, the magazine's dislike of the bombers intensified as the campaign continued until it reached a point where it began devising sadistic revenge fantasies of extermination:

As for the Dynamiters – well, the rule of doing to them as they would do to you might be followed with advantage. Any one of them caught with infernal machines in their possession should be secured on a harmless-looking box, containing an explosive compound, and with one of their clockwork adjustments to fire it. The

[30] 'Irish Agitators in Paris: Their Views on the Dynamite Warfare', *The New York Times* (22 April 1884), 3.
[31] 'District news', *The York Herald* (2 February 1885), 4.
[32] *The Standard* (26 January 1885), 5.
[33] 'The Irish Terror in London', *Funny Folks* (31 March 1883), 98.

time to which it would be set should be unknown to him. He would then have the privilege of sitting in a state of expectation for an uncertain period, cheered by a hope that the works *might* fail in their object, as they had done in some instances at the London railway stations. Such a mode of execution could not be considered a-bomb-inable as too violent a punishment. We blew men from guns during the Indian Mutiny, and the mode now suggested for the Dynamiter would be comparatively mild, as it would merely be giving him 'a good blowing up', and letting him go – say, to use an Irish term – to smithereens![34]

Other than provoking such viciousness the dynamite war scarcely achieved any significant purpose, although it can be argued that the fear it instilled in London kept the cause of radical Ireland somewhere near the forefront of political life. For a period, as the Fenian terrorist and leader of the 'Invincibles' Patrick Tynan recalls with only slight exaggeration, 'hotels were emptied of pleasure-seeking strangers, who feared to remain in a city that was practically in a state of siege, fearing that possibly the buildings they sojourned in might be blown up over their heads. Underground railway travel became risky, and the mysterious dread of unseen danger unhinged society'.[35] Alongside this the war forced a division between those in London who claimed Irishness and those that did not. Indeed, this was one of Rossa's intentions in mobilizing his Skirmishers in Britain in the first place. As Niall Whelehan has argued, the Skirmisher's campaign was to be of a scale 'sizeable enough to ignite a nativist backlash against the Irish population in Britain' with the aim of igniting a greater revolutionary conflict.[36] This was also predicted by Lomasney prior to the war's onset, who 'was deeply concerned about the terrible revenge which would be exacted upon the Irish living in England if such a campaign took place'.[37] A cartoon in *Moonshine*, a humorous London periodical that was usually conservative in its politics, captured something of the menace of this possibility in April 1884. Titled 'An Address to the Irish in England', it featured John Bull equipped with tar and feathers addressing a group of middle-class Irishmen (one holding an edition of the *Freeman's Journal*), while in the background a simian-featured dynamitard is led away by the police (see Figure 4). 'YOU do not dynamite me, you say. But the point is, does a single one of you raise his voice against the dynamiters? You live among us, share our work, accept our wages – are you going to speak soon, or will tar and feathers have to?' he threatens his audience.[38] *Punch* magazine was more perspicacious, seeking to reassure what it termed 'London Irish Working Men' in February 1885 that British retribution for the dynamite war would not be visited on them:

[34] 'The Man in the Street', *Funny Folks* (26 April 1884), 130.
[35] Patrick Tynan, *The Irish National Invincibles and Their Times* (London: Chatham and Co., 1896), 328.
[36] Niall Whelehan, 'Skirmishing, *the Irish World*, and Empire, 1876–86', *Éire-Ireland*, 42:1–2 (2007), 180–200, 185.
[37] Short, *The Dynamite War*, 57.
[38] 'An Address to the Irish in England', *Moonshine* (26 April 1884), 5.

It may surely be hoped that no employer of labour in England will so lose his head in a paroxysm of panic as to visit the atrocities of American-Irish miscreants on the heads of Anglo-Irish honest and good fellows. JOHN BULL is not the sort of Bull to go mad with fright, and behave with the unthinking fury of a frantic Bull in a China Shop. In the meanwhile, the Irish in our midst may well take note that the Dynamiters don't care a button what damage they may do them, whether by ruin of their means of living, or by blowing them up indiscriminately with their surrounding neighbours.[39]

Punch was largely correct. Alongside the seemingly random nature of its violence, one of the most important aspects of the dynamite war was that, despite its political rationale, it did not emerge from London's Irish community or respond to its specific problems and grievances. Indeed, if anything, the political tide of Irish London was receding from such extremism at this time and becoming, in Lynn Hollen Lees's phrase, 'domesticated [...] as extensions of the franchise gave Irish migrants and their descendants a place in the English political process'.[40] Most noticeably, this period was marked by an increasing confidence among the Irish middle class in the city, especially in the areas of journalism, politics and commerce. Such was the dynamism of this class that Irishness as a cultural (if not a political) entity was increasingly fashionable; a phenomenon that would peak with the Irish Exhibition of industries, crafts and culture at Olympia in West London in June 1888. For this class the dynamite war was little more than a source of embarrassment, as it constituted an impediment to their assimilation into wider London society. This period also witnessed significant cultural and social mobilization across the city among the (predominantly Catholic) Irish clerical lower-middle class. As I discuss in Chapter 4, while Yeatsean-focused narratives of the Irish cultural revival emphasize the establishment of the Irish Literary Society in 1891 as its genesis, a more plausible moment of origin for the movement – in London at least – can be traced to the founding of the Southwark Irish Literary Club by Francis Fahy, a civil servant for the Board of Works, in 1883, during the early years of the dynamite campaign.[41] The work of the Southwark Club was built on ideals of self-help, cultural improvement and social inclusivity and was broadly unsympathetic to Fenianism and the use of political violence. For these reasons it is hard to imagine it finding much in the way of common cause with Clan na Gael and its military strategy. Indeed, the key early ideologues of the revival were generally unimpressed with the campaign and particularly its seeming disregard for conventional codes of martial honour. Katharine Tynan, the tireless revival activist, visited London at the time of the bombings and in her memoirs noted the 'hostile atmosphere' they created in the city.[42] 'I remember wearing shamrock on St. Patrick's Day of that year [1884] in a London bus,

[39] 'Ireland's Worst Enemies', *Punch* (14 February 1885), 73.

[40] Lynn Hollen Lees, *Exiles of Erin: Irish Migrants in Victorian London* (Manchester: Manchester University Press, 1977), 233.

[41] W. B. Yeats, 'The Irish Dramatic Movement, a Lecture Delivered to the Royal Academy of Sweden', in *Autobiographies* (London: Macmillan, 1956), 559.

[42] Katharine Tynan, *Twenty-Five Years: Reminiscences* (London: Smith, Elder and Co., 1913), 131.

Figure 4 'An Address to the Irish in England', *Moonshine* (26 April 1884).

and being eyed by the occupants with positive hatred', she recalled many years later.[43] For Tynan, who at this time was, in her own words, 'very young, very simple, very enthusiastic, crammed to the lips with patriotic ardours, but just as much in sympathy with dynamite as any English person', Clan na Gael's strategy 'altogether departed from the ways of legitimate Fenianism'.[44] Indeed such was her distaste for the campaign that when an acquaintance (possibly the mysterious British spy 'Mrs Tyler'[45]) broached the subject she recoiled with visceral horror:

> Once she displayed to my amazed eyes a copy of the dynamite organ which was at that time being published in America – an infamous, ill-printed rag. She showed it to me as though on the edge of a confidence – that she belonged to the revolutionary party probably – and snatched it from my hands just when my first glance at it had revealed the loathsomeness of its contents. She was disappointed when I expressed

[43] Ibid., 117.

[44] Ibid., 134, 131.

[45] See Damian Atkinson's fascinating note about this extract in his *Selected Letters of Katharine Tynan: Poet and Novelist* (Newcastle: Cambridge Scholars Press, 2016, 38): 'Mrs Tyler was friendly towards those who aspired Irish nationalism and attempted to gather information for use to the British Government and also to entrap Irish nationalists. Apparently she acted in Ireland as well as England. She was mentioned as being a member of the Secret Service Department by Mr Healy in the House of Commons as reported in *Freeman's Journal*, 26 July 1884. There was speculation later that Mrs Tyler was a Mrs Lucille Yseult Dudley who attempted to murder O'Donovan Rossa in New York in 1885. However, nothing has been proved.'

my abhorrence of the dynamite propaganda; and after a pretended justification of it she dropped the matter.[46]

The extremity of Tynan's response was not unusual. In his *Autobiographies* W. B. Yeats noted approvingly that O'Leary, who was at this stage his mentor and confidant, 'would cast off his oldest acquaintance did he suspect him of rubbing shoulders with some carrier of bombs', because such activity contravened his deeply held sense of what constituted 'honourable warfare'.[47] As Tynan, who also knew O'Leary well at this time, observed, 'he was almost fanatically high-minded and clean-handed. He would have made war, but he would have abhorred murder and expediency was to him only another name for lying and dishonesty'.[48] Indeed, according to Marcus Bourke, 'so strongly did [O'Leary] feel on this topic that at least twice in 1885 he publicly referred to his old friend and associate in the movement, O'Donovan Rossa, as a madman'.[49] Part of Yeats's intention in writing *Autobiographies* was to integrate Fenianism into his vision of an evolving narrative of Irish self-determination but the zealotry of the dynamitards remained stubbornly beyond the ambition of this project. More generally there appears to have been considerable ambivalence on the part of Irish London towards the attacks, even if it was they who would endure the repercussions of the bombings through sporadic (although usually small scale) outbreaks of retributive violence. Indeed, the dynamite attacks established an atmosphere of living that would become the norm for the London Irish through much of the next century – the condition of existing between the poles of assimilation and prejudice, of being part of the city while also being held apart from it. As such it was their peculiar fate to be the target of both fetishization and suspicion, often simultaneously. As Fahy and O'Donoghue noted in 1889, as a result of the campaign the London Irish were 'more carefully studied, and their suffrages more sought after'.[50] It was this bifurcated existence that created the particular and easily distinguishable attitude that the Irish have held towards London since: the city is both a kind of home, a place of distinctive Irish settlement, culture and economy, and, at the same time, a site of strangeness, hostility and prejudice.

However, even though the political success of the dynamite war was limited, it is worth noting that it demonstrated considerable innovation in its methods. As Clutterbuck has argued, the operatives' 'strategy, operational methodology, tactics and targeting were innovative in both concept and execution and in turn they provided a blueprint for the conduct of terrorism that has not changed fundamentally for well over a hundred years'.[51] Most notably, they identified the propaganda benefit of attacking high-profile and symbolically significant targets and combining these operations with mass terror attacks on areas of high population density such as transport systems.

---

[46] Tynan, *Twenty-Five Years*, 136.
[47] W. B. Yeats, *Autobiographies* (London: Macmillan, 1956), 210, 100.
[48] Tynan, *Twenty-Five Years*, 131.
[49] Marcus Bourke, *John O'Leary: A Study in Irish Separatism* (Georgia: University of Georgia Press, 1968), 175.
[50] Fahy and O'Donoghue, *Ireland in London*, 7.
[51] Clutterbuck, 'Progenitors of Terrorism', 154.

Alongside this, the fact that both Clan na Gael and the Skirmishers were based overseas meant that it was more difficult for the British authorities to infiltrate their structures or to disrupt their established funding networks. As Whelehan has observed, they were 'manifestly transnational agents'.[52] Meanwhile, in an attempt to impede infiltration and informing, the operatives on the ground in Britain were organized around what we would now recognize as something close to a cell structure and thus they had only very limited access to (and therefore knowledge of) a restricted number of other agents. Finally, it is worth noting that in the realm of counter-insurgency the dynamite campaign led to the establishment of the Special Branch (initially called the Special Irish Branch) at Scotland Yard, the first unit dedicated to combating terrorism and political violence.

Given that the creation of spectacle was one of the campaign's primary objectives, it is unsurprising that the dynamite war itself became a product of popular media. London newspapers reported the attacks in exhaustive detail with endless witness statements, diagrams, maps and opinion pieces, and it is difficult not to perceive the extent of this information as a means of compensating for the one truly terrifying element of the campaign: its fundamental unknowability. Reports frequently described the attacks in the form of the then nascent detective story genre with the dogged Majendie usually cast in the role of hero. In turn, these reports were, to use Deaglán Ó'Donghaile's term, 'recycled' as popular fictions.[53] It is noticeable that in this recycling the dynamitards were often depicted as fearsome and yet also slightly ridiculous, a combination that naturally suited the excesses of the sensation genre then much in vogue. As the poem 'Guy Fenian' published in *Punch* in November 1883 put it: 'Oh pity the poor Fenian who has tried to wreck a train,/Or blow a public building up with dynamite in vain;/ He has wasted his materials, not created much alarm,/Done anything or anyone but very little harm.'[54] It was in these slightly contradictory terms that the war was also depicted in melodramas, comedies, sensation novels (of which Robert Louis and Fanny Van de Grift Stevenson's *The Dynamiter* of 1885 is the most well-known) and reams of political satire. It also offered itself as a topical and convenient plot device for more earnest 'condition of society' novels such as *After the Manner of Men: A Novel of To-Day* by Robert Appleton from 1894 and as a subject for topical theatre.[55] For instance, *Helter Skelter* by Walter Browne, a comedy performed at the Alexandra Opera House Sheffield in 1886, was a convoluted farce with a plot driven, in part, by a suspicion that a nearby jail is to be dynamited by Fenian agitators. The play featured the character 'Inspector Messiter' (a borderline incompetent version of Majendie) and used the notoriety of the dynamite campaign to bring topical urgency to what was otherwise a lacklustre venture. Of greater ambition was *The Nationalist* by J. W. Whitbread, produced at the Queen's Royal Theatre Dublin in 1891. A four-act political melodrama, the play was part of a series of Irish-themed historical productions staged

[52] Whelehan, *The Dynamiters*, 13.
[53] Ó'Donghaile, *Blasted Literature*, 3.
[54] 'Guy Fenian', *Punch* (10 November 1883), 220.
[55] Robert Appleton, *After the Manner of Men: A Novel of To-Day* (Boston: Franklin Publishing Company, 1894).

at the theatre that frequently provoked a feverish audience response.[56] *The Nationalist* combined grievance at agrarian evictions with the emergence of a new terrorist group, 'The Dynamitards', who lurk offstage as the unseen threat of physical force nationalism. Despite being, in Christopher Fitz-Simon's judgement, a 'fairly turgid example of stock in trade melodrama', the play was popular enough to be revived on a number of occasions, perhaps because, in the words of the Abbey Theatre chronicler, Joseph Holloway, it knew 'the pulse of the popular audiences'.[57]

Such representations indicate that the capacity of the dynamite war to create new and jarring juxtapositions in the fabric of modern urban life – its status as an act of modernity – was recognized at the time. And yet despite the immediate processing of the war as a form of spectacle, the speed at which Irish politics moved in this period in the wake of the Parnell crisis meant that it was soon superseded as an issue requiring urgent attention. Despite this, the campaign did not disappear entirely from political or cultural memory. Rather it would be alluded to with surprising frequency but in ways that were often encoded or deeply embedded in textual detail. In this way the war could be deployed as a useful metonym for indicating the extremities of political violence, even if it was a subject still too controversial to be faced head on. It is, for instance, a presence in Joseph Conrad's *The Secret Agent* of 1907 and an occasional shadowy threat in the Sherlock Holmes mysteries of Arthur Conan Doyle. More enticingly, it reappears in what is perhaps the greatest nineteenth-century Irish London text of all, Oscar Wilde's *Importance of Being Earnest* from 1895.[58] In this comedy the resolution of the drama revolves around the fact that in her earlier life a governess, Miss Prism, had absent-mindedly deposited a handbag containing her charge, the baby Jack Worthing, in the cloakroom of Victoria station – or, more precisely, the cloakroom for the 'Brighton line' as Jack is quick to confirm (this being the more upmarket part of the station). The conceit sharply satirizes middle-class ideas of what constitutes appropriate childcare in the period and the implications of Miss Prism's memory lapse propel the drama to its climax with an irresistible momentum. Alongside this, the moment also recalls the previous time that a deposited handbag in Victoria Station's cloakroom intruded into public consciousness: the handbag containing a clockwork-timed bomb that exploded in the early hours of 25 February 1884. As a result, for contemporary audiences the detonation of the play's comic climax had a very charged political fuse. Typically, Wilde is careful not to overemphasize the reference but it is notable that when she is asked to identify the handbag as her own, Miss Prism recognizes it in part because it bears the marks of an 'explosion' – although in this case, and as one would expect given her seemingly respectable status, it is the 'explosion of a temperance beverage'.[59] Such a reading reveals a further slyly subversive streak to the play – a work which was anything but the 'trivial comedy' he claimed it

---

[56] For more on this phenomenon see Cheryl Herr, *For the Land They Loved: Irish Political Melodramas, 1890–1925* (New York: Syracuse University Press, 1991), 9.

[57] Christopher Fitz-Simon, *'Buffoonery and Easy Sentiment': Popular Irish Plays in the Decade Prior to the Opening of the Abbey Theatre* (Dublin: Carysfort Press, 2011), 27, 115.

[58] Oscar Wilde, *The Importance of Being Earnest* (London: New Mermaids, 2004).

[59] Ibid., 142.

was – and accords with the way that Wilde elsewhere would allude to sympathy for the cause of radical Ireland while rarely quite stating it.[60]

It is in examples such as this that the dynamite war had an afterlife in culture. Despite the dubious legacy of the campaign, the indefatigable commitment of figures such as Lomasney and Clarke and their certainty about the integrity of their cause cast a long shadow. Indeed, the irreducible fanaticism they both embodied and demanded from others would become a constant and defining element in twentieth-century Irish republicanism. It is this imperative that James Joyce examines in his *Ulysses* of 1922, a work which, among many other things, can be described as an alternative history of Irish nationalism. Here Joyce returns to the subject of nineteenth-century Fenian terrorism in London at a time when it appeared to be almost entirely anachronistic and he does so as part of the high modernism of the 'Proteus' chapter, Stephen Dedalus's dense and allusive interior monologue on Dublin's Sandymount Strand. Attempting to remember what he can of the fragmented history of militant Irish nationalist activism, Stephen recalls his acquaintance with Kevin Egan, a fictionalized version of the Fenian Joseph Casey, in Paris. Casey had been one of the prisoners in Clerkenwell House of Detention whose attempted rescue by gunpowder-equipped Fenians in 1867 had been so badly mismanaged. On his acquittal he moved to Paris and found work as a printer. His brother Patrick was friendly with Joyce's father back in Dublin, and Joyce sought out Casey when he moved to Paris in 1903. Casey lent money to the perpetually impoverished young writer and Richard Ellmann notes that they would meet regularly for lunch at the Restaurant des Deux-Écus on the rue du Louvre. There, according to Ellmann, Casey 'drank absinthe without water while he talked about the blows that had been struck for Ireland'.[61] This recollection is lightly fictionalized in Stephen's recollection of Egan in *Ulysses*:

> Noon slumbers. Kevin Egan rolls gunpowder cigarettes through fingers smeared with printer's ink, sipping his green fairy as Patrice his white. About us gobblers fork spiced beans down their gullets.
> [...]
> The blue fuse burns deadly between hands and burns clear. Loose tobaccoshreds catch fire: a flame and acrid smoke light our corner. Raw facebones under his peep of day boy's hat.[62]

In an extraordinary moment of literary compression, Egan's cigarette morphs into the fuse that detonated the Clerkenwell bomb more than thirty years previously, yet, despite the implicit menace of this noir image, he is presented as an essentially tragic figure: one of the few surviving representatives of a political movement now rendered

[60] For more on what can be termed 'Hibernian Wilde' see Jarlath Killeen, 'The Greening of Oscar Wilde: Situating Ireland in the Wilde Wars', *Irish Studies Review*, 23:4 (2015), 424–50 and Sondeep Kandola, '(Re)Hibernicising Wilde? A Genetic Analysis of *The Picture of Dorian Gray*', *Irish Studies Review*, 24:3 (2016), 351–69.

[61] Richard Ellmann, *James Joyce* (Oxford: Oxford University Press, 1982), 125.

[62] James Joyce, *Ulysses* (London: Bodley Head, [1922] 2008), 3.216–18, 3.239–41.

obsolete, estranged from his wife and child, and, as Stephen dryly observes, 'unsought by any save me'.[63] As his life is now little more than the mundane routine of 'making his day's stations, the dingy printingcase, his three taverns, the Montmartre lair he sleeps short night in', so he is reduced to boasting to those who will listen of his past when he was a 'strapping young gossoon'.[64] Most notably he returns to the chaos and destruction of the failed prison escape when 'he prowled with colonel Richard Burke, tanist of his sept, under the walls of Clerkenwell and, crouching, saw a flame of vengeance hurl them upward in the fog. Shattered glass and toppling masonry'.[65] The image is vivid but it is also mythologized by self-regard, and ultimately little more than a symbol of the self-mutilation Joyce was inclined to see as ever-present in the nationalist narrative. If this were not devastating enough, Joyce makes clear that such retrospection also demands a price. In return for his hospitality, Stephen suspects that Egan wishes to 'yoke me as his yokefellow, our crimes our common cause'.[66] However, in this, as in the other aspects of his life, Egan will have no luck; Stephen has no intention of entering into such servitude. *Ulysses* recognizes both the determination and the futility of the Fenians' London campaigns, their manifest failures as well as their few inadvertent successes, and through this achieves a more complex, if untidy, understanding of pre-Revolutionary Irish political life.

The 1886 painting *Bad News in Troubled Times: 'An Important Arrest Has Been Made, That of a Young Man Named'* by Margaret Allen, (see Figure 5) the first female honorary member of the Royal Hibernian Academy, was another striking attempt to explicate the mysteries of the dynamite war and, like Joyce's later epic, place the campaign in its larger historical context. Depicting a distraught Irish farming couple reading in the *Freeman's Journal* of the arrest of their son in connection with the dynamite war, the piece responded to the inherent melodrama of the campaign in a manner similar to contemporaneous literary and dramatic representations. A narrative painting with impressive compositional balance, the pair is traumatized in grief while a kitten plays on the floor with a ball of wool the mother has dropped in her shock. Indeed, every detail of the image is freighted with meaning: a gun leans against a table, a ladder leads up to a loft and the stoic yet bewildered expression on the father's face as he gazes into the future speaks of further agonies ahead. On the wall in the background, and in balance with the kitten, an allegory depicts Ireland as a young maid about to be devoured by a (British) vulture. As Niamh O'Sullivan observes, 'the iconographic origins of this image are clearly Titian's *Rape of Europa*, and an illustration in *Punch* [titled "The Irish Vampire"] that was directly contemporaneous with the painting'.[67] The painting, then, declares its nationalism openly, but this is not the nationalism of the Irish-American dynamiters. Instead the image depicts the moment when the dignified self-reliance of a comparatively wealthy Irish farming class is shattered by

---

[63] Joyce, *Ulysses*, 3.250.

[64] Ibid., 3.245, 3.250–51.

[65] Ibid., 3.247–9.

[66] Ibid., 3.228.

[67] Niamh O'Sullivan, *Gorry Gallery Catalogue, an Exhibition of 18th–20th Century Irish Paintings* (Dublin: Gorry Gallery, 2008), 46.

Figure 5 Margaret Allen, *Bad News in Troubled Times: 'An Important Arrest Has Been Made, That of a Young Man Named'*.

events in the remote metropolitan centre and, as such, it becomes an image supportive of Home Rule. In this Allen's method was by no means as revolutionary as Joyce's, but it was arguably more pragmatic. As its title signposts, *Bad News in Troubled Times* captures a moment of both fear and possibility where a domestic crisis stands – or rather substitutes – for a looming national emergency. The afterlife of the painting adds further significance to this interpretation. In 1888 it was chosen as one of the exhibits in the Irish exhibition at Olympia, an event that, as the next chapter discusses, sought to present Ireland in an entirely positive, if largely non-political aspect. Among other less controversial pictures, the presence of a painting that referenced a recent campaign of Irish political violence in the very city in which the exhibition was held is notable. Perhaps it was permissible because Allen's image renders the trauma of the dynamite war as an issue of domestic family grief and so resolves at the level of aesthetic composition that which could not be resolved politically. In this way it could offer some degree for reassurance for the exhibition attendees while leaving the lives and motivations of the actual bombers in the shadows. As such the painting acknowledges the reluctance among the Irish middle class to countenance the obduracies of violent Irish nationalism. In the world of Irish London, specifically, this was a blindness that the events in the years leading up to 1916 would repeatedly and sometimes startlingly expose.

3

Hibernia exhibited: Irish London on display

*LIST-SLIPPER Makers and Learners Wanted: good hands, good pay. Apply 21
Blackmore Street, Drury Lane. No Irish need apply.*[1]

The first two chapters of this book describe a series of disaster narratives, grinding
hardships and acts of violence that, taken as a whole, form a story of nineteenth-
century Irish London that is in many ways disheartening. Although there were some
fleeting moments of encouragement, such as the victory of the matchwomen in the
1888 Bryant and May strike, Irish London was usually subject to the actions of others,
frequently lacked political and cultural agency and had only a limited sense of itself as a
collective. Indeed, at times even the idea of 'Irish London' as a recognizable entity could
not be asserted with great confidence. However, this state would not endure; during
the closing decades of the century the manner in which the London Irish began to
recognize shared experience, form identity positions from which politics could emerge
and adapt to what was often an abrupt and traumatized new reality was remarkable.
While the London Irish remained preoccupied by issues of status and reputation in a
city that could be deeply hostile to their presence, such grievances were increasingly
accompanied by a greater interest in matters of *self*-identification and a sometimes
angry rejection of the limited and prejudiced ways the Irish had previously been
depicted. For the London-based Irish comedian Tom Carey, for instance, this took the
form of a series of increasingly vociferous advertisements in the entertainment listings
newspaper, the *Era*, which declared, with ever greater certainty, the need for a new
authenticity in Irish performance to contest received national stereotypes circulating
in Britain:

> Tom Carey is not like those who think Irish comedy consists of appearing in a
> frieze coat and knee breeches, hopping about the stage and singing a few senseless
> words [...]. Tom Carey's dress, style, make-up, songs, music, jokes, dances, &c.,
> are his own and purely Irish. Tom Carey does not wear clogs, throw flip-flaps, or
> hand-springs. No grotesque fawning in his Irish sketches. Whoever saw an Irish
> peasant (male or female) wearing clogs, and tumbling about, as we often see them
> represented by our so-called 'Irish Comedians?' 'How Pat *is* represented.'[2]

[1] *Islington Gazette* (29 September 1892), 3.
[2] *Era* (9 November 1873), 5.

This strident assertion of national identity was a declaration increasingly sounded in popular Irish performance during this time and it was dependent on a notable self-confidence; Carey advertised himself as immersed in the matter of Ireland to such a degree that he became the embodiment of a national ideal. In this way, the 'Irishness' of his performance was derived solely from the revelation of his own inner resource. This was a markedly uncompromising stance and the insistent question posed by his advertisement – how should Pat be represented? – would become the crucial issue for Irish stage performance through the rest of the century and one that would be asked in increasingly forceful ways. We do not have an account of the specifics of Carey's act, but, according to the *Era*, he 'completely revived Irish business in the music halls'.[3] Clearly the 'grotesque fawning' that had previously been the accepted lot of the stage Irish would no longer do.

Following Tom Carey's lead, this chapter will argue that, while the idea of an 'Irish community' in London in this period would initially seem to be lacking in definition, ultimately it was willed into existence through modes of cultural performance that were contextually specific to the city and thus highly distinctive. These interventions could be textual (such as Hugh Heinrick's *A Survey of the Irish in England* from 1872 or Francis Fahy's and D. J. O'Donoghue's *Ireland in London* from 1889) or public (such as the Irish Festival at Alexandra Palace in 1876 or the Irish Exhibition at Olympia in 1888) and were not confined to one particular socio-economic group. Through this cultural production, previously inchoate Irish communities began to recognize that they shared a larger common experience and the idea of 'Irish London' was created as a meaningful entity for understanding social change and ethnic allegiance. Although the achievements of the later Irish cultural revival movement have tended to reveal some of the shortfalls of this activity – for instance exposing its blindness to the stratifications of class, its failure to account properly for the unique and complex status of Irish diaspora life in the city, and its tendency to fall back on a sentimental and erroneous view of conditions in Ireland itself – it still demonstrated a social and cultural endurance in the face of considerable hardship that refuses the condescension of posterity.

Any analysis of this activity is rendered significantly more complex by the unique characteristics of the London-Irish social context. As Gearóid Ó Tuathaigh has observed, 'the Irish in Britain constituted a somewhat peculiar minority' because they displayed two quite distinct types of minority consciousness:

> The first kind is that minority, usually immigrant, which seeks the maximum degree of assimilation and integration into the majority society, but which regards itself as the object of collective discrimination by the majority. In short, a minority whose urge to integrate is resisted. Secondly there is the European-type minority (based on religious, ethnic or linguistic grounds) which finds itself (through the accident of war or geography) in a minority status and which seeks to retain its distinctiveness and to resist assimilation into the majority community. The Irish

---

[3]   *Era* (16 March 1873), 7.

in nineteenth-century Britain [...] shared certain characteristics of both of these types, while fitting snugly into neither mould.[4]

This classification is slightly stark, but nevertheless it illustrates something of the convoluted dilemma which the London Irish were required to negotiate. In railing against discrimination and prejudice, occasionally seeking accommodation with the host community (an accommodation that was frequently rejected), asserting a distinctiveness based upon a national cultural inheritance and, at times, entirely and effectively assimilating into the fabric of the city, London-Irish identity can sometimes appear to be a contradictory and puzzling process of continual reversal and revision. Moreover, in important ways the cultural activity I describe in this chapter is not entirely coterminous with the expression of Irish nationalism, although such nationalism was frequently a major element. Instead, expressions of nationhood were filtered thought the complexities of an emigrant consciousness in which the homeland represented both the longed-for possibility of an eventual return and the site of an often-traumatic sense of personal rejection and failure.

The economic and social conditions of the London Irish were also changing. By the 1870s, as the long shadow of the Famine receded, Irish emigration to Britain declined and those that remained from the earlier post-famine wave were, as John Hutchinson and Alan O'Day have observed, 'older and increasingly tending towards assimilation.'[5] As a result of its sudden and often brutal deracination, many of the cultural practice of this group are now lost. Indeed, as Reginald Hall has noted in his foundational research on Irish musicianship in London, while there was 'limited activity in singing, instrumental music-making and dancing' and 'indications of some activity in households, kinship and friendship networks and the community', ultimately 'the extent and detail of the surviving rural practices of this immigrant population may [...] never be known.'[6] More positively, it is clear that from the 1880s onwards there was what Ó Tuathaigh terms a 'demonstrable improvement in the general status of the immigrant Irish in terms of both jobs and of living conditions.'[7] The London-Irish workforce was increasingly skilled and able to move into sectors such as manufacturing, the railways and municipal work that had previously been unattainable. With this they would play an important role in the city's nascent labour movement and were a significant presence in many trade unions.[8] In turn, these developments led to a general movement away from a ghettoized existence in the few remaining Irish slums

---

[4]   M. A. G. Ó Tuathaigh, 'The Irish in Nineteenth-Century Britain: Problems of Integration', *Transactions of the Royal Historical Society*, 31 (1981), 149–73, 150–1.

[5]   John Hutchinson and Alan O'Day, 'The Gaelic Revival in London, 1900–1922: Limits of Ethnic Identity', in *The Irish in Victorian Britain: The Local Dimension*, ed. Roger Swift and Sheridan Gilley (Dublin: Four Courts Press, 1999), 257.

[6]   Reginald Richard Hall, *Irish Music and Dance in London, 1890–1970: A Socio-Cultural History* (PhD thesis, University of Sussex, 1994), 56.

[7]   Ó Tuathaigh, 'The Irish in Nineteenth-Century Britain', 156.

[8]   John Hutchinson, 'Diaspora Dilemmas and Shifting Allegiances: The Irish in London between Nationalism, Catholicism and Labourism (1900–22)', *Studies in Ethnicity and Nationalism*, 10:1 (2010), 107–25, 109.

in central London to settlement across the city, with particular concentrations of Irish population south of the river and in the north-west.

Although the majority of Irish migrants coming to London at this time remained unskilled and limited to a narrow range of activities, from the 1870s, as Hutchinson notes, 'an increasing proportion [...] oriented to civil service and teaching positions in England (particularly London) because of the growth of secondary education and professional training in Ireland, combined with limited employment opportunities at home'.[9] John Denvir, writing in 1892, suggests that the catalyst for this was the introduction of the competitive examination system for the Civil Service, which led to an influx of Irish appointments and 'a greater proportion of them, perhaps, than of the other nationalities of the empire'.[10] Certainly, as R. F. Foster has noted, Victorian London 'was the magnet for generations of middle-class Irish *arrivistes* determined to make their mark' and this was especially discernible in the areas of publishing and journalism.[11] The reasons why ambitious Irish writers wanted to come to London in the 1870s and 1880s were compelling: the reading public in Ireland was small and often conservative by instinct while London, by comparison, offered a vast market, an established array of journals and newspapers, and a receptiveness to new ideas that could be intellectually intoxicating. One such, George Bernard Shaw, who moved to London from Dublin in 1876, articulated his motives for leaving forcefully: 'Every Irishman who felt that his business in life was on the higher planes of the cultural professions felt that he must have a metropolitan domicile and an international culture: that is, he felt his first business was to get out of Ireland. I had the same feeling.'[12] For Shaw, as for many others who made the move, this was a relocation without romance or sentiment: 'For London as London, or England as England, I cared nothing [...] but as the English language was my weapon, there was nothing for it but London,' he recalled bluntly. Others, however, were more enamoured of London's heritage. Francis Fahy, a major figure in this study, came to London as an eighteen-year-old from Kinvara, Co. Galway, in 1873 to work in the civil service and described the capital as 'the world-city of my readings and my dreams'.[13] His anticipation was intense:

> I was in the very heart of all I longed to explore. My readings of histories and novels had familiarised me with the London both of imagination and reality – Westminster Palace, the Abbey, the Tower, Ludgate, the Charterhouse, the Inns of Court. I already knew their position and appearance, and most of my early years in

---

9   Hutchinson, 'Diaspora Dilemmas', 108.

10 John Denvir, *The Irish in Britain from the Earliest Times to the Fall and Death of Parnell* (London: Kegan Paul, 1892), 399.

11 R. F. Foster, 'An Irish Power in London: Making It in the Victorian Metropolis', in *'Conquering England': Ireland in Victorian London*, ed. R. F. Foster and Fintan Cullen (London: National Portrait Gallery, 2005), 12–25, 14.

12 George Bernard Shaw, *The Matter with Ireland* (London: Rupert Hart Davies, 1962), 10.

13 Clare Hutton, 'Francis Fahy's "Ireland in London – Reminiscences" (1921)', in *Yeats's Collaborations. Yeats Annual, 15: A Special Number*, ed. Wayne K. Chapman and Warwick Gould (Basingstoke: Palgrave Macmillan, 2002), 233–80, 237.

14 Ibid., 238–39.

London were spent in roaming about its streets and parks, visiting the museums, churches and showplaces, and filling them with memories of historic or fictitious characters from the works of Ainsworth, Thackeray, Dickens and others.[14]

Fahy's romanticized vision would not survive entirely intact. Although London would always remain his home, the Land War of 1879 awakened his political sensibilities to such a degree that he would devote the rest of his life to the promotion of Irish culture in the city, galvanizing many future Irish revolutionaries in the process.

Alongside the civil service, Fleet Street was also greatly enriched by this new wave of Irish immigration. As Heinrick notes with a little hyperbole, by 1872 there was 'not a newspaper in London without its one, two, three and four Irish writers and Irish reporters on its staff – indeed, Irish reporters are not alone numerous, but are the best and the ablest who supply the daily papers with the Court and Parliamentary records of the day'.[15] Journalists such as Justin McCarthy (who had arrived in London from Ireland via Liverpool in 1860) and T. P. O'Connor (who came ten years later) were both deeply inspired by London's literary culture and would become influential figures in liberal and Home Rule politics during the final years of the century. McCarthy edited the *Morning Star* and wrote leaders for the *Daily News*, while O'Connor was subeditor on the *Daily Telegraph*, London correspondent for the *New York Herald*, and went on to found a number of papers including the *Star* (1887) and the *Sun* (1893). Both sat as MPs in the House of Commons for the Irish Parliamentary Party and combined nationalist beliefs with a deep assimilation into middle-class Liberal London society. The potential contradictions of these life choices were obvious and would become more marked as the century progressed. Little wonder, then, that both figures would be regarded with disdain by the many nationalist revivalists who came to London in the 1880s and 1890s, who viewed them as deeply compromised and essentially hypocritical in their politics.

Despite their increased numbers, London's Irish middle class remains slightly elusive in accounts of the period. This may be because, as Foster contends, for many writers and historians they are 'statistically invisible and ideologically unattractive', in that they were more prone to assimilation and further removed from the resources of a Gaelic culture that was still just about visible in the London-Irish working class.[16] Nevertheless Irish middle-class and aristocratic activity in London was certainly evident at the time, even if this was often only as an object of mild ridicule. In 1881 *Funny Folks* reported that London was 'full of Irish refugees, timid women, who have fled before the Land Leaguers, or have been despatched by husbands and fathers across the water to a place of safety'. As a result, the article continued, 'this influx of interesting Hibernian femininity will naturally exercise an influence on the fashions of the coming season', leading to such phenomenon as 'a run upon bog-oak ornaments

---

[15] Hugh Heinrick, *A Survey of the Irish in England*, ed. Alan O'Day (London: Hambledon Press, 1990 [1872]), 11.

[16] R. F. Foster, 'Marginal Men and Micks on the Make: The Uses of Irish Exile, c. 1840–1922', in *Paddy and Mr Punch: Connections in Irish and English History* (London: Penguin, 1993), 289.

[...] worn by all persons of fenny pretentions to *chic*.[17] As such satire indicates, the Irish middle class in London became more willing to self-represent in this period and were essential in the creation of large-scale cultural projects such as the Irish Festival organized at Alexandra Palace. In a similar manner, it is impossible to imagine more grass-roots phenomena such as the foundation of the Southwark Irish Literary Club in 1883 occurring without the energy of cultural activists trained in the civil service like Fahy and John T. Kelly.

Perhaps the most important account of Irish life in London from the beginning of the period under focus is Heinrick's *A Survey of the Irish in England* from 1872. A collection of articles originally written for the *Nation* newspaper to assess the state of the Irish franchise across England, Heinrick's work is neglected when compared to other nineteenth-century accounts of Irish life in London, and even O'Day, the book's most recent editor, suggests it is a source that should only be used advisedly. Nevertheless, despite its shortcomings its reportage is of value in that, as O'Day notes, it 'falls into a vital time gap between the flood of Famine era refugees and the second wave of Irish emigration consequent on the agrarian depression of the later Victorian age' and records what were a developing set of key ideologies and affiliations among the emigrant Irish at this time.[18] Heinrick, Wexford-born in 1831 but resident in England, was an enthusiastic nationalist and had been active in the amnesty campaign for Fenian prisoners in the 1860s, before becoming an energetic exponent of Home Rule. Described by John Denvir as a 'brilliant writer', he founded the first newspaper for Irish migrants in London, the *Irish Vindicator*, in 1871 (although this was not a success and closed after only four months).[19] His survey of the Irish in England, commissioned by Alexander Martin (A. M.) Sullivan, the sympathetic editor of the *Nation*, was his next project and would prove to be his major contribution to the cause of Irish Home Rule. Although, in many ways, a sentimental account beholden to many of the most insidious stereotypes about the Irish at this time, his central diagnosis of the maladies affecting the Irish in London was forceful:

> The prodigality of the landlord class and the poverty of the poor East-end outcasts are but evidences of cause and effect – the one of which must be arrested before the other can be checked. Till an Irish Parliament either holds out sufficient inducements to the Irish landlords to reside at home, or imposes a penalty on absenteeism, Irish wealth will be squandered in England.[20]

As this indicates, for Heinrick the conditions of the emigrant Irish in London were the inevitable symptoms of an economic and political sickness back in Ireland itself. The landlord class flaunted itself in London society, revealing nothing more substantial than its parasitism, while the Irish in the city's East End were sucked ever further into

[17] 'Hibernian Fashions', *Funny Folks*, 320 (15 January 1881), 12.
[18] Heinrick, *A Survey of the Irish in England*, xix.
[19] John Denvir, *The Life Story of an Old Rebel* (Dublin: Sealy, Bryers and Walker, 1910), 180. Heinrick, *A Survey of the Irish in England*, x.
[20] Ibid., 4.

the hopeless poverty that increasingly defined their life prospects. With this diagnosis Heinrick's is one of the starkest assessments of Irish life in the capital. 'There are thousands – tens of thousands of the Irish people in London alone who are lost – lost irretrievably. [...] Our people are crushed, physically debased, and morally ruined by the dreaded circumstances almost inseparable from their lot,' he lamented.[21] Heinrick did not deem the Irish themselves to be at fault for this state of affairs but instead blamed their association with the English: 'Everything good which the Irish in England have preserved is their own; their vices in nine cases out of ten are acquired,' the book insists repeatedly.[22] As a result, Heinrick's study argues strongly against assimilation and for the preservation of a distinctively Irish set of cultural attitudes in a manner that prefigures some of the de-Anglicizing rhetoric of the revival twenty years later.

Despite this pessimism, Heinrick's account balances his analysis of the dangers that the London Irish face with frequent reminders of the community's implicit cultural vibrancy, proclaiming that 'there is in London, as in nearly all the large towns in England, an immense force of Irish life, energy, and intelligence, which, if organized and united, would constitute a most valuable aid in accomplishing the national regeneration of their native land.'[23] Key to this potential was the energy of the city's Irish middle class and he argues enthusiastically for the political benefits that would accrue were it able to establish common purpose with 'the great army of Irish industry which swarms in the marts and docks, and whose voice is potent in the democratic council or popular assembly'.[24] As these sentiments indicate, in many ways the *Survey* was a propaganda piece for the Home Rule movement, and much of Heinrick's consideration of London discusses the prospects for the city's then rapidly growing Home Rule Association, which, as he reports, consisted of fifty branches, 'and the members to tens of thousands'.[25]

While the overall reliability of the *Survey* is debatable, elements of it are revealing. Most obviously, the text's very existence indicates that, while it is scarcely flourishing, there is clearly an Irish community that Heinrick can refer to; in other words, by the early 1870s an idea of 'Irish London' signifies as a meaningful term of social organization. Moreover, the survey provides useful information about the extent to which the Irish were deeply integrated into all sections of London's professional life. Although at this stage it was hardly mobilized in any meaningful way, the political potential of this grouping was palpable. Despite his rejection of any form of assimilation, it is also worth noting Heinrick's continual concern with the politics of representation and the manner in which the Irish community appeared and appealed to the rest of British society, an emphasis that was typical of pre-revivalist ideologies of national identity formation. In this spirit the book reserves its harshest condemnation for Irish journalists working on London newspapers who were willing to act as 'the mere mercenaries of the English interests – prepared to turn, metaphorically, on the spit their own kith and kin, at an

---

[21] Ibid., 28.
[22] Ibid., 129.
[23] Ibid., 4.
[24] Ibid., 5.
[25] Ibid., 13.

hour's notice at the usual stipulated prices of two or three guineas an article'.[26] Heinrick himself would not compromise in this manner, but, perhaps as a result of this refusal, the remaining years of his life were difficult. He died in poverty after a long illness in 1877 aged forty-six, leaving to his children 'little but the memory of a life devoted to the battle of Irish freedom', as one obituary observed.[27]

There were other indications of change in the manner in which the London Irish chose to self-represent at this time. By 1872 some of the wilder elements of the celebration of St Patrick's Day in the city – summarized by the *Graphic* as 'the temptation to tread on the tail of your neighbour's coat, and beat him to a jelly out of pure love and affection' – were coming under greater regulation or were replaced by more formal and respectable displays of nationality.[28] This was driven by the Catholic Church and took the form of a pledge (the 'Truce of God') which required abstinence over the period of St Patrick's Day 'so as not to have the anniversary of Irelands' patron disgraced by scenes of riot and debauch'.[29] Marking the establishment of a public holiday in Ireland on the Saint's day, a 1878 cartoon in *Funny Folks* titled 'St. Pathrick's Day by Act of Parliament' observed this transformation by juxtaposing past scenes of drunken violence with contemporary celebrations that consisted of nothing more riotous than a tea party presided over by the English temperance campaigner, Wilfrid Lawson.[30] St Patrick's Day was also the traditional date for Irish political demonstrations in the capital, a custom so firmly entrenched that when a year passed without one (in 1878) it attracted comment.[31] These rallies could be of a considerable scale – the *Morning Post* estimated that a Home Rule event at Hyde Park on the eve of St Patrick's Day in 1873 attracted 15,000 people from across the city – but they gradually declined in attendance after the 1870s and by 1882 had been abandoned entirely.[32] Despite this, interest in the commemoration of the day continued to grow, although the emphasis moved from politics to leisure. By the early 1880s the listing of Irish-themed events detailed in the *London Daily News* was remarkably extensive and encompassed nearly all areas of the city. The most significant event amidst these celebrations was an annual concert at the Royal Albert Hall, which usually consisted of military bands playing popular Irish music. Resolutely unionist in tone, this occasion encapsulated the extent of state-sanctioned engagement with Irish culture in this period and as such was the celebration of a national, if not a nationalist, day. Indeed, many years later such evenings would be pressed into more explicit national service, acting as fundraisers and recruitment events for the British war effort during the First World War.[33]

---

[26] Ibid., 11.

[27] 'Death of Mr. Hugh Heinrick', *Wexford People* (13 October 1877), 4.

[28] 'The Irish in London', *The Graphic* (21 March 1874), 266–7, 266.

[29] 'Patrick's Day in the Metropolis', *The Standard* (18 March 1872), 2.

[30] 'St. Pathrick's Day by Act of Parliament', *Funny Folks*, 172 (16 March 1878), 85.

[31] *The Standard* (18 March 1878), 2.

[32] 'Home Rule Demonstration in Hyde Park', *Morning Post* (17 March 1873), 2. 'St. Patrick's Day in London', *London Daily News* (18 March 1882), 3.

[33] 'Irish Concert at the Albert Hall', *Middlesex Chronicle* (20 March 1915), 3.

There were, however, other forms of Irish political identity which demanded to be heard. Most notably, a series of monster meetings in support of the amnesty campaign for Fenian prisoners held in Hyde Park constituted a significant landmark in the political mobilization of Irish London. The largest of these was held on 3 November 1872 when, according to the *Morning Post*, there 'could not have been less than 20,000 persons assembled', with 'Piccadilly and Oxford Street [...] thronged with people of all classes and both sexes hastening to the park'.[34] The article speculated that the gathering was so large because of four reasons: 'the strong appeal made to the working classes by the Fenian Amnesty Committee', the Home Rule association mobilizing the London-Irish community as a whole, the fine weather and (tellingly) 'the expectation of a scene consequent upon the anticipated interference with the meeting by the police'. Processions to the meeting originated from areas across the city including Paddington and Hammersmith, with the largest, representing the East End, from Clerkenwell Green. This parade 'was headed by a brass band, and accompanied by a number of flags, conspicuous amongst them being a green silk one with the inscription "God save Ireland," and carried by a young Irish woman dressed in green silk'. Similarly prominent was a large banner with the inscription: 'Disobedience to tyrants is a duty to God.' The composition of the meeting was heterogeneous, with the report noting many women, English working men, and, what it termed, 'higher classes' represented. The rally passed a series of resolutions including one which was noteworthy because of its determinedly internationalist perspective on Irish affairs: 'The treatment of Fenian prisoners, considered in conjunction with the Algerine-like rule of the Government in Ireland, and the treatment of so-called rebels in Jamaica and India, combine to exhibit the true spirit of British policy, and contrasts most strikingly and unfavourable with that of the United States of America after the suppression of a protracted and sanguinary civil war.'[35] Despite the anticipation of police violence the meeting was conducted peacefully, and at its conclusion the crowd dispersed from the park singing 'God save Ireland'.

Alongside its willingness to place Ireland's national question in the context of other international liberation struggles, there were a number of other significant aspects to this event. These include the participation of a nascent Irish labour movement including a number of female activists, the involvement of sympathetic non-Irish working-class marchers, a militancy that was at least prepared to countenance resistance to oppressive policing and, perhaps most notably, a high degree of organization. This ability to mobilize was important for the political life of the city as a whole. Indeed Denvir's study of the Irish in Britain observed that the 'Irish may be said [...] to be the backbone of other popular movements in London', noting that:

> Not only do you find them in the ranks of the purely Catholic and Irish societies, with their bands, banners, and patriotic emblems, but in connection with other political and temperance organisations – if one may judge from the handsome

---

[34] 'The Amnesty Demonstration in Hyde-Park', *The Morning Post* (4 November 1872), 6.
[35] Ibid.

banners, on which you often see depicted such subjects as 'Sarsfield', 'The Irish Parliament House', and 'O'Connell', with quotations from Tom Moore and harps and shamrocks galore.[36]

Even accounting for the propagandist element of Denvir's perspective, the organization of Irish labour which he identifies was a major factor in the history of popular protest in London. Most vividly a series of large demonstrations in Hyde Park and Trafalgar Square (a location which was perceived as the symbolic interface between the wealthy west of the city and the poor east) in 1887 united London's Irish and English working class in protest at a series of grievances including unemployment, the Coercion Act (which banned 'seditious' gatherings in Britain and (most contentiously) Ireland) and the incarceration of the Irish MP William O'Brien who had been arrested on charges of incitement. On 13 November, a day that became known as 'Bloody Sunday', the police deployed considerable violence while dispersing a rally at Trafalgar Square. There were mass arrests and many protestors were seriously injured, including three who subsequently died. This brutality provoked condemnation in the liberal press and, albeit briefly, brought the attention of the media to the wretched living conditions of London's Irish poor.

The Irish Festival organized at Alexandra Palace in north London in March 1876 was another determined statement of presence. Held on the Saturday after St Patrick's Day, the event brought together many diverse Irish groups from across the capital and the south of England including Home Rule associations, Irish language enthusiasts and temperance societies. According to the *Daily News*, its significance lies in the fact that it 'afforded an opportunity of bringing for the first time the Irish organisations of London conspicuously to the fore'.[37] Despite some logistical problems including a request by the organizers to 'come early' which left many 'drifting about the Alexandra Park and Palace in a helplessly unemployed condition', eventually the band of the St Anne's Total Abstinence Society struck up and the celebrations commenced.[38] The numbers in attendance were large – estimated at 20,000 by the *Daily News* and 25,000 by the *Freeman's Journal* – and the tone was good humoured; as the *Freeman's Journal* observed absurdly, 'no one knows better how to enjoy a day's outing than an Irishman, full of frolic, high spirits, and good humour, except it be the rosy-cheeked, blue-eyed, daughters of Erin'. The programme for the day included 'a performance of Irish music on the grand organ, followed by more Irish music from the band of the 1st Middlesex Engineers, and, the most Irish of all, [...] an entertaining contest between half a dozen national pipers'.[39] Later there was a production of Dion Boucicault's *The Colleen Bawn*, followed by further recitals, while in the grounds a hurling match was 'played with the greatest zest and good humour', and a series of Irish jig dancing contests were held.[40] The celebrations culminated in the early evening when a grand march past of the

[36]   Denvir, *The Irish in Britain*, 395.
[37]   'St Patrick's Day at the Alexandra Palace', *London Daily News* (20 March 1876), 2.
[38]   Ibid.
[39]   'Patrick's Day's Celebration in London', *Freeman's Journal* (20 March 1876), 6.
[40]   *The Times* (20 March 1876), 6.

various organizations took place on the Palace's East Terrace with a spectacular host of banners and around twenty bands. Following this parade most of the crowd dispersed although the festival atmosphere stayed with them; even those who later found themselves stranded at King's Cross station waiting for connections were entertained by an impromptu concert of Irish musicians with 'the more youthful and energetic of the company dancing a jig on the platform'.[41] Meanwhile back at Alexandra Palace the day concluded with a banquet at which the chairman of the event, Mitchell Henry, the Home Rule MP and industrialist, proposed a toast to the Queen and then spoke passionately (and at some length) on the subject of Irish history and the endurance of national character. 'Ireland has erected her alters to religion and patriotism, and has refused to bow the knee to the grim and blind idols of the new materialistic faith,' he thundered. As his speech illustrated, while the tone of the event was for the most part celebratory, it was also politically resolute. Although short on detail, Henry's call for the Irish to 'throw off the chains of intellectual, moral, and physical debasement' entertained a level of political radicalism that was unusual for such events at this time.[42]

The ambition of the festival, then, was impressive, and as an early instance of the kind of quintessentially Irish event that would become increasingly frequent in London through the rest of the century its importance is clear. At one level the festival was notable because it recognized that there was a degree of common cause among the London-Irish middle and working classes, although in reality this confluence was more of a loose coalition of Irish-orientated groups seeking to assert their presence rather than an overt political strategy. Certainly the temptation to see the festival as a proto-revivalist event should be resisted, if only because of the manner in which its preoccupations were in contradiction with some of the major tenants of revivalism. As Henry's speech vividly illustrated with its insistence on Ireland's 'religious fervour and undying patriotism', the foundation of Irish unity and national selfhood remained its Christian faith (however variously that faith was conceived), and in few of the speeches that followed the banquet was there any sense that Irish identity might be otherwise conceived or represented. Moreover, while the great possibilities of Home Rule were touched upon a number of times, the dominant themes of the banquet were instead the obduracy of national survival, the necessity of resisting assimilation and the ultimate endurance of Irish identity when cast adrift from Ireland itself. In his speech Michael Francis Ward, member of the Home Rule League and MP for Galway Borough, developed the implications of this in striking ways:

> If any other nation sends out a colony to another country it is rapidly merged into the life of the other country and is lost but an Irish colony is never lost (applause). They had planted an Irish colony long ago in France when they were driven out of Ireland by overwhelming power – that Irish colony to a certain extent still exists to-day, and its head is the ruler of France (cheers). In late times they had sent Irishmen all over the world when they were driven forth by England, driven

---

[41] 'St Patrick's Day at the Alexandra Palace', *Daily News* (20 March 1876), 2.
[42] 'Irish Demonstration at the Alexandra Palace', *Standard* (20 March 1876), 3.

forth to colonise, sometimes at the point of a bayonet, frequently at the point of a crowbar, and as a result he asked was not there now an Irish nation in America and in Australia bigger than in Ireland? (cheers) That Irish nation had been driven forth dishonestly by the strong right arm, but driven forth as it were providentially, for in every large colony of England it stands up against England's crushing power (hear, hear). Ireland had to congratulated herself on the fact that wherever she sent her sons they never ceased to be Irishmen, and never ceased resisting oppression (hear, hear, and applause).[43]

As this indicates, the Irish Festival looked forward to the possibilities of an Irish future in both Ireland and the diaspora, but in so doing it returned repeatedly to the disaster narrative of nineteenth-century Irish experience. To put this differently, the threat of national cultural annihilation which had arisen repeatedly during the previous century remained vivid.

It was through such events that the Irish would become increasingly visible in the city during the remainder of the century. This raised profile was, in part, allied to the progress of the Home Rule cause, but, more broadly, it is important to recognize the manner in which Irish personal identity (and with this a commodified idea of 'Irishness') was increasingly mobilized as a way of structuring urban leisure activity. From the growth of interest in Irish literature among the burgeoning clerical class to the phenomenal popularity of the Irish cockney comedian, from the itinerant Irish musician playing jigs for step dancers on Hampstead Heath to middle-class parlour concerts of Irish harp music, Irishness in London in the 1880s was highly visible and unusually fashionable. Central to this was the increasing influence of elite Irish middle-class and aristocratic society, alongside those who did not necessarily possess Irish nationality but whose liberalism made them sympathetic to the Irish cause, such as the prominent power couple John and Ishbel Hamilton-Gordon (Lord and Lady Aberdeen). An evangelical Christian aristocrat driven by the ideal of public duty, John Hamilton-Gordon would serve twice as Lord Lieutenant of Ireland (1886 and 1905–1915) and as the Governor General of Canada (1893–1898). The typical activities of this class on behalf of Ireland included charity work, direct interventions in Irish economic development projects, consciousness-raising activities about Irish social conditions and related publishing and journalism. Usually from the Anglo-Irish Ascendency, they exerted influence through small coteries and friendship groups and, in a slightly more formal manner, through attendance at a range of weekly salons across the city at which Irish affairs were discussed alongside other domestic and colonial issues. Significantly these salons were usually organized by women and thus were a key way in which they could exert political influence.

A prime example of this activity was the long-running salon of the historian Alice Stopford Green, which she organized with her husband and fellow historian John Richard Green, and then solely following his death in 1883. Stopford Green, born in Kells in Co. Meath in 1847, had a long and often dramatic life as an activist on behalf

---

[43] 'Patrick's Day's Celebration in London', *Freeman's Journal* (20 March 1876), 6.

of Irish nationalism (according to P. S. O'Hegarty, 'she helped everything cultural, everything patriotic and everything intelligent') that culminated in her crucial role as chairman of the committee that planned the importation of arms for the Irish Volunteers in 1914.[44] In this position she acted as a major funder and organizer for the Howth gun-running operation which landed 1,500 Mauser rifles at Howth harbour on 26 July 1914. Her husband's death left her wealthy and with a degree of independence that was unusual for the time and from her exclusive address at 14 Kensington Square she dedicated herself to her historical studies and her weekly salons, creating what Angus Mitchell identifies as one of London's 'most dynamic intellectual coteries'.[45] Described as 'a salon for a brilliant and diverse group of friends', attendees included Florence Nightingale, Mary Kingsley, Mary Augusta Ward, Sydney and Beatrice Webb, Arthur Conan Doyle, Henry James and Winston Churchill.[46] A gifted speaker and wit – according to *AE* (George Russell) she was 'a genuine artist in conversation' – Stopford Green was at the centre of this circle and thus was a key figure in the circulation of often radically nationalist ideas among London's liberal society and Irish middle class.[47] According to her first biographer, a typical meeting would include 'a large and heterogeneous assortment of guests – liberal politicians, journalists, men of letters, dons, foreign refugees, Irish nationalists, colonial administrators', while Stopford Green would insist that they were all seated on hard-backed chairs 'believing they talked better if they were not too comfortable'.[48] Following a trip to a prisoner of war camp on St Helena during the Boer War she became a founder member and vice president of the Africa Society in 1901 and the Congo Reform Association in 1904, where what would prove to be an important friendship with Roger Casement developed. Indeed, in a manner reminiscent of Casement, she was always instinctively inclined to interpret Irish nationalism in the wider context of anti-imperialist struggle.

Stopford Green's republican beliefs deepened as the Home Rule crisis loomed, and she eventually relocated to Ireland in 1918, ending a forty-one year sojourn in London during which she had been a major figure representing and advancing Irish nationalist ideas in London's elite metropolitan circles. Younger Irish women like Dora Sigerson and Katharine Tynan would learn much from her example, not least how to make the transition from what were essentially domestic roles to direct political activism. Indeed Sigerson, along with her husband, the journalist and literary critic Clement Shorter, followed Stopford Green in hosting dinner parties for influential figures in Irish society every Wednesday night at their home in St John's Wood. The conversation at these gatherings was expected to be political or cultural in nature, and the guests frequently included prominent members of the literary revival – for instance on St Patrick's Day 1901 W. B. Yeats and George Moore attended. Sigerson also hosted one

---

[44] P. S. O'Hegarty, BMH Statement: 839 (17–31 December 1952).

[45] Angus Mitchell, 'Too Dark Altogether', *Dublin Review of Books* (July 2018). Available online:http://www.drb.ie/essays/too-dark-altogether (accessed 7 May 2019).

[46] 'Alice Stopford Green', in *Dictionary of National Biography: 1922–1930*, ed. J. R. H. Weaver (Oxford: Oxford University Press, 1937).

[47] R. B. McDowell, *Alice Stopford Green: A Passionate Historian* (Dublin: Allen Figgis, 1967), 49.

[48] McDowell, *Alice Stopford Green*, 48.

of the more important regular salons of *fin de siècle* London and was a member of the Irish Literary Society and the Lyceum Club in Piccadilly, a weekly meeting inaugurated by Constance Smedley in 1903 intended to develop the work and education of women in the areas of medicine, science, art and literature.[49] It was through these that she was able to propagate revivalist ideas and to maintain contact with old friends from Ireland such as Tynan and Yeats.

The literary salon of Lady Jane Wilde, which she established in 1879 when she left Ireland to join her sons Willie and Oscar in London following the death of her husband, Sir William Wilde, was less overtly political in nature but equally influential. Although a figure of some fame in Ireland, she was practically unknown in London and was forced to live in much-reduced circumstances for reasons which were partly due to the family's previous profligacy. According to Yeats, while in London she expressed the desire 'to live on some high place, Primrose Hill or Highgate, because I was an eagle in my youth', but she was obliged instead to take rooms 'near her son in level Chelsea'.[50] Undeterred, she recommended the Saturday evening salon she had previously hosted in Dublin and it soon became something of a phenomenon and so popular that she supplemented it with a 'literary Wednesday' gathering. Guests included Eleanor Marx, John Ruskin, Yeats (who gained his introduction through Tynan), Charles Gavan Duffy, friends and associates of Oscar (who, at least in its early days, was assiduous in attending), and a young and impoverished George Bernard Shaw, who was especially grateful for the emotional and practical support it gave him. There was also a significant international dimension. 'All London comes to me by way of King's Road', she boasted, 'but the Americans come straight from the Atlantic steamers moored at Chelsea Bridge'.[51] Jane Wilde's rooms, which she shared with Willie, were small and cluttered and as a result the soirees could get uncomfortably crowded. This claustrophobic atmosphere was enhanced by the particular ambience she created. Tynan, who had declared to Father Matthew Russell in 1884 that 'to get into a London literary circle is my earthly ambition',[52] was certainly impressed:

> One Saturday Miss Skeffington Thompson took me to see Lady Wilde, who at that time used to hold Saturday receptions at her house in Park Street, W. I remember that it amazed me to find a little house wedged in between another little house and a big public-house at the corner. I did not understand that Park Street, Grosvenor Square, W., was a place to live, even if one could not swing a cat in the rooms and the public-house was cheek by jowl with one. The first day I went there, there was a beauty of the hour present, Miss Craigie Halkett; and there was Miss Fortescue the actress, just fresh from her breach of promise case against Lord Garmoyle, and

[49] Parejo Vadillo, 'New Woman Poets and the Culture of the *Salon* at the *Fin de Siècle*', *Women: A Cultural Review*, 10:1 (1999), 22–34, 23.
[50] W. B. Yeats, *Autobiographies* (London: Macmillan, 1956), 138.
[51] Anna de Brémont, *Oscar Wilde and His Mother: A Memoir* (London, Everett and Co., 1911), 58.
[52] Whitney Standlee, 'A World of Difference: London and Ireland in the Works of Katharine Tynan', *Irish Writing London: Vol. 1: Revival to the Second World War*, ed. Tom Herron (London: Bloomsbury, 2013), 73.

very much the fashion of the moment. Lady Wilde, in a white dress like a Druid priestess, her grey hair hanging down her back, received us in a couple of narrow London rooms, with open folding doors, in a gloom illumined only by a few red-shaded candles. All the blinds were down; and, coming in from the strong sun outside, the gloom was the more impenetrable. Lady Wilde shook hands with me and motioned me to a seat. I went in the direction she had indicated to me blindly. A soft hand took mine, and a soft voice spoke. 'So fortunate,' said the voice, 'that no one could suspect dear Lady Wilde of being a practical joker! There really is a chair.' The soft hand drew me to it. […]

The few shaded candles at Lady Wilde's afternoons were arranged so as to cast the limelight on the prominent people, leaving the spectators in darkness. Lady Wilde did not forget the spectators. She discovered one in the darkness to draw attention in a loud voice to the points of the exhibits. 'Such a beautiful long neck!' she would say: or 'Do you see the glint on her hair as she turns? I wish Oscar were here to see it.'[53]

Through this period of her life Yeats believed that Jane Wilde 'longed always perhaps, though certainly amid much self-mockery, for some impossible splendour of character and circumstance', and it was certainly the case that her salons were often treated as something of a pantomime, or little more than a stop-off for well-heeled American tourists eager to see the Wildes perform in their native habitat.[54] However, as with Oscar's aesthetic strategies, there was method in her studious eccentricity. Although she had toned down her Irish nationalist sympathies following her departure from Ireland, Jane's feminist views had become more forthright and, despite (or, perhaps, because of) its deliberately obfuscatory interior, it is no exaggeration to see her weekly salon as an important location for the circulation of sometimes radical ideas about women's role in society. The salon also played a significant role in developing the network of middle-class Irish cultural activists in London. Tynan's recollection that she was introduced to the salon by Emily Skeffington Thompson is notable not least because the latter would be one of the initiators of the Southwark Junior Irish Literary Club in October 1881, a foundational moment in the history of the Irish literary revival. Indeed, the presence of figures like Tynan, Skeffington Thompson, Yeats and Gavan Duffy suggests that the salon helped maintain Irish émigré interest in the national question and inhibited the process of assimilation into British society. In this pre-revival period, such opportunities in London were rare. Ultimately Jane Wilde's salon faded in popularity due to its host's relative poverty, the changing fashions of elite London society and, most damagingly, the fact that its major attraction, Oscar, was increasingly distracted elsewhere and so rarely attended. In the summer of 1890, one of its regulars, Anna de Brémont, paid a visit after a period in South Africa and was 'conscious of a subtle change in the atmosphere of the dim old room'. As she records,

[53] Katharine Tynan, *Twenty-Five Years: Reminiscences* (London: Smith, Elder and Co., 1913), 127–8.
[54] Yeats, *Autobiographies*, 138.

'there was no longer the joyous spirit of intellectual camaraderie that had made the dingy surroundings bright with the interchange of wit. Lady Wilde no longer shone forth in her wonted brilliant manner. She said little, and more than once I fancied I heard her sigh softly. A cloud seemed to have fallen upon the house in Oakley Street.'[55] The age of the salons was fading and, for the London Irish at least, they would be replaced by revival organizations that offered more structured opportunities for the expression of national identity with a clearer ideological focus. This was not entirely positive, however, as these organizations often discouraged precisely the kind of wide-ranging political and cultural discussion and the formation of loose coalitions of shared interests that salon culture encouraged.

Alongside the cultural and social work of the salons, the Irish middle class in London sponsored substantial economic activity. Irish industries and crafts were heavily promoted in the city and these commodities were often entirely reliant on an explicit Irish identification for their appeal. The highpoint of this activity was the Irish Exhibition held at Olympia in West London from June to October 1888 (see Figure 6). This extensive and ambitious event interpreted its brief broadly and offered (for an entrance fee of a shilling) displays of Irish manufacturing and arts, performances of Irish music, military manoeuvres, galleries of visual arts, fabrics, and ceramics, and exhibitions detailing Irish history, nature and culture. Although avowedly 'non-political' in its remit ('those who imagined that the "resources of Ireland" were mainly whiskey and dynamite, will be pleased to see Irish muslin instead of muzzling' sniped one London periodical), the event could hardly avoid enmeshing itself in the intensity of Irish politics at this time.[56] As Brendan Rooney points out, 'one might view the Irish exhibition as a rather extravagant public relations exercise, designed to appease the English public and amend their image of Ireland and the Irish in general'.[57] The event also reflected the popular prejudices of London itself; the *Freeman's Journal* reported that at one point the organizer's felt obliged to evict 'a few Jews who had improperly got possession of stalls, though some Jewish and a large number of English exhibitors remain'.[58] Such unconcealed anti-Semitism sat alongside the general mismanagement of the event as a whole. The delays in construction were such that building work was still in process long after the exhibition opened, while the project overall made a substantial loss with the debts passed on to the members of the organizing committee. 'There is no harm in saying that up to the present time the enterprise has not been exactly a marvel of management,' remarked the *London Daily News* drily.[59]

The scale of the event was not perhaps remarkable when compared to other trade exhibitions in London at a time of confident imperial expansion but was certainly significant in the context of Ireland and Irish manufacturing. In the exhibition hall there were nine avenues of displays, while a subway led from the hall to a six-acre outdoor

[55] de Brémont, *Oscar Wilde and His Mother*, 122–6.
[56] 'The Irish Exhibition', *Moonshine* (16 June 1888), 4.
[57] Brendan Rooney, 'The Irish Exhibition at Olympia, 1888', *Irish Architectural and Decorative Studies*, 1 (1998), 100–19, 103.
[58] 'The Irish Exhibition', *Freeman's Journal* (10 July 1888), 7.
[59] 'The Irish Exhibition', *London Daily News* (17 July 1888), 5.

Figure 6 The Irish Exhibition at Olympia. Illustration for *The Graphic* (9 June 1888).

site containing reconstructions of particularly compelling Irish scenes. The centrepiece of the exhibition was undoubtedly the 'Donegal Industrial Village', a mock-up of a rural Irish settlement designed by Alice Hart, the founder of the Donegal Industrial Fund. A heavily idealized version of a typical Donegal settlement, the village consisted of twelve thatched cottages (which burned Irish peat), a large cross imported from Ireland at its centre, a holy well and a ruined Irish tower. The cottages were populated by actual Donegal peasants, who were employed in demonstrations of their native crafts such as weaving and embroidery.[60] Other spectacular exhibits included a reconstruction of Blarney Castle, a Celtic round tower, and even a fully functioning dairy complete with sixty cows and attendant milkmaids in costume at which there was daily production of butter and cheese.[61] Alongside these, the *Belfast News-Letter* reported that 'fountains, a switchback railway [an early form of roller coaster], and a tobogganing slide have been added to gratify and amuse visitors to this unique exposition of Irish industries'.[62] In addition to the permanent displays, the exhibition hosted a number of individual events including an attempt at a balloon voyage to Vienna (which was abandoned at Margate), horse jumping competitions and an elaborate sham battle (which created 'an abundance of noise and smoke') representing 'an engagement during the Indian Mutiny, between the Sepoy rebels and several Irish regiments'.[63] Most notable was the 'Fancy Fair' in July at which famous women whose 'potent influence may be said to regulate fashion and govern "Society"' replaced the 'Irish peasants' on the craft stalls in the area known as the 'Old Irish Market Place' (an area modelled on a market in Belfast).[64] Dressed in Irish fabrics and jewellery, society personalities that took part included Lady Aberdeen, Countess Tolstoy, Constance Wilde and Lady Gladstone.[65] The first day of the fair was extremely crowded and feverish with excitement; as the *Belfast News-Letter* reported 'the rush of people was enormous and the limited space quickly became uncomfortably warm'.[66] Certainly it energized an exhibition which had previously appeared worthy but slightly dull, lacking 'the indispensable touch of the professional showman's hand', as the *Daily News* put it.[67] It also indicated not only how fashionable Ireland was at this time, but also something of the sympathy felt for Ireland's cause among London elites. The *Belfast News-Letter* stated that 'about 400 ladies of rank have expressed their willingness to take part' and this figure is corroborated by the detailed daily schedules published by the *Morning Post*.[68] Certainly if these numbers are correct, then the Fancy Fair can be judged as something close to a phenomenon of its kind.

---

[60] For more information on these crafts and who undertook them see Janice Helland, *British and Irish Home Arts and Industries 1880–1914: Marketing Craft, Making Fashion* (Dublin: Irish Academic Press, 2007), 50–7.

[61] It is of interest that Francis Fahy, founder and president of the Southwark Irish Literary Club and a foundational figure in the history of the Revival, visited the Olympia exhibition and noted that: 'The special feature of which for us was an Irish produce section, and of that produce, most Irish and most attractive, a group of some dozen dairymaids from Kerry, whose dark hair, blue eyes and dazzling complexions had become the talk of London. Good Heavens, the quantities of milk and butter and "barmbrack" we consumed at their stall, and the difficulty it was to drag us away from it' (Clare Hutton, 'Francis Fahy's "Ireland in London"', 252).

[62] *Belfast News-Letter* (2 June 1888), 5.

[63] *The Graphic* (18 August 1888), 7 and *The Graphic* (4 August 1888), 6.

[64] *Belfast News-Letter* (18 July 1888), 5.

[65] A full list of the women attending and the stalls on which they worked appears in the *Pall Mall Gazette* (17 July 1888), 13.

[66] *Belfast News-Letter* (18 July 1888), 5.

[67] *London Daily News* (17 July 1888), 5.

[68] *Belfast News-Letter* (2 July 1888), 3 and *The Morning Post* (20 July 1888), 1.

If such patronage indicated enthusiasm for the cause of Irish economic renewal after the disasters of the previous decades, the event also resonated with contemporary Irish politics in more contentious ways. As Janice Helland observes, 'the exhibition was meant to be strategic and compensatory as Home Rule debates proliferated; in retrospect, it represents a microcosm of tensions on the eve of Parnell's fall from grace'.[69] Indeed, Parnell himself was positively inclined towards the event, attending the opening of the exhibition and contributing a range of marble stones from his quarry at Avondale to the display hall. But the complex mixture of accommodation, dialogue and stern refusal which typified much of pro-Home Rule strategy at this time, was also evident at the exhibition. Alongside the educative and illustrative element of the event – its liberal commitment to enabling a better understanding of Ireland's situation – there were also clear indications as to where the limits of that appeal might lie. Most dramatically, a visiting group of musicians, the Barrack Street Band from Cork, refused to play 'God Save the Queen' after the conclusion of their performance, choosing instead to leave the stage with their instruments. The *Belfast News-Letter* reported that 'this behaviour was of so unexpected and startling a nature that the public appeared unable to realize the state of affairs until a Nationalist Member of Parliament began to applaud the retreat'.[70] A military band was summoned from a recital elsewhere in the grounds to perform the necessary anthem and the organizers banned the band from performing again at the exhibition. In explanation, the musicians themselves claimed that 'they dared not go back to Ireland if they had played "God Save the Queen"'.

Perhaps the most notable aspect of the Irish exhibition was the manner in which it refracted an idea of Ireland in crazed and multiple ways, creating an image of the homeland that seemed to mirror the distortions and selective ellipses of the emigrant consciousness. As such it was a manifestation of what Foster has termed '"Virtual" Ireland' and was only the most extravagant example of a phenomenon that could be identified in different forms and media across London during this period.[71] For instance, Fahy's and O'Donoghue's *Ireland in London* from 1889, a key text of codification for the London-Irish and the first substantial cultural and historical survey of it as a specific group, frequently veered towards the hyperreal, dramatically compressing and intensifying the Irish experience of the capital. Originally a series of articles for the *Dublin Evening Telegraph* that were edited and reprinted as a single volume, the book is a dense and allusive history that weaves Irish experience into the fabric of London's streets and buildings to such an extent that the city is rendered unthinkable without its Irish component:

> Perhaps no city out of Ireland has been so much influenced by Irish genius, Irish character, and Irish achievement. The inquiry: 'How far has that influence been exercised, and to what purpose?' can only be answered – first, by a glance at their position among the other various races in England, and its tremendous

---

[69] Helland, *British and Irish Home Arts and Industries 1880–1914*, 56.
[70] *Belfast News-Letter* (22 August 1888), 5.
[71] Foster, 'An Irish Power in London', 18.

difficulties: and, secondly, by a study of their achievements in literature, art, science, military genius, and statesmanship, as exemplified in the metropolis of the world. London teems with memories of Irishmen – famous in all the various walks of life – and of their works, and the truly great part they have taken in making London what it now is – the most extensive as well as the most solidly intellectual city of the world – can be unerringly traced through every step of its history, literary and otherwise, from the remotest period of its literary and mechanical activity down to the present day.[72]

As the emphatic tone of this indicates, Fahy and O'Donoghue effectively willed a coherent idea of Irish London into existence. At a time when the poorer Irish were, as they note, 'obliged to settle in the low-rented neighbourhoods, where the scum and dregs of London generally live', the book's relentless narrative of Irish achievement offered an overt message of encouragement and consolation that returned repeatedly to the historical endurance of the Irish in London and insisted that 'though compelled to dwell in the midst of the concentrated villainy of London, it may happily be said that they escape almost unscathed from the fierce ordeal'.[73] For this reason, and as Peter Van de Kamp has observed, in an important way *Ireland in London* was as much a guide *for* as well as *to*, the London Irish. The book recorded its history and spatial distribution across the city, insisted on the longevity of Irish experience at a time when the fractures of modernity and mass emigration could easily obscure such knowledge and offered a rebuke to the persistent anti-Irish prejudice that saw their presence in the city as indubitably alien.[74] Indeed, rather than repeating the disaster narrative of Irish history that was frequently rehearsed at this time, *Ireland in London* insisted that the London Irish embodied a 'Celtic genius [that] could not be repressed', and (when compared to their 'English neighbours in the courts and alleys') a 'greatly superior morality'.[75] As a result it judged the London Irish to be 'more honest, more chaste by far, and less brutal'.[76] As the next chapter will discuss in greater detail, at this time Fahy and O'Donoghue were leading figures in the Southwark Irish Literary Club and would eventually become founder members of the Irish Literary Society alongside Yeats in 1892. With its hopeful vision for the future of the London Irish, *Ireland in London* certainly complemented the values of the Southwark Club, which Fahy envisaged as a means of mobilizing Irish culture for social improvement. O'Donoghue was similarly driven. Described by Yeats as 'an obstinate little man', he was born in Chelsea of working-class Irish parents and had effectively self-educated at the British Museum Library.[77] A dedicated bibliophile throughout his life and possessing a 'remarkable

---

[72] F. A. Fahy and D. J. O'Donoghue, *Ireland in London* (Dublin: Evening Telegraph, 1889), 3.

[73] Fahy and O'Donoghue, *Ireland in London*, 9.

[74] Peter Van de Kamp, 'Whose Revival? Yeats and the Southwark Irish Literary Club', in *Tumult of Images, Essays on W. B. Yeats and Politics*, ed. Peter Van de Kamp and Peter Liebregts (Amsterdam: Rodopi, 1995), 154–81, 163.

[75] Fahy and O'Donoghue, *Ireland in London*, 4.

[76] Ibid., 9.

[77] Yeats, *Autobiographies*, 208.

memory for the minutest details', he made his living as a bookseller and writer and, among other publishing achievements, compiled a substantial biographical dictionary, *The Poets of Ireland*, which identified 2,000 Irish writers living and dead.[78] Like many of his generation he would relocate from London to Dublin in what Yeats called 'a fit of patriotism' in 1896 and would eventually become the librarian at University College Dublin, although it appears that with his thick 'Cockney dialect' he was often regarded with some suspicion as too Anglicized (a fate shared by many London Irish on their return to the homeland).[79]

Overall, *Ireland in London* is captivated by the city's history, scale and achievements. It insists on the centrality of Irish experience to this and delights in detailing the specifics of that contribution. At the same time, however, it recognizes (sometimes uneasily) that this experience has to be circumscribed; that while Irish achievements in London can be celebrated, they should not be regarded as a gateway for the process of assimilation. For this reason, the authors maintain a dogged resolution that the London Irish should never be 'absorbed into the general population, but preserve their national characteristics through all circumstances'.[80] This, in turn, leads to a significant volte-face in the book's concluding remarks:

> In its entirety, we think that we may fairly claim that this book, despite its many imperfections, affords proofs of the most convincing character, if such were needed, that the sons and daughters of Ireland, despite grievous disadvantages, and almost unique persecution, are capable of the highest intellectual development; and whilst marvelling at the enormous share which their genius has enabled them to take in the literary, scientific, and artistic life of Britain, we may fervently hope that the day is not far distant when those brilliant attainments may be utilised for the benefit of their widowed motherland, no longer a province, but, in all its essentials – 'A Nation Once Again!'[81]

Ultimately, then, the book bids farewell to the city and insists that the London-Irish gaze should be turned back to Ireland itself. This is a demand that others would also voice in increasingly insistent ways as the revival movement gained traction through the 1890s and, as such, *Ireland in London* can be understood as a bellwether for a larger cultural shift. This was not the only development that the book would prefigure. Thanks to Fahy and O'Donoghue's considerable efforts, it is certainly clear that by 1889 the Irish in London were visible, but it was a visibility created by the light cast from a small number of stellar individuals – figures celebrated in the book's lengthy sections on Irish dramatists, actors, writers, politicians and journalists. By contrast the existence of the Irish poor down among the 'the scum and dregs of London' was noted but left unexplored; they remained, as O'Day puts it in his discussion of Heinrick's 1872 survey of the Irish in Britain, 'shrouded'.[82] As this suggests, despite Fahy's and O'Donoghue's

[78] *The Globe* (7 February 1893), 4.
[79] Ibid.
[80] Fahy and O'Donoghue, *Ireland in London*, 9.
[81] Ibid., 163.
[82] Heinrick, *A Survey of the Irish in England*, xx.

insistence that there was a shared Irish experience of the city, it is clear that this class remained adrift from the economic and cultural resources of an increasingly mobile and vibrant Irish middle class. Indeed, the Catholic Church remained the one major institution providing any degree of social relief for large areas of Irish settlement in the city. For this reason, *Ireland in London*'s repeated reference to a shared national 'genius' was never more than a rhetorical ploy that in its essential emptiness acknowledged a wider failure. The revival, at least in its early stages, saw the rectification of this as one of its most pressing tasks, and it would attempt to bring cohesion to an idea of 'Irish London' through offering the opportunity to acquire shared cultural knowledge. For the most part it would fail in this ambition, but the aspiration was certainly notable and, perhaps most significantly for what was to occur, it would lead a few farsighted individuals to a profound understanding of the ways in which culture could be mobilized for radical political ends.

4

'Those tumultuous days': London's Irish cultural revival

These are a few of the people whom I recollect, who played a great part in those tumultuous days, and much of whose work for the movement has drawn no attention to itself. There were many others, and many whose names are known and, whose work is recognised. And behind them are many, the unknown warriors of the rank and file, who scorned delights and lived laborious nights in small ill-lit rooms and halls, working for the poor old woman. Blessings on them all.
– P. S. O'Hegarty[1]

However else it has since been mythologized, traduced or revised, it is clear that the Irish cultural revival broke upon the social structures of late nineteenth-century Irish London like a wave. Led by a modernizing (usually Irish-born and Catholic) intelligentsia, and frequently characterized by a refusal to countenance any form of assimilation with the British host community, the aim of this movement was nothing less than the creation of what John Hutchinson and Alan O'Day have termed 'an autonomous modern nation capable of competing in the international economic and political order'.[2] In this they functioned alongside the other recognizable type of revivalist from this time: the romantic (often middle/upper class and Protestant) Irish poet, diarist or scholar. These figures often had longer-term familial and social connections to London. These two types of revivalists would make common cause when expedient, but were also careful to draw a clear distinction when it was otherwise deemed necessary. Certainly in their political determination, the modernizing intelligentsia were much more hard line about the possible ways in which culture might be mobilized in the service of national renewal. As such, they were the 'shock troops of the cultural revival', absolutely dedicated to their objectives and determined to create new structures for Irish national life.[3]

As this distinction indicates, it is constructive to see the revival – and especially the revival in London – as a form of culture war between competing political and

[1] P. S. O'Hegarty, BMH Witness Statement: 839 (17–31 December 1952).
[2] 'The Gaelic Revival in London, 1900–1922: Limits of Ethnic Identity', John Hutchinson and Alan O'Day, *The Irish in Victorian Britain: The Local Dimension*, ed. Roger Swift and Sheridan Gilley (Dublin: Four Courts Press, 1999), 259.
[3] Ibid., 264.

generational interests and, as with most wars, this could become both messy and confusing. While the revivalists liked to imagine their activity in terms of clear demarcations between political positions, between Irish and British culture and between nativism and assimilation, in reality there was much blurring, negotiation and compromise. This was especially true in the movement's earliest manifestations in the late nineteenth century. It is not until around 1905 that the aims of the movement are clarified, as organizations with a distinct cultural agenda, such as the Gaelic League, gain popularity. It is perhaps because of this emerging singularity of purpose that much of the scholarly interest in Irish London has been focused on this period. Certainly, the dynamism of the revival, with its intense attachment to an ideal and its complex networks of friendship groups and coteries, makes it a compelling subject. Moreover, the professionalization of the movement created a record of achievement that remains visible. The quotidian work of London's revival organizations required the management and recording of membership lists, and the documentation of accurate minutes, accounts, and publication subscriptions. Such activity was second nature for the new generation of cultural revivalists who were often civil servants, teachers or journalists by day. As the tireless activist Patrick Sarsfield (P. S.) O'Hegarty recalled of his time working for many such organizations in the city, 'they had local committees, and central executives, and special committees, and masses of minute books and account books to be kept, and everybody who was willing to work at all worked to the pin of his collar'.[4] Many of these individuals – typically unattached young men living alone for the first time – had benefitted from an education in the national school system in Ireland and they become a highly visible subclass in London, working in the vast administrative machines of the Civil Service or Post Office. Michael Collins, the one-time London Post Office clerk and future revolutionary leader, was a representative example of this group and someone who gained important political and organizational skills through his deep immersion in London's revival movement. London also attracted more unusual specimens too, such as the Belfast Presbyterian and Irish language enthusiast Robert Lynd, who moved to London in 1902 as a freelance journalist and lived a bohemian life with the Belfast artist Paul Henry in a studio in Kensington. As with many others, the atmosphere of Irish London radicalized his politics although, unlike many of his acquaintances, he consistently opposed the use of physical force. Lynd's later house in Hampstead was one of the centres of Irish cultural activity and (more covertly) political mobilization in the city. He delivered Irish classes for the Gaelic League and helped edit its journal *Inis Fáil*, taught the language to his friend Roger Casement and seemingly knew everyone of influence (including James Joyce, who held his wedding reception at Lynd's house in 1931).

As might be predicted, this new generation of activists frequently found the pre-existing political and social organization of the Irish community in London to be entirely inadequate. By the late 1880s, the Home Rule movement in London was both lacking in dynamism and a cause that was gradually losing its galvanizing effect on the political life of the Irish community. Alongside this, the influence of the Catholic

---

[4] P. S. O'Hegarty, 'Personal Recollections', *Sunday Independent* (26 August 1945), 7.

Church in the capital was frequently either fitful or reactionary, and many of the Irish poor remained locked in squalid and desperately overcrowded slums, with little opportunity for education or economic advancement. They also remained the victims of much overt anti-Irish prejudice. That said, if the new generation of revivalists found Irish London to be morally and politically paralysed, it can be argued that, initially at least, the lack of appeal was mutual. As R. F. Foster has observed, in general 'the new, Anglophobic, culturally separatist organizations did not, unlike the old Home Rule structures, appeal to the Irish in Britain'.[5] Certainly a key effect of the revival was that it ultimately forced people to decide which side they were on, making distinct affiliations which previously had been comfortably (or sometimes less comfortably) imprecise. This political polarization engendered a new stringency about classification, and many who had previously considered themselves securely Irish would find themselves dismissed as mere 'West Britons', a term of abuse that assumed a particular waspishness among the circles of elite Irish London.[6]

In London, then, the revival is not merely a retrospective label used to demarcate a series of emerging attitudes towards culture and politics, but rather was a phenomenon that declared itself with a self-conscious insistence, transforming (and often rendering anachronistic) previous ideological conceptions of what Irishness was and how it might be utilized. Indeed, even as early as 1894, the London-based Irish journalist William Patrick (W. P.) Ryan, in his *The Irish Literary Revival: Its History, Pioneers and Possibilities*, was historicizing the movement, emphasizing those elements of it that were distinctive to London, and anticipating its revolutionary potential. 'Its aim is to teach Ireland to see herself, to be herself, to set her in her true place, realizing her nature and her mission. It is an effort to bring knowledge, books, brave hopes, Celtic idealism as her ministering spirits', the book's conclusion proclaimed with a certain breathless intensity.[7] This self-awareness of itself as a cultural phenomenon often lent the movement a slightly performative air and a sense that its key mobilizers embarked on activities with half an eye on how history might judge them. Certainly, it is striking to note how quickly a specific historical narrative for the revival was created. Following the accounts by Ryan in 1894 and Cornelius Weygandt in 1904, Ernest Boyd confirmed the position of the Southwark Irish Literary Club as the foundational moment for the revival movement as a whole in his influential work of literary history of 1916, *Ireland's Literary Renaissance*, and this version of events proved remarkably enduring.[8] However, more recent academic work has challenged this perspective in striking ways. Most powerfully, Ian Sheehy's work on the Southwark Club and its successor the Irish Literary Society (ILS) decentred W. B. Yeats and, by implication, his mythologization of these events and focused instead on the remarkable activities of Ryan himself, an

5   R. F. Foster, 'Marginal Men and Micks on the Make: The Uses of Irish Exile, c. 1840–1922', *Paddy and Mr Punch: Connections in Irish and English History* (London: Penguin, 1993), 299.

6   Foster, 'Marginal Men and Micks on the Make', 291.

7   W. P. Ryan, *The Irish Literary Revival: Its History, Pioneers and Possibilities* (London: Ward and Downey, 1894), 183.

8   Cornelius Weygandt, 'The Irish Literary Revival', *The Sewanee Review*, 12:4 (October 1904), 420–31, 424. Ernest Boyd, *Ireland's Literary Renaissance* (Dublin: Maunsel and Co., 1916), 84–5.

activist in both organizations and later a vocal critic of the ILS.[9] This research helps us to see more clearly just how peripheral Yeats became in the activities of the ILS after its heady early few months, but it also enables a clearer view of the movement and its achievements as a whole. Indeed reading the ILS through Ryan's sometimes embittered perspective allows it to be seen almost as a betrayal, rather than a continuation, of the founding ideals of the Southwark Club and as an organization that never fulfilled its potential to act as a radical body for the enabling of Irish culture. As such, it can be argued that, if anything, the ILS evolved to the point where it became subtly antagonistic to the revival spirit.

The ILS was not the only revival organization in London to be affected by such tensions and it is notable how rapidly the movement as a whole would shape-shift. These transformations were often politically expedient, but, as Irish London remained a small pond, they could also be triggered by something as mundane as the arrival of new and energetic individuals or friendship groups. Indeed even an institution which superficially can appear as stable as the Gaelic League endured dramatic swings in fortune; its popularity tended to increase when the prospects for Home Rule receded and vice versa. As this suggests, the revival was always ideologically contested territory; just as new initiatives and organizations announced their presence in a deliberately self-conscious fashion, so ideas and individuals from previous generations would frequently return to positions of influence long after it appeared their moment had passed. These shifts were often provoked by London itself and by Irish attitudes towards it. For many, London was a city of possibility, hope and expectation, and a place where Irish migrants could find common cause and friendship with fellow émigrés, such as in the case of the Rhymers' Club. But London was also a place of corruption, assimilation (these two terms often being unhelpfully conflated by nationalist radicals), and 'the most indifferent, if not the most inimical, city in the world' for an Irish language movement, as Tom Barclay, the remarkable second-generation Irish memoirist and labourer, labelled it.[10] In this context, the work of the revivalists is particularly striking. Even allowing for the fact that this sudden upsurge of activity was concentrated around a comparatively small number of people – effectively the emergence of a number of elite groupings within a more diffuse constellation of interests and attitudes – it remains the case that because of their commitment to the movement much of our sense of the cultural life of Irish London moves from a period of hazy indefinability to sudden sharp relief. However, the seeming clarity of this moment can also be misleading. The autonomous nature of the revival project and its attachment to just one goal makes it easier to overlook those parts of the movement that were less clearly defined, those that were more open to assimilation rather than adhering simply to the cultural influences of 'Irish Ireland', and those revival initiatives that simply failed in their objectives or misjudged their influence. Such instances are important because they indicate some of the necessary compromises London life would continue to demand of its Irish

[9] Ian Sheehy, *Irish Journalists and Littérateurs in Late Victorian London c.1870–1910* (DPhil. thesis, Hertford College, University of Oxford, 2003), 200–53.

[10] Tom Barclay, *Memoirs and Medleys: The Autobiography of a Bottle Washer* (Leicester: Coalville Publishing, 1995), 96.

population. Alongside this, it is necessary to cast a cold eye on some of the movement's own cherished myths. Most notable among these is Yeats's account of the revival which began, according to his 1923 Nobel lecture, 'when Parnell fell from power in 1891' and a 'disillusioned and embittered Ireland turned away from parliamentary politics'. Such was the significance of this 'stir of thought' that he argues it effectively created the conditions for the Anglo-Irish War twenty-eight years later.[11] As this chapter will discuss, Yeats had his own reasons for wanting to advance this historical interpretation, but even a cursory glance at the range of Irish cultural activity in London from the early 1880s onwards reveals that much notable work that was recognizably revivalist in tone was taking place long before the Parnell crisis. Indeed, as I previously discussed, Gladstone's embrace of the Home Rule cause in 1886 and the subsequent Government of Ireland Bill was equally, if not more, significant as it legitimated the expression of nationalist aspirations and thus encouraged the establishment of Irish cultural organizations across the city. As such, rather than arising out of a despair at the impossibility of meaningful political process, Irish cultural activity was often triggered by what Foster identifies as 'the apparent imminence of Home Rule and a triumphant constitutional nationalism'.[12] This revision of Yeats's revival narrative is not new – in 1904 Weygandt's summary of the movement for the *Sewanee Review* queried Yeats's version of the revival for similar reasons – but in the context of Irish London it is especially valuable as it allows the movement to be seen (in part) as a continuation of the general metropolitan enthusiasm for all things Irish that occurred in the late 1870s and 1880s, which I discussed in the previous chapter.[13] Certainly, while many revivalists liked to present their activities as constituting a clean break with the past, there were, in fact, always continuities and gradual transformations. As Ryan put it in 1894, 'what really happened in 1891 was not that strong cleavage, that ending of an epoch, that beginning of a new one. [...] Forces that were in training through a whole decade now found the broad stage'.[14]

The specific context of London also qualifies and complicates the broader terms of Yeats's model of the revival movement as a whole and the manner in which it effectively placed political mobilization and cultural activity in a self-cancelling binary. While in this interpretation the cultural life of the revival was seen implicitly as a response to political failure and thus a form of inevitable compromise, this chapter will argue that this seriously underplays quite how profoundly an ideal of 'Irish Ireland' was lived among revivalists in London at the time. Indeed, to turn the opposition on its head, if Irish political life in London in the final years of the nineteenth century had lodged within it a willingness to contemplate compromise and accommodation, the Irish cultural identity that superseded it was much more absolute in spirit and very wary about the dangers of possible assimilation. In other words, the revival attained a state

[11] W. B. Yeats, 'The Irish Dramatic Movement, A Lecture Delivered to the Royal Academy of Sweden', in *Autobiographies* (London: Macmillan, 1956), 559.
[12] R. F. Foster, *W. B. Yeats: A Life, Vol. 1: The Apprentice Mage 1865–1914* (Oxford: Oxford University Press, 1997), 41.
[13] Weygandt, 'The Irish Literary Revival', 425.
[14] *United Ireland* (28 April 1894), 1.

that was reminiscent of Raymond Williams's sense of culture as 'a whole way of life' because for many individuals its texts, events and organizations became synonymous with lived experience itself.[15] The scale of this achievement was impressive; by 1902, as the journalist Charlotte O'Conor Eccles observed, the structure of an entire Irish social world was in place as 'the Irishman finds in London his own literary, athletic, political and social institutions'.[16] It was in such ways that the revival made its appeal to Irish London; it could provide a coherent political rationale, structured leisure time, education and self-improvement, and, to some degree, a support network able to provide a form of social security.

The importance of the Southwark Irish Literary Club is frequently recognized only in the context of its successor, the ILS, but this considerably misrepresents the significance of the earlier initiative. Southwark had long been a centre of Irish political activity in London partly due to the number of lower-middle-class Irish engaged in clerical work who had made it their home in the 1870s. One of these, Francis Fahy, a civil servant for the Board of Works, had moved there in 1873 and, in a lecture of reminiscences delivered to the ILS in 1921, he emphasized the extent of Irish political mobilization in the locality and especially the role of the Land League as an inspiration for his work. Fahy founded the club in January 1883 as the logical development of a pre-existing organization, the Southwark Junior Irish Literary Club, which had commenced its work in October 1881. This was the creation of two Irish sisters: Catherine (Kate) Rae, the wife of the famous Scottish polar explorer John Rae, and Emily Skeffington Thompson. Given the importance of their initiative to the history of the revival, it is surprising that more is not known about these figures, although Fahy recalls them as 'ladies of means, living and moving among the best circles of London Society'. As he continued (a little obsequiously), 'to see these two delicately nurtured ladies sitting there teaching history and songs to some score of poor little Irish boys and girls was certainly a lesson in self-abnegation and devotion to the motherland'.[17] According to Ryan, 'thousands of Irish children in London were growing up Irish in nothing but in name' and so the club's mission was to 'teach them Irish history and many things kindred, to brighten their minds with national songs, stories, and traditions, to develop their now dim Celtic talents'.[18] Alongside history, the Junior Club provided classes in Irish geography, recitation, song and literature, with Fahy taking a more prominent role in its management as it gained in popularity. The club also developed a publishing operation in collaboration with John Denvir, the Liverpool-based Irish journalist and political mobilizer, and this produced Irish-themed children's literature which the club circulated to its members. Its success was notable; according to Clare Hutton, by 1884 there were 359 members distributed across branches in Southwark, Bermondsey, Kensington and Peckham.[19]

[15] Raymond Williams, *Culture and Society: 1780–1950* (New York: Anchor Books, 1960), 250.
[16] Roger Swift, ed., *Irish Migrants in Britain, 1815–1914* (Cork: Cork University Press, 2002), 191.
[17] Clare Hutton, 'Francis Fahy's "Ireland in London – Reminiscences" (1921)', in *Yeats's Collaborations. Yeats Annual, 15: A Special Number*, ed. Wayne K. Chapman and Warwick Gould (Basingstoke: Palgrave Macmillan, 2002), 233–80, 247.
[18] Ryan, *The Irish Literary Revival*, 12.
[19] Hutton, 'Francis Fahy's "Ireland in London"', 236.

The Junior Club, then, constituted one of first glimmers of the movement that would eventually become the Irish literary revival and as such it is worth emphasizing two of its distinctive features: firstly, that it was initiated by female activists and, secondly, that it was a response to the cultural needs of second-generation Irish migrants. As the revival gained in momentum the movement would become increasingly dominated by men and focused on the idea of an 'Irish Ireland', but it is salutary to note that neither of these elements were present in this early manifestation. The subsequent Southwark Irish Literary Club was equally innovative and was defined by its commitment to the principle of adult education. Operating under the motto 'Sgar an solus' ('spread the light'), according to Ryan, 'its objects were the cultivation of Irish history, art, and literature, and the providing of a medium of social and intellectual intercourse for Irish people of both sexes'.[20] Fahy's description of the Club's early days is compelling:

> The original members, about 40 in number, were the teachers and helpers, male and female, of the Children's Classes, but a little active canvassing soon brought this number up to 100. We met on successive Wednesdays, at first in the Surrey Rooms, then 2 years later in a hall or chapel hard by belonging to the Peculiar People, in Bath Street, London Road, a street so dark and gloomy that one of our humorous lecturers dubbed it 'Cut-throat Lane' and hearing who our landlords were, prophesied that we should one day become absorbed in that Sect and die without benefit of doctor or clergy. I have often since then passed that street at night to find it forbidding beyond belief and to marvel at the power of youth, hope and enthusiasm to ignore and set at nought the most glaring defects and inconveniences.[21]

The activities of the club were diverse, including Gaelic nights, recitations, lectures, debates and concerts. It invited notable speakers such as the prominent Home Rule MP John Redmond, and the barrister and historian Richard Barry O'Brien. The club also hosted 'Original Nights' where 'good Irish work in poem, story, sketch and ballad' could be presented to a usually sympathetic audience.[22] Similar events would become a feature of many Irish societies both in Ireland and beyond, but the particular vibrancy and creativity of the Southwark nights were marked. As Fahy recalls, 'many of our members discovered their literary vein on these nights and were able to test on a small circle of friendly critics productions, grave and gay, that appeared later in the Irish press'.[23] As this suggests, a commitment to creativity was at the heart of the Southwark Club and was one of its major principles of organization. According to reports of its meetings in the local press, the club was 'strictly national, but non-political and non-sectarian', although it was generally sympathetic to Home Rule and optimistic about the possibilities for Irish self-government.[24] Fahy was the energizing

---

[20] Ryan, *The Irish Literary Revival*, 16.
[21] Hutton, 'Francis Fahy's "Ireland in London"', 248–9.
[22] Ryan, *The Irish Literary Revival*, 22.
[23] Hutton, 'Francis Fahy's "Ireland in London"', 251.
[24] *South London Press* (24 September 1887), 5.

force behind this activity and a crucial figure, not least because of his ability to hold the 'disparate elements of the various London-Irish societies together'.[25] That said, he remains something of a mysterious figure or, as Hutton puts it, 'shadowy'.[26] Described by Ryan as an 'enthusiast and a tireless worker', he was clearly deeply committed to the Irish community in London and, with his 'equable nature', was able to motivate others in a similar fashion.[27] Yeats's view was a little more ambivalent, describing Fahy as 'a king among his own people' and the Southwark Club as nothing less than a 'Fahy cult'.[28] However, where Yeats saw a cult, Fahy himself saw what he termed a 'Happy Family', and he delighted in the fact that alongside the educational aspects of the club 'many a soirée of dance and song relieved the heaviness of our programme, [and] many an outing into the woodlands of Kent and Surrey gave some of us our first delightful picture of the English countryside'.[29] In a manner that would eventually define the revival as a movement, the Southwark Club attempted to provide a complete social world for its members and it is not hard to understand why slightly adrift figures such as Ryan (according to O'Hegarty 'an exotic figure, with long dark hair, a small goatee, and a slouch hat' wrapped in 'a dreamy and mystical atmosphere') became entirely immersed in its activities.[30]

Despite this, the club appears to have flared brightly in its early days and then slowly waned in popularity. Just two years after its foundation attendance at its meetings was reported to be 'meagre' and membership had stalled at just eighty-six members.[31] However, the club still hosted notable events. For Fahy, the 'most memorable of all' took place on 21 September 1887 when Justin McCarthy, the Irish Parliamentary Party MP, lectured on 'The Literature of '48', with Sir Charles Gavan Duffy, the veteran Young Ireland leader, chairing.[32] The hall was packed for the event, and the speakers 'loudly cheered on entering'.[33] Ranging widely beyond its ostensible subject, McCarthy's address was remarkable both for the confidence of its political predictions and their inaccuracy, asserting that 'the question of Home Rule was settled. (Cheers) They had only got to arrange terms and draw the treaty. The battle was virtually over, and the whole question had come to an end'.[34] With this seemingly inevitable triumph secured, McCarthy praised the role of the 'poets and the dreamers', 'who raised Ireland from her national slumber'. Misplaced though this assurance would prove, his lecture is intriguing in that it imagines in microcosm what was, effectively, an alternative (if

---

[25] 'Francis A. Fahey', in *Dictionary of Irish Biography*, ed. James McGuire and James Quinn (Cambridge: Cambridge University Press, 2009), 691.

[26] Hutton, 'Francis Fahy's "Ireland in London"', 233.

[27] Ryan, *The Irish Literary Revival*, 12. Hutton, 'Francis Fahy's "Ireland in London"', 233.

[28] Peter Van de Kamp, 'Whose Revival? Yeats and the Southwark Irish Literary Club', in *Tumult of Images, Essays on W. B. Yeats and Politics*, ed. Peter Van de Kamp and Peter Liebregts (Amsterdam: Rodopi, 1995), 154–81, 162.

[29] Hutton, 'Francis Fahy's "Ireland in London"', 252.

[30] P. S. O'Hegarty, BMH Witness Statement: 839 (17–31 December 1952).

[31] 'Southwark Irish literary Club', *Dublin Weekly Nation* (11 July 1885), 5.

[32] Hutton, 'Francis Fahy's "Ireland in London"', 250.

[33] *South London Press* (24 September 1887), 5.

[34] Ibid.

rogue) cultural history, one in which nineteenth-century land reform and a cultural revival had led to the peaceful attainment of Home Rule. Among those in attendance for McCarthy's lecture was an 'exquisitely dressed' Oscar Wilde, who concluded the evening with a vote of thanks to the speaker and a promise to present the club with a copy of *Ancient Legends, Mystic Charms, and Superstitions of Ireland*, which his mother, Lady Jane Wilde, had recently edited.[35] Observing that 'he had ever held as sacred the names of those distinguished countrymen of his mentioned by the lecturer', he too was cheered by the enthusiastic audience.[36] Fahy recalls of this moment, 'I need not say with what curiosity we looked and listened to him, happily ignorant of the terrible destiny hidden for him in the future.'[37] Arguably, this night was the zenith of the society's activities, just as it was also perhaps the high-water mark for Irish London's optimism about the likely success of the Home Rule project.

Although it would be subsequently compromised by events, the idealism of the Southwark Club was crucial not just to the revival as a movement but even to the *idea* of a revival itself. As Ryan commented in 1894, 'the Southwark strain in one way or another ran through the whole revival. Southwark had some share in the inspiration of the Pan-Celtic Society, it led directly to the formation of the Irish Literary Society, London, it had even something to do with the Dublin National Literary Society'.[38] It is necessary, also, to understand the significance of the club in the context of London, in that it demonstrated some of the possibilities for migrant community organization within the city. The Southwark Club proved that it was possible to nurture an Irish cultural project within the city and that, as such, London was not entirely coterminous with Britishness. As Irish writers and organizations began to affirm the values of cultural independence, so it became clear that London, by dint of its sheer size and diversity, could enable this aspiration to a degree that was simply not possible in smaller British towns and cities; in other words, sheer critical mass ensured that assimilation was no longer an inevitability. More prosaically but just as importantly, as one of its founding committee, John T. Kelly, asserted, the club 'educated hundreds of young Irish children in a knowledge of Ireland, its history and its songs; it kept score of young Irish men in London away from the pot-house and the music-hall; and it did something in a small way to encourage the study of Irish Literature'.[39]

Yeats first visited the club in March 1888 and delivered a lecture on 'Irish Fairy Lore' in June of that year. He was, however, miserably unimpressed by the proceedings, dismissing its members as 'young people, clerks, shop-boys, and shop-girls' and its procedures as repetitive and inane. Indeed, he claimed that by 1889 'it had ceased to meet because the girls got the giggles when any member of the Committee got up to speak'.[40] Notwithstanding the fact that by this stage of its existence the club had indeed lost much of its energy and had ceased regular meetings – its relocation away from its

---

[35] *Freeman's Journal and Daily Commercial Advertiser* (23 September 1887), 5.
[36] *South London Press* (24 September 1887), 5.
[37] Hutton, 'Francis Fahy's "Ireland in London"', 250.
[38] *United Ireland* (28 April 1894), 1.
[39] *Flag of Ireland* (12 May 1894), 1.
[40] Yeats, *Autobiographies*, 199.

heartland in Southwark, a difficulty in finding engaging lecturers and the fissures in Irish society created by the Parnell crisis being some of the major difficulties it faced – Yeats's criticism of the club also justified his intervention in effectively taking it over and remaking it as the ILS on his return to London in the autumn of 1891. In December he called a meeting at his new family home in Bedford Park, Chiswick, inviting the remnants of the Southwark Club, as well as T. W. Rolleston and John Todhunter, a figure he considered to have useful organizational talents. Significantly perhaps, Fahy was unable to attend, claiming he had been given, what Ryan terms, 'insufficient notice', although he would be involved in subsequent discussions.[41] At the meeting the broad principles of what would become the ILS were agreed as well as, in Ryan's words, 'a scheme for the publication and circulation of Irish books', a project which would eventually prove contentious.[42] In Yeats's version of events it is at this point that the Irish revival proper commences, although others involved in the creation of the ILS did not view it as quite so momentous. Indeed, as Fahy makes clear in his reminiscences, for him the ILS was simply a continuation of the principles of the Southwark Club on a more ambitious scale. Eventually, however, the new organization would move away from the 'missionary spirit' of creativity so prized by Ryan, a departure that would dismay some of its Southwark veterans.[43]

Alongside the Southwark faction, other coteries had an important role in the formation of the ILS and the revival in London more broadly. There was, for instance, considerable overlap with the 'Rhymers' Club', an informal gathering of poets formed in May 1890 that was much mythologized by Yeats in the years that followed.[44] Despite this, its origins had been pragmatic: according to Yeats, its purpose was to introduce poets to each other, prevent jealousy, and 'feel a share in each other's triumph'.[45] While the club met in a number of venues – famously Oscar Wilde would only attend when the location was not a Public House – it was closely associated with 'Ye Olde Cheshire Cheese' on Fleet Street, and the 'Companions of the Cheshire Cheese', as Yeats would name them many years later, included such talents as Ernest Rhys, Ernest Dowson, Lionel Johnson, Francis Thompson, Lord Alfred Douglas and Victor Plarr (who was Librarian of King's College London).[46] As Yeats's affectionate appellation suggests, the Rhymers' Club did not take itself too seriously, but his declaration in the same poem that these were 'poets with whom I learned my trade' was a serious acknowledgement of creative debt. Certainly his experience of the Rhymers' Club would remain key to his understanding of his individual development as a poet and aesthetician. The club met on alternate Friday evenings, and its usual format followed, what Yeats termed, 'a round table of rhyme': each member of the club would read work in progress and

[41] Ryan, *The Irish Literary Revival*, 52.
[42] Ibid., 55.
[43] Ibid.
[44] For more on the difficulty of dating the Rhymers' Club with accuracy see R. K. R. Thornton, 'Dates for the Rhymers' Club', *English Literature in Transition, 1880–1920*, 14:1 (1971), 49–53.
[45] W. B. Yeats, *The Trembling of the Veil* (London: T. Werner Laurie, 1922), 52.
[46] W. B. Yeats, 'The Grey Rock', in *Responsibilities and Other Poems* (London: Macmillan, 1916), 3.

a group critique would follow.[47] During this discussion critical judgement could be unsparing, as Dowson noted in February 1891:

> Thursday at Horne's was very entertaining: a most queer assembly of 'Rhymers'; and a quaint collection of rhymes. Crane (Walter) read a ballad: dull! One Ernest Radford, some triolets and rondeaus of merit: 'Dorian' Gray some very beautiful obscure versicles in the latest manner of French symbolism; and the tedious Todhunter was tedious after his kind. Plarr and Johnson also read verses of great excellence; and the latter, also read for me my 'Amor Umbratilis': and Oscar arrived late looking more like his Whistlerian name, in his voluminous dress clothes, than I have seen him.[48]

Describing the same meeting Johnson was no less blunt, writing to Campbell Dodgson that 'eighteen minor poets of our acquaintance [...] all inflicted their poems on each other, and were inimitably tedious, except dear Oscar'.[49] As his qualification suggests, Wilde was a celebrity by this point and his visits to the club provoked what a disapproving Plarr recalled as a 'kind of idolatry'. 'The simple-minded were as much puzzled and overawed by his vogue as they have been puzzled and overawed by other vogues in later days,' he continued, sniffishly.[50] Johnson's acknowledgement that at times the Rhymers' Club could be something of an ordeal concurs with other contemporary accounts – Plarr noted an atmosphere of 'gloom' and 'reticence' – and this contrasts oddly with the determinedly hearty note the Rhymers were keen to strike in their hospitality.[51] As Rhys recalls:

> Our custom was to sup downstairs in the old coffee-house boxes, something like high double-seated pews with a table between. After supper at which we drank old ale and other time-honored liquors, we adjourned to a smoking-room at the top of the house, which we came to look upon as our sanctum. There long clays or churchwarden pipes were smoked, and the Rhymers were expected to bring rhymes in their pockets, to be read aloud to the club for criticism.[52]

As this account indicates, the Rhymers' Club was overwhelmingly male in composition and a certain self-regard was its signature element. This bonhomie was codified by Rolleston in his 'Ballade of the "Cheshire Cheese" in Fleet Street',[53] a humorous if banal

---

[47] W. B. Yeats, *Letters to the New Island*, ed. Horace Reynolds (Cambridge, MA: Harvard University Press, 1970), 143.

[48] Thornton, 'Dates for the Rhymers' Club', 49.

[49] Ibid.

[50] George Mills Harper and Karl Beckson, 'Victor Plarr on "The Rhymers' Club": An Unpublished Lecture', *English Literature in Transition, 1880–1920*, 45:4 (2002), 379–85, 388.

[51] Mills Harper, Beckson, 'Victor Plarr on "The Rhymers' Club"', 390.

[52] Ernest Rhys, 'Yeats and The Rhymers' Club', in *W. B. Yeats: Interviews and Recollections*, ed. E. H. Mikhail (London: Macmillan, 1977), 41.

[53] T. W. Rolleston, *Sea Spray: Verses and Translations* (Dublin: Maunsel, 1909), 33–4. The poem concludes: If doubts or debts thy soul assail, If Fashion's forms its current freeze, Try a long pipe, a glass of ale, And supper at the 'Cheshire Cheese'.

effort intended to commemorate the meetings of the club in what he called that 'sacred spot'.[54] As time passed, meetings would more usually be held in member's homes, although Joann Gardner's assertion that through this relocation 'the group gradually gained a sense of sobriety and purpose' is debateable.[55]

Despite these efforts at homosocial bonding, the Rhymers' Club remained diverse in its poetic interests and even Yeats, who was skilled in finding common cause among disparate talents, could identify little more than a 'search for new subject matter, new emotions, which so clearly marks the reaction from that search for new forms merely' as a unifying factor.[56] Indeed, according to George Mills Harper and Karl Beckson, in 'the Club's diversity of interests lay a major cause of its disbanding'.[57] The passing of time, however, allows for alternative critical perspectives and Nicholas Daly's more recent assessment of the group glimpses shared preoccupations that appear to have eluded Yeats himself. As he observes, 'the regulars at the Cheshire Cheese were interested in interiority, in the evanescence of consciousness, in love, in the city, and above else in literary form.'[58] Certainly for this group of nomads and émigrés the experience of London life was an essential common denominator, and there remain grounds to agree with Plarr's assertions that they remained 'a distinct and independent group'.[59] The publication of two anthologies of Rhymers' Club verse in 1892 and 1894 enhances this perception.

For Yeats, at least, one of the most attractive elements of the Rhymers' Club was that it offered Celticism by another name in that its cooperative and coterie-forming energies were inimical to what he saw as England's 'land of literary Ishmaels'. 'It is only among the sociable Celtic nations that men draw nearer to each other when they want to think and dream and work,' he continued, slightly fancifully, in a puff piece for the club published in the *Boston Pilot* in 1892.[60] The argument is slightly forced, but certainly it is difficult to imagine the ILS succeeding without its more raffish twin, not least because of the number of poets who were active in both organizations. As Ryan noted in his early account of the revival movement, 'in addition to Rolleston, Yeats, Dr. Todhunter, Lionel Johnson, the "Rhymers' Club" gave the Society some promising poets. Among them was George Arthur Greene [...] Victor Plarr and A. C. Hillier were also attracted from the little Parnassus of the "Rhymers," and mean, I hope, to "hammer the ringing rhyme" on a Celtic anvil henceforward.'[61] That John O'Leary, the veteran Fenian and Yeats's friend, also attended on occasion only deepens the importance of the Rhymers' Club for an understanding of the rise of cultural nationalism in London during this period. Given the intensity with which it burned the Rhymers' Club was always destined to be a time-limited venture, and by the time enthusiasm for the club

[54] Mills Harper and Beckson, 'Victor Plarr on "The Rhymers' Club"', 380.
[55] Joann Gardner, *Yeats and the Rhymers' Club: A Nineties Perspective* (New York: Lang, 1989), 9.
[56] Yeats, *Letters to the New Island*, 144.
[57] Mills Harper and Beckson, 'Victor Plarr on "The Rhymers' Club"', 382.
[58] Nicholas Daly, 'Britain', in *The Fin-de-Siècle World*, ed. Michael Saler (London: Routledge, 2014), 123.
[59] Mills Harper and Beckson, 'Victor Plarr on "The Rhymers' Club"', 387.
[60] Yeats, *Letters to the New Island,* 143.
[61] Ryan, *The Irish Literary Revival*, 119.

waned around 1894 many of its poets were established in their own right (or were clearly not likely to achieve success at all) so there was less need to identify as a coterie. Clearly for Yeats the club provided a crucial stage in his development. As Beckson has noted, 'Yeats emerged from his Rhymers' Club experience with a deepened sense of artistic commitment to what he later called "the artifice of eternity"' and, in this, 'Dowson and Johnson were Yeats's emblem of that raging in the dark from which legends are made'.[62]

It is clear, then, that the Rhymers' Club and the Southwark Irish Club shaped the nascent ILS in crucial ways. The society came into formal existence on 12 May 1892 when its first meeting was held at the Caledonian Hotel on the Strand. Sir Charles Gavan Duffy agreed to act as president with the energetic Rolleston as secretary and de facto prime organizer. The committee as a whole had a number of representatives from the old Southwark Club including Fahy, Ryan, D. J. O'Donoghue, Sophie Bryant and James O'Keeffe; while the Rhymers' Club provided Yeats, Johnson, Plarr and Todhunter. Beyond these organizations, other significant figures were invited to take part including Barry O'Brien, who would act as the ILS's Chair until 1906 (ruling over it, according to Katharine Tynan, with 'a rod of iron').[63] Other notable members of the society at its inception included Maud Gonne, Douglas Hyde, Oscar Wilde, Bram Stoker and Stephen Gwynn, the journalist, poet and nationalist politician, who became its secretary in 1902. Overall, Yeats's recollection that the ILS 'was joined by every London-Irish author and journalist' is not a huge exaggeration.[64] Early meetings were held at a number of venues (including, as might be expected, the Cheshire Cheese), and Stopford Brooke had the honour of delivering the inaugural lecture on 'The Need and Use of Getting Irish Literature into the English Tongue' in March 1893. Although it was not apparent at the time, as Sheehy has demonstrated in impressive detail, in the different factions and interest groups that were brought together to form the first ILS committee were the seeds of what would become subsequent conflict. Indeed, the difficulties which assailed the ILS reflected in microcosm many of the broader tensions apparent within Irish-London society as a whole. These problems were overdetermined in origin, but included the interpersonal politics implicit to literary and cultural coteries, disciplinary tussles between creative writers and historians (broadly represented by the Southwark faction on one side and Barry O'Brien and Duffy on the other), the continual aftershocks from the great political events of the time (of which the Parnell crisis was the most profound) and the usual low rumble of sectarianism. Alongside these points of tension, and of equal importance, was the generational struggle between a younger cohort of revivalists and older Irish Londoners who tended to be more deeply assimilated into the life of the city and were usually more sympathetic to the Home Rule agenda. To further complicate matters, it is also necessary to account for Yeats's sometimes complex motivations for engaging with the ILS and with the revival movement in London more broadly. In Warwick Gould's view

---

[62] Karl Beckson, 'The Legends of the Rhymers' Club: A Review Article', *Victorian Poetry*, 19:4 (Winter 1981), 397–412, 406.

[63] Katharine Tynan, *Memories* (London: Eveleigh Nash and Grayson, 1924), 327.

[64] Yeats, *Autobiographies*, 199.

this involvement was largely strategic, in that Yeats's priority was to create an 'English or an Irish expatriate reading community to buy books, in order to begin to build the reputation at home which might reinvigorate Dublin culture'.[65] For this reason, as Gould continues, 'in London Yeats had to learn to roll literary logs, to lecture, and, in the Irish Literary Society, to create his own audience'. Given this, it is of little surprise that through the 1890s Yeats's main interests would revert to Dublin, although he would always remain an enthusiastic log roller in literary London and a broadly sympathetic friend of the ILS (and this despite the fact that, according to Foster, ultimately 'it never greatly appealed to him').[66]

The potential difficulties apparent in the constitution of the ILS's first committee would reveal themselves gradually in the manner in which the society organized its events, attracted new recruits to committee positions and advanced its plans for the dissemination of texts. Most damagingly, the society was consumed in a protracted and often bitter dispute over the management and editorial control of the 'New Irish Library', a long-cherished plan driven by Yeats to produce a series of Irish books, both original and reprinted. As an attempt to provide some foundation to a national literary canon that remained in many ways precarious, the project was idealistic and seemingly influenced by the spirit of the earlier Southwark Club. Indeed, initially former Southwark figures such as Ryan were energetic in helping to advance its ideals. However, during the summer of 1892, Duffy, who had a very different vision for the project, wrested control of the initiative from Yeats, an act which would infuriate the younger poet and which he would later consider 'the failure of our first attempt to create a modern Irish literature'.[67] Despite this anger and the wider turbulence it caused in the ILS, Duffy managed to keep the scheme afloat and, with Hyde and Rolleston as subeditors, published twelve volumes in the series between 1893 and 1887. Their reception, however, was lukewarm, and Yeats delighted in savaging the dullness of the first set of volumes in *The Bookman*:

> Lord Beaconsfield once said that the way to give a successful supper party was never to ask anybody who had to be explained, and the advice is good for more important matters. The members of 'The Irish Literary Society' of London and 'The National Literary Society' of Dublin, and the other persons responsible for the present Irish literary movement, had done well to have taken it to heart and avoided anything so desperately in need of explanation as three out of the four books already published in this *New Irish Library*. Their first volume, *The Patriot Parliament*, was an historical tractate which, if modified a little, had done well among the transactions of a learned society, but it bored beyond measure the unfortunate persons who bought some thousands of copies in a few days, persuaded by the energy of the two societies, and deluded by the name of Sir

---

[65] Warwick Gould, 'Yeats and His Books', in *Essays in Honour of Eamonn Cantwell: Yeats Annual No. 20: A Special Number* (Cambridge: Open Book Publishers, 2016). Available online: http://books.openedition.org/obp/3448 (accessed 12 March 2019).

[66] Foster, *W. B. Yeats: A Life*, Vol. 1, 124.

[67] Yeats, 'Ireland after Parnell', *Autobiographies*, 218.

Charles Gavan Duffy and Thomas Davis upon the cover. Pages upon pages of Acts of Parliament may be popular literature on the planet Neptune, or chillier Uranus, but our quick-blooded globe has altogether different needs.[68]

Although the 'New Irish Library' row initially appears to be a conflict about genre, in that it pitched Yeats's ideas for an imaginative national literature against Duffy's desire to promote foundational texts of Irish history, it was also (and probably more profoundly) an argument across generations as Duffy, a veteran of the Young Ireland cultural nationalist movement, the co-founder of *The Nation*, and, most pertinently, the initiator of 'The Library of Ireland' series of Irish biography, poetry and criticism in 1845 from which the New Irish Library took its inspiration, sought to impose his ideas on the younger voices in the ILS. This was not something that Yeats could countenance; he condemned Duffy's 'domineering obstinacy' and declared that he possessed, in a revealing phrase, 'an entire lack of any culture that I could recognise'.[69] For Yeats, Duffy's choices for the New Irish Library were an attempt to impose, what Helen O'Connell calls, 'the vulgarity of middle-class Ireland over the imaginative depths of both oral culture and Yeatsian high Revivalism' and as such they antagonized his aristocratic as well as his nationalist instincts.[70]

Aside from these internecine conflicts, the annual general reports of the ILS provide a detailed record of its other interests, listing committee membership and attendance, reports from subcommittees, and donations. For instance, the report for 1897–98 (when the ILS had been in existence for five years) records some important tendencies, including Yeats's waning involvement in the society and the founding of the allied organization, the Irish Texts Society.[71] The great popularity of the Gaelic League classes hosted by the ILS in their rooms at 8 Aldephi Terrace indicates the continued inclusivity of the society's work, although other initiatives, such as the series of 'House dinners' held at the St James Restaurant and the number of private 'At Home' house parties organized by ILS members, indicate, perhaps, a more exclusive tendency. By this stage of its existence, the socially desirable aspects of ILS membership were becoming recognized in London society and events such as its fund-raising 'Cinderella Dance', held at Westminster Hall in February 1895, were widely reported beyond the boundaries of Irish London.[72] Other elements of the ILS continued in a manner that was still recognizably indebted to the example of the Southwark Club, even though

[68] W. B. Yeats, *The Collected Works of W. B. Yeats Volume IX: Early Art: Uncollected Articles*, ed. Richard J. Finneran and George Mills Harper, John Frayne and Madeleine Marchaterre (New York: Scribner, 2004), 245–6.

[69] Cyril Pearl, *Three Lives of Charles Gavan Duffy* (Sydney: New South Wales University Press, 1979), 226.

[70] Helen O'Connell, *Ireland and the Fiction of Improvement* (Oxford: Oxford University Press, 2006), 190.

[71] General report of the Irish Literary Society, London (1897–98), NLI: EPH C44. Such were Yeats's commitments in Ireland during this period that he attended only four out of twenty-five meetings. He was also greatly preoccupied with plans to mark the centenary of the 1798 uprising.

[72] Handbill organized by the Irish Literary Society, London to take place on 18 February 1895 in Westminster Town Hall (MS EPH B337, National Library of Ireland). Tickets for this event were a not inconsiderable five shillings.

most of those from the former organization were no longer closely involved. Most notably the 'Original Nights' continued in much the same form as in their Southwark manifestation and five were held during the year. The report notes that they were so 'attractive and popular' that 'they have latterly somewhat overtaxed the accommodation at the Society's rooms'. In total fifty-four individuals contributed to these nights over the year, and it is significant that of these 60 per cent were women. While the outward-facing activities and committee work of the ILS remained dominated by men, it is notable that women were the major contributors to what remained of the ILS's commitment to creative work.

The 1898 report, then, paints a picture of the ILS in vigorous health and such was its continued growth that by 1902 it was, according to O'Conor Eccles (who was an energetic propagandist for the Society), 'the chief centre of social intercourse for the Irish in London'.[73] Given the often ephemeral nature of Irish organizations in London at this time this was no small achievement (indeed the society is still in existence), yet the impression remains that the ILS was something of a missed opportunity in that the ideals of creativity, inclusivity and self-help which it inherited from the Southwark club were gradually compromised until it was scarcely recognizable as a revival organization at all. Fahy appears to have recognized the reality of this transformation with his usual equanimity and stayed on good terms with the society but other activists were vocal in their criticism. Chief among these was Ryan, who launched a series of increasingly bitter denunciations of what he saw as the ILS's elitism and anti-literary tendencies, culminating in an extended article for the *New Ireland Review* in March 1895 under the pseudonym 'O. Z.'. Provoked by the relocation of the headquarters of the ILS from Bloomsbury to the more salubrious Adelphi, the piece was bitingly sarcastic in its denunciation of the ILS's aristocratic pretensions and its desire to give 'style and tone to Irish intellectual products' while leaving others to 'supply the creative spirit, the humdrum commodity of inspiration'.[74] As part of this argument, the article focuses on what it terms the 'leading (active) lady members' and provides detailed pen portraits of Emily H. Hickey, Elsa D'Esterre Keeling, Sophie Bryant, Tynan and O'Conor Eccles. Seemingly a satire on a society piece from the popular press and written in a style similar to *Literary London: Its Lights and Comedies*, his miscellany of literary criticism from 1898, Ryan (who according to O'Hegarty 'was like a rapier in argument or in controversy'[75]) is stridently misogynistic:

> The women members have not done a very great deal towards intellectual impulse within it; less even than might be expected, in the way of encouraging Irish studies. And yet they have been a gracious and enlivening, though sometimes a subdued element in the organisation, or whatever else it is. Like placid or winning faces looking down from the pictured walls upon the student, they acquire a moving guise and grace, and even spell, as the Society's life-day lengthens. They have moved

[73] Swift, *Irish Migrants in Britain, 1815–1914*, 191.
[74] O. Z., 'From a Modern Irish Portrait Gallery VI: An Adelphi Group', *New Ireland Review*, 3 (March 1895), 24–32, 24.
[75] O'Hegarty, BMH Statement: 839.

in and out, sometimes with a questioning, almost a lonely air, as if wondering whether the ground would ever become homely, or restful, or spirited.[76]

In a piece that despaired of the manner in which the ILS had ceased to be a creative organization rooted in community work, its focus on the role of women in the society aligned increased female involvement with the loss of dynamism and purpose. At such moments the gendered unconscious of London's revival was starkly revealed: for activists such as Ryan the movement was at its most dynamic when, as in the Southwark Club, women's involvement was minimized and male homosociality prioritized.

Ryan was not alone in his criticism of the ILS. In 1900 David Patrick (D. P.) Moran, the political journalist and leading advocate of Gaelic Catholic nationalism, condemned the society as fatally compromised by its attachment to the idea that an Irish national literature in English was viable, and its concomitant failure to embrace, or even properly understand, the ideals of Irish Ireland:

> The Irish Literary Society is in the main composed of a very superior collection of West Britons; for in London, where to be Irish is to be foreign – and amongst all mean people it is highly respectable to be foreign – it is extraordinary the number of lineal descendants of prosperous shopkeepers who do not disdain to flock to the watery-green standard that floats over the society.[77]

Moran's language is typically inflammatory, but as a one-time member of the ILS and a figure closely woven into the activities of Irish London in the 1890s, his identification of the general political and cultural shift of the Society at this time was accurate. Indeed, such was scale of this gradual transformation that by 1921 the ILS could be considered, in Mo Moulton's phrase, 'a microcosm of Anglo-Irish culture in England', illustrative of nothing more than 'the tenuous survival of a kind of Anglo-Irish hybrid culture in the capital'.[78] Others took a less critical view. O'Hegarty, looking back in 1952, recognized that its members were 'not as conscious of the bitterness of the bread of exile as the members of the Gaelic League or the political clubs', but argued that the society still had a 'legitimate function' as 'a meeting ground where writers and artists, professional men, upper civil servants, members of the Irish Party, and leaders of the Gaelic League and of the political clubs, could, and did meet and interchange opinions and arguments about things of general national interest'.[79] As he recognizes, such a shared space was vulnerable and proved to be 'ill-fitted to withstand the stresses of the war and of Easter week'. But despite this, it was still a very long way from the idealistic first meetings of the Southwark Irish Literary Club in the Surrey Rooms in 1883.

---

[76] O. Z., 'From a Modern Irish Portrait Gallery VI', 25.
[77] D. P. Moran, 'One Hundred Years of Irish Humbug', *An Claidheamh Soluis* (19 December 1900), 149–51, 149.
[78] Mo Moulton, *Ireland and the Irish in Interwar England* (Cambridge: Cambridge University Press, 2014), 228.
[79] O'Hegarty, BMH Statement: 839.

At this point, it is useful to recall the distinction between different types of revival organizations in this period as drawn by Clare Hutton in her pioneering work on Irish cultural history. As she notes:

> As the 1890s wore on, revivalism itself had begun to stratify into a range of disparate (though still interrelated) cultural constituencies. On the one hand, there were increasing numbers of people with a revivalist *mentalité*, such as Gaelic Leaguers, Irish Irelanders, and individuals who were committed to economic revivalism; on the other, there was a much smaller and more elite group of 'Literary Revivalists'.[80]

This divide can also be identified in London's revival institutions. While the ILS was increasingly associated with the activity of a literary elite and had, as Alex Davis notes, 'considerable overlap with the embryonic London avant-garde', elsewhere there was a burgeoning number of organizations with a more distinctively 'Irish-Ireland' outlook.[81] These bodies were markedly less interested in the cultural paradoxes faced by the Anglo-Irish and their hyphenated dilemmas and much more inclined to direct intervention in the social lives of the Irish in London. Indeed (in the context of London at least) it is possible to see these two types of organization as not simply offering parallel versions of Irish identity, but rather to recognize that they were frequently ideologically opposed. For this reason it became increasingly difficult for individuals to maintain an interest in both groupings and, as with Ryan, it is notable how many activists deserted the former type of movement and committed their energies instead to the emerging organizations. There were also a number of literary societies across the city that either had been inspired directly by the example of the Southwark Literary Club or were built on similar principles, a typical example being the North London Irish Literary Society, which met at Camden Hall in Camden Town. Like the Southwark Club, this society offered a series of recitations, readings, songs and soirées, but, according to its advertised programme, it was less exclusive than the Southwark and was occasionally willing to include non-Irish material.[82]

Irish dancing or, more specifically, ceili dancing was also an increasingly significant activity and one which had a distinctive London character. Organized by the London civil servant and Gaelic League secretary, Fionán MacColuim, it is generally considered that the first recognizable Irish ceili – meaning general participation figure dancing rather than an exhibition of step-dancing – was held in the Bloomsbury Hall in October 1897, following a more traditional concert of Irish music and dance. With the expertise of Patrick Reidy (or Professor Reidy as he was known), an Irish dance master living in Hackney (and, according to Reginald Hall, 'a national icon'), MacColuim then refined the format and devised new group dances such as 'The Walls of Limerick' and 'The Siege

[80] Clare Hutton, 'Joyce and the Institutions of Revivalism', *Irish University Review, Special Issue: New Perspectives on the Irish Literary Revival*, 33: 1 (Spring/Summer 2003), 117–32, 123.

[81] Alex Davis, 'Whoops from the Peat Bog? Joseph Campbell and the London Avant-garde', in *The Irish Revival Reappraised (Nineteenth-Century Ireland)*, ed. Betsey Taylor FitzSimon and James H. Murphy (Dublin: Four Courts Press, 2004), 145–53, 147.

[82] *Weekly Freeman's Journal* (18 February 1888), 6.

of Ennis' with the intention of increasing the number of participants (spectating was discouraged) and ensuring that the movements and sequences remained respectable.[83] Such dances, as well as new eight- and four-handed reels and jigs, were variants on what Reidy insisted were much older Irish forms and they proved extremely popular both in London and back in Ireland. As Gwynn described, following the conclusion of evening Irish classes in the Athenaeum Hall, Tottenham Court Road, 'with the greatest alacrity, the floor is cleared, and the young people fall to dancing Irish dances to Irish airs'.[84] At the 1901 Gaelic League Oireachtas in Dublin, enthusiastic London members, including MacColuim, Art O'Brien (who would eventually become London League president and a member of the Irish Revolutionary Brotherhood (IRB)), Eileen Drury and Una Ni Dubhda, demonstrated these new dances in a performance at the Mansion House, although there was significant resistance to their introduction as sanctioned League activities due to what was perceived as their synthetic and un-Irish origins. The publication in 1902 of *A Handbook of Irish Dances* by James O'Keeffe (a prominent London League activist originally of the Southwark Club) and O'Brien offered itself, at least in part, as a rebuttal of these objections in its assertion of the historical legitimacy of the dances it described.[85] Such arguments about cultural authenticity are rarely resolved to the satisfaction of all parties, but certainly it is true that without the work of the London Gaelic League modern Irish dance would have taken a very different form.

Alongside these essentially cultural initiatives, it is also important to recognize the presence of other Irish organizations across the capital that were less avowedly nationalist in their outlook but which still played a substantial role as nodes in the Irish-London network. These included the Four Provinces Club in the Inns of Court, the Union of the Four Provinces of Ireland, and, most significantly, the Irish Club in Charing Cross Road. The latter was a key location for both political debate and theatrical gossip, and, in the words of Diarmuid O'Leary (the Clapham IRB member), a venue 'frequented by artists looking for employment'.[86] As it was a location where the worlds of Irish drama, literature and politics mingled in a slightly more louche atmosphere than revivalists would usually tolerate it constituted a unique space. Finally, there were also a large number of Irish political organizations which flourished and faded with remarkable frequency. These were not exactly revival bodies as Hutton defines them, but they were certainly sympathetic to revival ideals and included many overlapping individuals. Many of these organizations were located at the Fenian headquarters at 55 Chancery Lane and included, as David Fitzpatrick lists them, 'the Young Ireland Society (founded in 1882), Parnellite Leadership Committee (1891), Parnellite Irish National League of Great Britain (1891), Amnesty Association (1892), Gaelic League (1896), Gaelic Athletic Association (1895), O'Donovan Rossa Reception Committee, John Daly Reception Committee, '98 Centenary Association, Irish National Club (1899),

---

[83] Reginald Richard Hall, *Irish Music and Dance in London, 1890–1970: A Socio-Cultural History* (PhD Thesis, University of Sussex, 1994), 112.

[84] Stephen Gwynn, 'Gaels in London', *Westminster Gazette* (3 June 1902), 3.

[85] J. G. O'Keeffe and Art O'Brien, *A Handbook of Irish Dances: With an Essay on Their Origin and History* (Dublin: O'Donoghue, 1902).

[86] Jeremiah J. (Diarmuid) O'Leary, BMH Witness Statement: 1108 (2 March 1955).

Cumann na Gaedheal (1903) and Sinn Féin (1905)[87] 55 Chancery Lane was one of the medical practices occupied by the veteran Fenian Mark Ryan, a sometime member of the IRB's Supreme Council and a vital figure in the political mobilization of Irish London through this period. Ryan was the inspiration for these organizations and was on all but one of their committees, but rather than an indication of vigour, their sheer number spoke more accurately of what M. J. Kelly has described as 'the fragility of Irish nationalist organisation in this period.'[88] That said, 55 Chancery Lane was a location of deep importance and was described by the IRB member Thomas Barry as nothing less than the 'centre of Irish National life in London.'[89] Alongside Ryan, who had stepped down from frontline involvement in the organization at this point, the IRB organizer Anthony McBride (the brother of the prominent republicans John and Joseph) was also a doctor at the practice and for a period it was the hub for all IRB activity in Britain.[90] As a result nearly all the ostensibly outward-facing political organizations that were headquartered there were IRB fronts, and it was also the location from which the infiltration of organizations such as the Gaelic Athletic Association (GAA) was directed.[91] The police were well aware of this activity; Richard Connolly, who would eventually become the London Representative on the Supreme Council of the IRB in 1913, was sworn into the organization at Chancery Lane in 1902 and his recollections of this period emphasize the heavy surveillance they had to negotiate.[92]

The Gaelic League, which reorganized in London in 1896 after a brief period as a subsidiary body of the ILS, also had strong links with the Chancery Lane IRB, and for a period it was startlingly successful in mobilizing Irish Ireland in the capital with around 1,500 members in its numerous regional centres.[93] These 'Local Schools', as the League called them, were distributed evenly across the capital in locations such as Barking, Islington, Kew, Vauxhall, Haverstock Hill and Fulham. There was also a second branch at Forest Gate in East London, which remained autonomous from the central London League until a merger in 1904. At the peak of the League's success, the scale of its gatherings was certainly impressive; O'Conor Eccles reported in 1902 that 'the visitor to the Athenaeum Hall, Tottenham Court Road, will find on any Monday evening some two hundred young men and women assembled to study Gaelic'.[94] Not unreasonably, then, the League in London would think of itself as 'suggestive, at its best, of the beginnings of a national university', committed to the creation of 'an awakened,

[87] See Mark F. Ryan, *Fenian Memories* (Dublin: Gill and Son, 1945), 172 and David Fitzpatrick, 'A Curious Middle Place: The Irish in Britain, 1871–1921', in *The Irish in Britain 1815–1939*, ed. Roger Swift and Sheridan Gilley (London: Pinter Publishers, 1989), 34–5.
[88] M. J. Kelly, *The Fenian Ideal and Irish Nationalism, 1882–1916* (Woodbridge: Boydell Press, 2006), 24.
[89] Thomas Barry, BMH Witness Statement: 1 (22 February 1947).
[90] Ibid.
[91] Richard Connolly, BMH Witness Statement: 523 (5 June 1951).
[92] Ibid.
[93] According to Mark Ryan, Fahy 'never joined the Fenian movement, but was on terms of friendship with those of us who believed in physical force' (Ryan, *Fenian Memories*, 157).
[94] Swift, *Irish Migrants in Britain, 1815–1914*, 192.

trained, alert, enlightened people, with a clear consciousness of its strength'.[95] While the primary work of the League was focused on the Irish language, it interpreted its brief more broadly and played an important role in such related activities as regulating the definition and teaching of Irish step dancing in the capital, working with its closest ally, the GAA, in promoting joint cultural and sporting events and organizing many ceilis, Irish music recitals, St Patrick's Night Festivals, *Feiseanna,* and, eventually, an annual *Aonach* (or trade fair) at the Royal Horticultural Hall in Westminster. There was clearly significant demand in London for such Irish entertainment, and it is notable that on St Patrick's Day in 1906 the League filled the Royal Opera House in Covent Garden for both matinee and evening performances of Irish music. For these reasons, the London branch gained a reputation for dynamism and innovation within the overall organization; it was zealous in its recruitment, 'intensely earnest and intensely sincere', and continually looking to deploy new technology such as the phonograph and gramophone to enhance its work.[96] In these heady early days, enthusiasm for the League's work could become evangelical. As Ryan observed, 'the Gaelic League is the story of ourselves: our better selves tuned up to co-operative effort in the intellectual, the artistic, and to some extent the spiritual order'.[97] As such it was 'related to elements in our subconscious, or supra-conscious, natures'.[98] Ryan was not alone in responding to the spiritual elements of the League's message. For O'Hegarty the League enabled him 'to be put into touch with something far back in the Race'.[99] As he continued, 'unknown depths in me were stirred, and across the centuries I seemed to be in touch with days when Irish speech and Irish manners and traditions were in every valley and on every hill and by every river'. Certainly, it is impossible to fully account for the work of the League in London or the devotion it inspired without acknowledging the power of this mystical element and the manner in which it galvanized many otherwise mundane lives. More prosaically, as Gwynn observed after his initial immersion into the work of the organization, the London Gaelic League contained many fanatics, 'but no movement goes far without its fanatics'.[100]

However, despite the intensity of the League's appeal for individual activists, it remained subject to dramatic fluctuations in membership. Numbers tended to decline when prospects for Home Rule appeared most favourable but would climb again as such hopes inevitably receded. For this reason the League was most vibrant around 1902–6, then endured a period of steady retraction, before being galvanized again by the revolutionary events of 1916. Many of the 'Southwark strain' who were no longer at the heart of the ILS, such as Fahy, Ryan and O'Keeffe, would find themselves working together as early League mobilizers, with Fahy, who believed that 'the only distinction

[95] *Inis Fáil: A Magazine for the Irish in London* (September 1904), 1.
[96] 'The Emigration Play at Hampstead', *Inis Fáil: A Magazine for the Irish in London* (June 1906), 2. 'London Notes', *An Claidheamh Soluis* (22 June 1901), 231.
[97] W. P. Ryan, 'Twenty-Five Years of the London Gaelic League', *Guth na nGaedheal: Half-Yearly Magazine of the Gaelic League of London* (March 1924), 7–11, 11.
[98] Ibid., 7.
[99] O'Hegarty, BMH Statement: 839.
[100] Gwynn, 'Gaels in London', 3.

between an Irishman and an Englishman was a knowledge of the tongue of his sires', acting as its first president.[101] Their social backgrounds were indicative of the profile of the League as a whole. Although the organization liked to praise its classlessness, stressing that at its meetings 'the gay Lothario from Somerset House or Whitehall rubbed shoulders with the man who wielded a pick on the Embankment' while the 'the young lady from the Savings Bank Department' would 'share her O'Growney with the waitress who served her occasionally with a glass of milk and a bath bun at the ABC', in reality the lower-middle-class London Irish dominated the membership lists. More distinctive was the fact that a greater number of women were active in the League both as teachers and students than was the case with other revival organizations of the time.[102] Indeed, according to Jennie Wyse Power, it was 'the first Irish national society which accepted women as members on the same terms as men'.[103] Indeed, a provable Irish descent and an annual subscription of five shillings were the only requirements for membership, although the latter was a serious deterrent for those who were not financially secure. Perhaps for this reason the League was essentially middle-class in its tastes. The venues it chose for its social events were aspirational, and it policed the manners and etiquette of its members assiduously.[104] In this case, however, 'aspiration' was not a euphemism for social integration, and the League was distinct from earlier revival organizations in being much more absolute in its politics and stern in its opposition to cultural assimilation. This was clearly evident in the League's half-yearly magazine, *Guth na nGaedheal*, which first appeared in 1904 – in many ways the revival's annus mirabilis. Despite its London-Irish focus, the magazine was determined in its absolute refusal to countenance that there could be anything positive about life in the capital at all. Indeed, it considered the continued presence of Irish people in London as little short of a national tragedy. As M. E. L. Butler (aka Mary Butler) wrote:

> To none of our exiled kindred does my heart go out in such passionate pity as to those who are obliged by stress of circumstances, and entirely against their will, to remain in England. It must be an unending trial to live in such uncongenial surroundings; among those who are alien to them in race and creed, hostile to their national aspirations, and incapable of entering into their inner thoughts or of sharing their deeper emotions.
>
> We at home watch with intimate sympathy the brave efforts which are being made by the Gaelic League of London to save the Irish of that city from losing their national self-consciousness, and from being merged in the British populace,

---

[101] *Freeman's Journal* (29 August 1899), 6. In this context, it is interesting to note that it was not until he was in London that Fahy gained fluency in the language ('Irish Literary Celebrities, no. VII', *Dublin Weekly Nation* (29 December 1888), 3–4, 3).

[102] *The Irishman* (May 1913), 6. 'O'Growney' refers to Eugene O'Growney's *Simple Lessons in Irish: Giving the Pronunciation of Each Word* (Dublin: Gaelic League, 1901).

[103] Jennie Wyse Power, 'The Political Influence of Women in Modern Ireland', *The Voice of Ireland: A Survey of the Race and Nation from All Angles*, ed. W. G. FitzGerald (Dublin: John Heywood, 1923), 158–61, 159.

[104] 'The Manners of Gaelic Leaguers', *Inis Fáil: A Magazine for the Irish in London* (June 1906), 11.

by re-knitting the bonds which bind them to their own land: the bonds formed by national traditions, and customs, and history, and, above all, national language.[105]

An enthusiastic national organizer for the League and the woman who suggested to Arthur Griffiths that he might call his new organization 'Sinn Féin', Butler's area of interest tended to be on the duties of Irish women in the home, what Frank A. Biletz terms her 'domestic nationalism'.[106] In this her appeal to Irish women living in London was austere; as nothing positive resided in London itself, it became 'an Irish woman's duty to steep her home in an Irish atmosphere' and to 'furnish our homes from attic to cellar in Irish manufacture', until such a time as a return to Ireland itself could be enabled.[107]

This was not the extent of *Guth na nGaedheal*'s anti-London editorializing. P. T. McGinley's article 'Over Here in England' was more forthright again, fulminating against the assimilation of the Irish into British life, a process which 'jars upon our sense of poetic justice as well as upon our national instincts'.[108] McGinley, better known as Peadar Toner Mac Fhionnlaoich, would become president of the League in 1922 and was an important figure in steering language policy in the new Irish state. Although he was based in Ireland at the time he wrote the article, he had previously spent nineteen years in England as a member of the British Civil Service during which time he nuanced his Anglophobia and developed a distaste for both the Irish in Britain ('who frequently despise everything belonging to the race from which they have sprung'), and 'the influence of the Catholic Church and the Catholic schools in Great Britain'. For McGinley, then, the task of the League in London was nothing less than to wage cultural war, 'to retard the Anglicising process', and 'to induce Irish people resident in Great Britain to return to Ireland'. Although it may not have been obvious to McGinley due to the fact that he was no longer living in the city, there was a certain contradiction implicit to this position: the more the Gaelic League in London emphasized the vibrancy of its social activities and the range of cultural and educational possibilities it was creating within the capital – it was, in its own words, 'a virile and growing organisation' – the more stridently it urged Irish Londoners to abandon the city and return to Ireland.[109] As *Inis Fáil*, another magazine produced by the London Gaelic League, noted in 1905, 'the return of the Wild Geese from London is becoming a constant and mixed source of pleasure and sorrow to us. Unfortunately for the Gaelic League in London the flight generally takes place from among our best workers'.[110] Indeed, many would make the journey back at this time, one such being

---

[105] M. E. L. Butler, 'Irishwomen and the Home Language', *Guth na nGaedheal: Half-Yearly Magazine of the Gaelic League of London* (1904), 18–21, 21.

[106] Frank A. Biletz, 'Women and Irish-Ireland: The Domestic Nationalism of Mary Butler', *New Hibernia Review/Iris Éireannach Nua*, 6:1 (Spring, 2002), 59–72.

[107] Butler, 'Irishwomen and the Home Language', 20.

[108] P. T. McGinley, 'Over Here in England', *Guth na nGaedheal: Half-Yearly Magazine of the Gaelic League of London* (1904), 21–2, 21.

[109] Editorial, *Guth na nGaedheal: Half-Yearly Magazine of the Gaelic League of London* (1904), 7.

[110] 'Still They Go', *Inis Fáil: A Magazine for the Irish in London* (September 1905), 7.

the long-time activist W. P. Ryan who returned to Ireland in 1905 to begin a new life as editor of *The Irish Peasant*. One wonders what Fahy, who remained president of the League in London until he retired from ill health in 1908, made of these departures. Fond of taking his Southwark Literary Club for walks in the 'delightful [...] English countryside' in the 1880s, he was, despite his politics, deeply enmeshed in London's culture and history.[111] In this he was perhaps better able than many of his fellow League members to synthesize new realities from seemingly contradictory positions, and, as such, had more in common with the majority of Irish Londoners than with the non-integrationist position of the organization he headed. Unlike many of his fellow League members, he would resist the lure of Ireland and remained in London for the rest of his life, dying at his house in Clapham in April 1936.

Inis Fáil, which carried the subtitle 'A Magazine for the Irish in London', appeared monthly and with its emphasis on the minutiae of the organization, its slightly fussy obsession with branch housekeeping, and its fondness for gentle satire, appears to bear more of O'Hegarty's imprint than did the stern entreaties of *Guth na nGaedheal*. For example, in its first issue it carried a humorous piece lightly mocking Yeats's assertion that 'someday we shall fight dragons among blue hills' at a time when the Irish language itself was undergoing a rapid modernization of its technical vocabulary, and reprimanded members' habitual lack of punctuality for League events. This element of mild censure became one of *Inis Fáil*'s signature elements; a report on the west London Feis at Feltham in September 1905 criticized the half-hearted efforts of the entrants, complaining that 'we expected more spirit, more courage and dash in the competitions. The whole, while very agreeable, was not our ideal of a social and intellectual rally of the Gael'. 'We do not write in a carping spirit, but just to remind our friends that they did not quite do themselves justice,' the report continued to seemingly no great effect.[112]

IRB influence in the London Gaelic League was deep-rooted and had been present since the organization's inception. Indeed, according to Connolly, in some branches the League was effectively run by IRB operatives for its own purposes. As he recalled in 1951, 'we had a section in Peckham which was called the Davis Section. We had a branch of the Gaelic League there called the Thomas Davis Branch and we used that as a cover for our activities'.[113] The same was true of the GAA which had, in Barry's words, 'developed into a powerful organisation, the officers of which were all IRB men'.[114] At its peak the GAA had ten clubs across the city and in its promotion of Gaelic football, hurling, athletics and camogie it could reach parts of Irish London (typically younger men and women newly arrived from Ireland) which the Gaelic League found more difficult to attract. That said, numbers were never large and the organization was always in competition with the many other sports played across the capital in its search for participants, but it was successful in acting as the gateway for many who would

[111] Hutton, 'Francis Fahy's "Ireland in London"', 252.
[112] 'West London Feis', *Inis Fáil: A Magazine for the Irish in London* (October 1905), 2.
[113] Connolly, BMH Statement: 523.
[114] Barry, BMH Statement: 1.

subsequently become deeply involved in Irish politics and the promotion of Irish culture. The task of converting GAA enthusiasts into IRB members fell to Frank Burke (later de Burca) who had joined the IRB in London in 1893. In his own words, his brief was to make 'as big a splash as possible and, by activities in [the] GAA Organisation, to collect possible recruits for the IRB'.[115] Although, according to Denis McCullough, president of the IRB in 1915–16, Burke was little more than 'a fool', he had some success, and it is striking how many men were radicalized through this method.[116] John Shouldice was a typical example: he had left Ballaghaderreen in Ireland in 1899 aged seventeen to join the Civil Service in London, was immediately fostered by the GAA and was sworn into the IRB in 1901 at Chancery Lane. He would return to Ireland in 1907 and would have a significant role in the Easter Rising in 1916.[117]

For all the achievements of the Gaelic League and the revival in London more generally – the social structures it put in place, its rejuvenation of an ideal of Irish culture that was both dignified and meaningful, its ability to counter anti-Irish racism in a city which remained deeply prejudiced, and, perhaps most importantly, its profound radicalization of a significant number of individuals who would shape the course of Irish history during the following fifty years – it is necessary to remember that in the context of the Irish population of London as a whole it remained the activity of a small minority drawn from a limited social class. As O'Hegarty noted, despite its best efforts, 'the average Irish working man who comes to London would not come into the Gaelic class on any conditions, and you cannot force him'.[118] In itself this is not a criticism as to reach beyond this limited community and so engage with the vast majority of the London Irish – many of whom were poor, suffered from widespread illiteracy and had little leisure time for the kind of activities the revival encouraged – would have required resources far beyond those that were available. Moreover, the Catholic Church in London, while content to recognize the distinctive contours of Irish ethnic identity and its own role in shaping it, was frequently less than sympathetic to what it perceived as the political motivations of revival bodies. As a result, and despite the best efforts of individuals such as Fahy, the reach of the revival in the city was always going to be limited. However, this is not to imply that those London Irish who were largely untouched by the revival ethos lost their sense of Irish nationality – as Lynn Hollen Lees notes 'although a certain amount of cultural diffusion took place over time in London, the Irish resisted assimilation' – but it does suggest that the type of Irish identity that developed was of a kind not sanctioned by the Gaelic League with its aspirations to respectability and a certain engrained prudishness.[119] The next chapter of this study will look in greater detail at these alternative modes of cultural Irishness and the manner in which they circulated around London during this period.

---

[115] F. de Burca, BMH Witness Statement: 105 (undated).
[116] Denis McCullough, BMH Witness Statement: 915 (11 December 1953).
[117] John Shouldice, BMH Witness Statement: 162 (16 November 1948).
[118] P. S. O'Hegarty, 'Are We Democratic?', *Inis Fáil: A Magazine for the Irish in London* (March 1910), 4.
[119] Lynn Hollen Lees, *Exiles of Erin: Irish Migrants in Victorian London* (Manchester: Manchester University Press, 1979), 249.

One benefit of viewing the revival from the perspective of those that were excluded from it is that it enables some of its blind spots and elisions to be more clearly revealed. While the stratifications of class provide one effective way of understanding how participation in the revival's work was self-limiting, another can be perceived by a consideration of the way in which the role of women in revival organizations shifted over time. This chapter has already noted the manner in which the ILS was dominated by men in outward-facing committee positions despite the high number of women involved in the work of the society in other ways, most notably as part of the 'Original Nights' programme. In this, as in Ryan's attack on ILS women members who 'have not done a very great deal towards intellectual impulse', much of the revival's appeal was predicated on a belief in the vigour of male homosociality and, as with related organizations such as the Rhymers' Club, an enjoyment of its pleasures.[120] This tendency can be identified even in proto-revival organizations such as the Southwark Club, which in its transformation from a junior to an adult organization appeared to sideline the role of women as mobilizers. Once this change was effected, the hierarchy of the organization was rigid; Fahy recalls a committee member, P. J. Keawell, presenting notes for the efficient running of club meetings which included the following entreaty:

> Ladies – They should be got to work more – they are of little use at present, and what with our *new blood and talent* they will be nowhere shortly if they don't look up. If we could get our Post Office lady clerks to act they might have sufficient cheek to shame others.[121]

It is left unrecorded what work Keawell – who would eventually return to Ireland and become a senior figure in the national Gaelic League – expected of the club's female members, but the vituperative nature of his attack is notable given that women had been the primary organizers of the Southwark Junior Irish Literary Club only a few years previously.

Such exclusions cannot be explained simply by recourse to the broader social context of the time. As the presence of ILS activists such as O'Conor Eccles, who campaigned for women's education, and Sophie Bryant, who was prominent in the National Union of Suffrage Societies in 1908, indicates, revival organizations in London were part of a wider and diverse political landscape where progressive ideas could cross-pollinate. The measures taken by the Gaelic League to guarantee equality of membership between men and women also indicate an awareness of other political issues beyond the national question, although in practice the efficacy of this awareness was limited. Moreover, alongside these essentially social revival organizations, it is necessary to recognize the importance of, what Hutton describes as, 'institutions which promoted revivalism to communities through the written word (for example, publishing houses, journals and newspapers, libraries, and bookshops)'.[122] It is notable that women were more centrally

---

[120] O. Z., 'From a Modern Irish Portrait Gallery VI', 25.
[121] Hutton, 'Francis Fahy's "Ireland in London"', 256.
[122] Hutton, 'Joyce and the Institutions of Revivalism', 118.

involved in these types of organization. Initiatives such as *The Irish Home Reading Magazine*, published under the banner of the Irish Literary Society and jointly edited by Eleanor Hull and Lionel Johnson in 1894, or the 'Irish Texts Society', founded in 1898 and steered by Hull and Norma Borthwick, were in many ways complementary to social revival organizations but they also indicate a subtle shift in priorities. *The Irish Home Reading Magazine* was an ambitious project designed around a four-year programme of study, beginning with the early history of Ireland before the Norman invasion and concluding with Catholic emancipation. Perhaps as a result of this it never established itself and lasted only two issues. However, the 'Irish Texts Society', which was 'instituted for the purpose of promoting the publication of Texts in the Irish Language, accompanied by such Introductions, English translations, glossaries and notes as may be deemed desirable', was more successful and by 1900 it had 470 members in London alone.[123] Borthwick, another alumna of the Southwark Literary Society in the 1880s, would go on to be a major revival mobilizer, becoming chairman of the Drumcondra Gaelic League branch in Dublin in 1900 and, with Mairéad Ní Raghallaigh, founder of the *Irish Book Company* in 1901.

As these examples indicate, through this period reading was a key element of the process of political self-formation and another means of creating networks of common cause across the city. Indeed, if Irishness in London in the 1870s and 1880s was typically associated with performance, exhibition and parade, it is noticeable how the revival instead privileged individual contemplative acts such as reading, creative work and the study of the Irish language. This shift did not mean of course that public and formal displays of Irishness were no longer apparent, but it does perhaps indicate that such performative moments were now used to reinforce a sense of individual Irish identity which was often primarily imagined through the private consumption of texts and the acquisition of key knowledges. This indicates something of the breadth of the revival's appeal but also its limitations. Despite the efforts of bodies such as the Gaelic League to circumscribe the political and cultural agency of its members, in London at least such an aspiration would only ever have partial success. The revival's stern warnings about the dangers of assimilation, voiced most insistently through the pages of *Guth na nGaedheal* and *Inis Fáil*, could not prevent the reality of the fact that the shifting and conditional nature of ethnic identification among the London Irish allowed for integration with many host practices, even while it protected the primacy of other cherished native habits and observances. Indeed, although the revival in London offered itself as a design for life, coherent and self-contained, it can be argued with the benefit of hindsight that its real achievement was to create, through a series of insistent rhetorical strategies, the idea of the Irish subject as an agent of political change. And, as this book will discuss, in the years leading up to 1916, it is in this way more than any other that the movement in London would prove seismic.

[123] Irish Texts Society General Rules May 1898 (NLI: EPH C238).

5

'Ria's on the job': Irish popular performance in London

Walter Sickert's painting 'Little Dot Hetherington at the Bedford Music Hall' (see Figure 7) from 1888 is one of the most stunning images of popular performance in nineteenth-century London. Depicting the evening's entertainment of 24 November 1888, the work features Dot, centre stage at the Bedford in Camden, cast in a vivid white light and gesturing up to the gallery. Indeed, as the subtitle to the image that Sickert would sometimes add indicates, the song she is performing is the music-hall standard 'The Boy I Love Is Up In The Gallery', originally performed by Nelly Power and later to be made famous by Marie Lloyd. Framing Dot in her pool of light is the (almost entirely male) audience, the Chairman, Joe Haynes, to the right, and what appear to be boxes on either side of the stage. Her command of the space is total and she holds the audience's attention with absolute certainty, a confidence that sits (perhaps uneasily) with her obviously childlike form.

On closer examination, Sickert's painting further complicates our sense of Dot's performance. In the lower section of the image, above what appears to be the backs of vacant chairs, what could possibly be a balustrade gradually resolves itself to be, in fact, the frame of one of the heavy gilt mirrors that were a dominating feature of the Bedford's ornate interior. The image of little Dot is, then, all reflection. Moreover the reflected image on its left-hand side reflects back the image of the mirror on the right, creating an effect that the art historian Wendy Baron has described as a 'physical impossibility'.[1] Sickert's technique allows us to see the hall, the performer, and the audience but places these elements in a complex and disrupted relationship. Ultimately, even with our recognition of his use of the mirror, the image simply will not settle into coherence. Moreover, little Dot herself, the painting's subject, is not as guileless as she first appears. As was frequently the case with child performers at this time, the material she is performing is basically adult in content and, alongside this, as John Stokes observes, as she gestures upwards, she is 'teasing the gallery with the fancy that she can see them as they can see her'.[2] In this manner she presents the illusion of clear

Wendy Baron, *Sickert: Paintings and Drawings* (New Haven: Yale University Press, 2006), 20.
[2] John Stokes, *In the Nineties* (London: Harvester Wheatsheaf, 1989), 74.

Figure 7 Walter Sickert, 'Little Dot Hetherington at the Bedford Music Hall' (1888).

vision that the painting in other ways denies. Either way, the object of Dot's adoration, the boy in the gallery, is out of view and off limits both to her and to us, while the men that do appear in the picture seem to embody less innocent passions. Taken as a whole, then, the painting powerfully illustrates a perception of the music hall as a constantly disorientating place, the manner in which, as Lenin famously observed to Maxim Gorky in 1907, the British music hall takes the commonplace and 'attempt[s] to turn it inside-out, to distrust it somewhat, to point up the illogicality of the everyday'.[3]

Of Dot's subsequent career there is little we can assert with confidence, although we do now have a few more details than were available to Anna Gruetzner Robins, who stated baldly in 1992 that 'nothing is now known of her life'.[4] Born Florence Louise

---

[3] 'V. I. Lenin to Maxim Gorky, 1907', in *Collected Works, XVII* (Moscow: Progress, 1952), 16.
[4] Anna Gruetzner Robins, 'Sickert "Painter-in-Ordinary" to the Music-Hall', in *Sickert, Paintings*, ed. Wendy Baron and Richard Shone (New Haven: Yale University Press, 1992), 13–24, 16.

Hetherington in 1879 (she died in 1934), she is first advertised in the music-hall trade journal the *Era* in May 1887. Later that year the same newspaper noted approvingly that she was 'very clever and graceful in her movements'.[5] She would continue to perform in a steady, if unspectacular, fashion for the next fifteen years, mostly in the provincial theatres and pantomime. By 1900 her act had changed to the extent that she was described as a 'pleasing comedienne', and, on occasion, 'a soubrette and skipping rope dancer'.[6] Her career, then, was clearly not unsuccessful, but it was also mostly unremarked and unremarkable – like thousands of other performers who passed through the halls at this time. Certainly Dot's starring role in Sickert's painting would prove to be her one lasting claim to posterity. As such, she is a resonant symbol of the essential anonymity of much music-hall performance.

Looking beyond little Dot, Sickert's painting contains another unexpected detail. In the background of the image, peering around the stage curtain awaiting her turn, is a dark female figure in a black dress and hat. Her figure is half obscured by the curtain and her presence forms an uncomfortable (or even perhaps a little sinister) relationship with the angelic Dot in the foreground. As Baron has identified, this is Bessie Bellwood, the Irish Cockney singer, and at this time one of the biggest stars of the halls.[7] Well might she be displaying some apprehension at having to follow what is clearly a mesmerizing performance by the child singer. The effect of the juxtaposition is striking and a little troubling. Moreover, as with its optical complexities, Sickert's painting is misleading in its denotation of historical significance. Little Dot is the star of Sickert's canvas but would never achieve headline billing, while the shadowy Bessie – the figure who seems to elude Sickert's art – was in reality the phenomenon. Or perhaps it can be argued that Sickert's painting is telling us this too; Dot is the star of the moment, her performance flaring briefly before disappearing, but Bellwood, the next turn, is the older, larger, and more knowing presence. Indeed the moment of the painting is so intense simply because it is a moment – because it does not gesture to any larger narratives. As such it symbolizes one of the key and most affecting mythologies of music-hall performance: its momentary brilliance and its immediate obsolescence. Sickert's painting makes a fetish of little Dot and, in so doing, is implicitly mistrustful of Bellwood's backstage role and the professionalization of the halls which she appears to represent. Such a casting is unfair at one level, but at another astutely recognizes the significance of Bellwood as one of the first generation of newly professional music-hall stars at the forefront of the evolution of the form into a mode of mass entertainment.

These contexts transform Sickert's painting into a representation of a complex historical moment. In this the elusive and the allusive merge in the mysterious figure of Bessie, half visible, central to the painting's meaning, but also peripheral. Interpreted as such she becomes a powerful image for Irish London as a whole, a community which, as I have previously discussed, was often considered shrouded or secretive by

---

[5] *Era* (24 September 1887), 10.
[6] *Era* (29 September 1900), 21, and *Era* (15 December 1900), 17.
[7] Baron, *Sickert: Paintings and Drawings*, 178.

those who sought to explicate its mysteries. In fact Bellwood had a more substantial relationship to Sickert's work than her marginal role in the painting suggests. The two became friends around this period and Sickert sketched her on a number of occasions in 1888.[8] These repeated spectral images, depicting her in profile or three-quarter length, in different outfits, sometimes veiled and sometimes singing, indicate something of her typical mannerisms.[9] More mystifyingly, on the same sheets as the images of Bellwood are sketches of a policeman, and an undefined (although clearly genteel) man. Another individual image that survives is dated 21 June 1888 and titled 'Bess-ay ... ', and this forms the basis for the representation of Bellwood that appears in the Little Dot Hetherington painting.[10] But ultimately all these images of Bellwood remain unrealized, or give an impression of having been abandoned.

Despite her one-time notoriety, Bellwood too is now a largely forgotten figure. Born Elizabeth Ann Catherine Mahoney in 1857, her family was originally from Monkstown in Co. Cork, but her upbringing was among the Irish community of Bermondsey where she worked in local industry and, as was often reported in numerous hagiographic pen portraits, as a rabbit puller (or fur dresser), an exhausting and hazardous profession memorably described by George Sims in *How the Poor Live*.[11] Like many Irish families in London, in the summer they would relocate to Kent to work in the hop fields. It was as Mahoney, rather than Bellwood, that she began her career by singing Irish ballads in the early years of music hall, and posing, in M. Willson Disher's words, as 'the guileless daughter of Erin' at venues such as the Star in Bermondsey and the Jolly Tanners in Southwark.[12] 'Finding that line of business scarcely remunerative', as the *Era* put it, the transformation from Irish singer to Bessie Bellwood, Cockney comedienne, happened early in her life – twenty-five of her thirty-nine years of life were spent on the stage – and by 1876 she was playing large halls such as the London Pavilion.[13] Her personal reinvention immediately anticipated the development of the music halls from smaller venues (typically tavern rooms) to much larger purpose-built sites; what Stokes has described as 'a process of rapid expansion as the shabby, suburban establishments, with their "chairman", their rough and ready "turns" and their local clientele were challenged by the big West End theatres'.[14] As a result, Bellwood was at the vanguard of profound structural changes in urban popular entertainment during this period and was one of the first acts to refine and codify the idea of 'cockney performance'

[8] Matthew Sturgis, *Walter Sickert: A Life* (London: Harper Collins, 2005), 155. See also, Robert Emmons, *The Life and Opinions of Walter Richard Sickert* (London: Faber, 1941), 49.
[9] See, for instance, Ruth Bromberg, *Walter Sickert: Prints, A Catalogue Raisonné* (New Haven: Yale University Press, 2000), 95.
[10] Wendy Baron, et al., *Walter Sickert: 'Drawing Is the Thing'* (Manchester: Whitworth Art Gallery, 2004), 38.
[11] 'Floor, walls, ceiling, every inch of the one room these people live and sleep in, is covered with fluff and hair. How they breathe in it is a mystery to me'. George Sims, *How the Poor Live* (New York: Garland, 1984 [1889]), 14.
[12] M. Willson Disher, *Winkles and Champagne: Comedies and Tragedies of the Music Hall* (London: B. T. Batsford, 1938), 22. Bellwood was still occasionally describing herself thus in 1891, aged thirty-four.
[13] *Era* (24 September 1876), 8.

as a popular element of music hall's appeal, paving the way for later (and ultimately more enduring) female singers. The typical London musical-hall audience of the time was challenging at best and openly aggressive at worst and in response Bellwood's act became increasingly confrontational. As the *Pall Mall Gazette* observed in its obituary notice in 1896, Bellwood 'took that phase of life which suited her powers best – THE LOW, ROWDY, FIGHTING, HAIR-TEARING GIRL of the lowest courts in the East-end, a creature all fringe and mouth, and into her, as into all her characters, she thrust her own strong individuality'.[15]

Such confrontation was central to the appeal of cockney performance in its early manifestation. Indeed, much of what passed for entertainment in the halls at this time was framed as a running conflict between the act and audience, and the ability to understand this and respond spontaneously to hecklers was vital to the success of many turns. Although recent research on music hall has concentrated on the subtly choreographed nature of this relationship, it is also true that, as the comedian Arthur Roberts observed, 'it was all uproar whether they liked you or not'.[16] Bellwood's stagecraft was particularly adept at – and indeed dependent on – responding to audience interventions. As 'the coster's laureate', Albert Chevalier, who frequently performed on the same programmes as Bellwood, observed: 'the wittiest "god" that ever hurled satire at a stage favourite, from the security of Olympian heights, would only attempt it with Bessie, knowing full well that he would come off second best'.[17] Similarly her obituary in the *London Daily News* praised her ability to 'rout such "Johnnies", as she would call them, with great slaughter'.[18] The other key aspect of her historical significance was that (along with her close contemporary Jenny Hill) she 'broke with the gentility of the lady duettist to create racy and original solo character acts'.[19] In Bellwood's case these characters included a number of late nineteenth-century stereotypes such as the 'knowing' barmaid, the sexually precocious maiden, and the prim bluestocking. However, it was in the inability of these characters to in any way disguise the actual substance of what was presented as Bellwood's own abrasive personality that the success of her act resided. As an obituary astutely observed, 'her songs served only as skeletons, round which, and in the middle of which, and, indeed, at both ends of which, she could interpolate her "patter"; and in this "patter" was the secret of success. She possessed an inexhaustible fund of slang, which flowed from her lips in an incessant stream'.[20] For this reason, Bellwood's performance was both fluid, in that it depended on the dynamics of the hall and the audience on any particular night, and yet curiously static in that its function was the revelation of Bellwood's own synthetic 'personality' (which was made manifest as a fixed and instantly recognizable

---

[14] Stokes, *In the Nineties*, 54.

[15] *Pall Mall Gazette* (25 September 1896), 7.

[16] Arthur Roberts, *Fifty Years of Spoof* (London: Bodley Head, 1927), 28.

[17] Willson Disher, *Winkles and Champagne*, 60.

[18] *London Daily News* (26 September 1896), 6.

[19] Martin Banham, ed., *The Cambridge Guide to Theatre* (Cambridge: Cambridge University Press, 2000), 488.

[20] *Pall Mall Gazette* (25 September 1896), 7.

series of preoccupations and responses). In this the obsessively parodic repetitions of her act revealed something of the fragility of music hall's class and gender archetypes.

Alongside Bellwood's willingness to confront the audience directly and the often choking sentimentality of many of her songs, the other crucial element in her appeal was her reputation for what, at the time, was considered shocking vulgarity. For H. Chance Newton, Bellwood was 'one of the sauciest serios ever seen in even the "saucy" halls of her time', while George Le Roy was more direct again: 'Vulgar she undoubtedly was', he notes, 'and greatly addicted to use of "The Blue Bag" in her act'.[21] This was implicit to her work even in the early years of her career; a review of her performance at the South London Palace in April 1882 noted her '*Chic* and vivacity', and added 'we think it must be said that Miss Bellwood sails as close to the wind as possible in the way of suggestiveness; but nobody seems to find fault with her, and the "faster" she becomes the more she appears to be appreciated'.[22] Her material at this time (which included 'impersonations of a forward young lady who offers to all comers apparently "A kiss on the cocoanut [sic] mat"') certainly pushed at the limits of what was permissible.[23] That said, the issue of music-hall vulgarity was multi-layered. While much censure of it in the popular press was little more than salacious, it was also celebrated on the grounds that, as Barry Faulk puts it, 'vulgar expression was the natural outcome of the bracingly bad taste of "the people"'.[24] As such, vulgarity was also redolent of a vernacular authenticity and could be accepted accordingly. Either way, although it was obvious to most that the seemingly endless streams of vapid innuendo provided by Bellwood and the other music-hall performers of risqué material were essentially harmless, the mounting pressure on the halls to attain a level of respectability during the late 1880s and 1890s meant that if anything she became a more, not less, controversial figure as the century progressed. Charges of indecency pursued her throughout her career, culminating in a libel case she brought against A. G. Crowder, a Middlesex Magistrate, in April 1889. Crowder had written to the manager of the Canterbury Music Hall in Lambeth accusing Bellwood of 'indecent performance' and stating that she had been dismissed from the Royal, the Cambridge, and the Pavilion as a result. Bellwood, claiming only to be interested in saving her reputation rather than any financial gain, decided to take legal action. The anticipation in the popular media for 'a libel case more sensational that Mr Parnell's' was intense; as the *Pall Mall Gazette* smirked, 'what will fall to the lot of the twelve men and true whose duty it will be to judge of the delicacy and refinement of Miss Bessie Bellwood'.[25] The newspaper was to be disappointed; when the case came to court Crowder accepted that his information had been incorrect and apologized, while Bellwood was awarded full costs. But this did not mark an end to concerns about the morality of her act. In September 1889 the Police sent an officer to question the manager of Day's Concert Hall in Birmingham, where

[21] H. Chance Newton, *Idols of the 'Halls' Being My Music Hall Memories* (London: Heath Cranton, 1928), 171. George Le Roy, *Music Hall Stars of the Nineties* (London: British Technical and General Press, 1952), 42.

[22] *Era* (29 April 1882), 4.

[23] *Era* (5 January 1884), 19.

[24] Barry J. Faulk, *Music Hall and Modernity: The Late Victorian Discovery of Popular Culture* (Athens: Ohio University Press, 2004), 3.

[25] *Pall Mall Gazette* (21 August 1888), 9.

Bellwood held a short residency, to investigate whether her songs were 'more or less of an improper character.'[26] Again no action was taken. Despite frequently expressed statements of outrage, the dynamics of live performance meant that pursuing such cases against music-hall acts was very difficult and usually futile.

In spite (or because) of these controversies Bellwood became an early 'star of the halls' and was one of a relatively small group of artists that through their sheer popularity were able to drive the hall syndication process that was taking place at this time. As Roberts notes, for a period she 'was drawing all London to any hall at which she was appearing and was sending all London into ecstasies of mirth and happiness by her inimitable art.'[27] Her advertising catchphrase in trade papers at this time, 'Our Bessie, Everybody's Bessie', indicates something of the manner in which she made her appeal. One of Bellwood's early enthusiasts was the novelist and proto-Irish revivalist George Moore, whose *Confessions of a Young Man* from 1886 warmly praised the culture of the music halls and particularly their 'communal enjoyment and its spontaneity' that 'set us thinking of Elizabethan England.'[28] Moore set the vibrancy of the halls against the artificiality of London bourgeois culture and its often anxious quest for respectability, symbolized by the productions of the actress and theatre manager Madge Kendal at the St James Theatre. In contrast Moore found in music hall a 'delightful unison of enjoyment', 'unanimity of soul' and 'communality of wit', in a manner that prefigured the ways T. S. Eliot would locate music hall in the nexus of the national culture in his tribute to Marie Lloyd in 1922.[29] For Moore, it was Bellwood, 'that inimitable artist', who encapsulated these qualities most profoundly:

> [Bellwood's] native wit is so curiously accentuated that it is no longer repellent vulgarity, but art, choice and rare – see, here she comes with 'What Cheer, Rea! Rea's on the job.' The sketch is slight, but it is welcome and refreshing after the eternal drawing-room and Mrs Kendal's cumbrous domesticity; it is curious, quaint, perverted, and are not these the *aions* and the attributes of art?[30]

Bellwood performed 'What Cheer 'Ria' from the early 1880s onwards and it is the song most closely associated with her, not least because she composed its tune (see Figure 8). With its knowing references to the protocols of the hall space and audience, it is an important work in the music-hall canon. Indeed, alongside 'The Boy I Love Is Up In The Gallery', 'What Cheer 'Ria' is one of the earliest examples of this mode of self-reflexivity. In the song, Maria (or 'Ria'), a coster girl, decides to spend some of the money she has earned from her work in the 'wegetable line' to buy some 'toggery' and a better seat at the music hall ('where I'd often been before') next to the Chairman. The transgression is obvious to all in attendance, most obviously Ria's 'pals in the gallery' who cry out 'Wotcher 'Ria? 'Ria's on the job/Wotcher 'Ria? Did you speculate a bob?' Because the typology of cockney performance in the music hall at this time

[26] *Pall Mall Gazette* (26 September 1889), 6.
[27] Roberts, *Fifty Years of Spoof*, 30.
[28] George Moore, *Confessions of a Young Man* (London: Heinemann, 1929 [1886]), 151–2.
[29] T. S. Eliot, 'London Letter', *The Dial*, LXXIII: 6 (December 1922), 659–63.
[30] Moore, *Confessions of a Young Man*, 153.

Figure 8 Bessie Bellwood, London-Irish music hall singer and comedienne, on the score cover of 'What Cheer 'Ria'.

required any attempt at social elevation or the denial of one's essential nature to end in downfall and repentance, so 'Ria's attempts at social improvement are destined to fail. After a series of increasingly unfortunate and farcical mishaps she is manhandled out of the hall secure only in the knowledge that in future she must remain within her class position or face social humiliation. Alongside the harshness of this message lodged within a supposedly comic turn, the song's constant awareness of its status as self-conscious performance created a series of disruptive contexts for the audience, an apprehension intensified by the fact that, as Tracy C. Davis notes, Bellwood sang the chorus with 'selective elisions to sound like "watch your rear"'.[31] J. S. Bratton has noted that the music-hall auditorium 'contained a constantly shifting audience that was not one group but many, the old divisions of box, pit and gallery fragmented into class, sex, money and age-based distinctions'.[32] 'What Cheer 'Ria' took this sense of flux as its starting point and tested the limits of the social distinctions at work within the space. In this the song recognized that the music hall was both a world in its own right while also reflective of the hierarchies and exclusions in wider society. As Faulk has observed, a crucial element of music hall was its role as 'a broadcast medium circulating subtle ways of knowing'. In this context, to 'know' about the subtleties of the halls' many social codes constituted a form of cultural capital.[33] Few performers of the time manipulated this knowledge and its attendant tensions more effectively.

By the early 1890s Bellwood had reached, in the *Era*'s words, 'the zenith of her popularity' and her appearance was frequently met with scenes of wild enthusiasm.[34] 'What Cheer 'Ria' was the most famous song of the day and she enjoyed the distinction of having both a coursing greyhound and a racehorse named after her. Despite this much of her private life remained mysterious. Described by Harold Scott as having 'superabundant vitality', away from the stage Bellwood was a complex and often contradictory figure, or 'a strange compound of wildness and gentleness', as the *London Daily News* described her.[35] Possessing an 'uncontrollable temper' and prone to violence, she featured frequently in newspaper court reports through the 1880s and 1890s.[36] At the same time posthumous accounts of her life invariably noted her unusual kindness and generosity. Le Roy observed that 'she literally gave away her earnings and frequently performed the most menial of tasks, even to scrubbing the floors when visiting some of her sick protégées'.[37] Puzzled by this seeming contradiction, the *Pall Mall Gazette* proposed that it was because 'she was Irish [...] and she possessed all the capacity for friendship and enmities instinctive in her race'.[38] Bellwood's final years were

---

[31] Tracy C. Davis, *Actresses as Working Women: Their Social Identity in Victorian Culture* (London: Routledge, 1991), 119.

[32] J. S. Bratton, ed., *Music Hall: Performance and Style* (Milton Keynes: Open University Press, 1986), xii.

[33] Faulk, *Music Hall and Modernity*, 12.

[34] *Era* (17 October 1891), 16.

[35] Harold Scott, *The Early Doors: Origins of Music Hall* (London: Nicholson and Watson, 1946), 284. *London Daily News* (26 September 1896), 6.

[36] S. Theodore Felstead, *Stars Who Made the Halls: A Hundred Years of English Humour, Harmony and Hilarity* (London: T. Werner, 1946), 68.

[37] Le Roy, *Music Hall Stars of the Nineties*, 42.

[38] *Pall Mall Gazette* (25 September 1896), 7.

mostly triumphant and included two seasons in America in 1893–4 and 1896 as part of the general exchange of artists and songs between British music hall and American vaudeville that gained in frequency during this period. However, her life offstage was increasingly difficult and typified by 'many strange vicissitudes and pathetic incidents'.[39] Trapped in an estranged marriage, constantly pursued for the non-payment of debts, and dogged by a protracted legal action for fees brought against her by her long-term manager and agent Hugh J. Didcott, her circumstances were invariably chaotic. There were other indications of a turbulent domestic life. Midge Gillies in her biography of Marie Lloyd notes the numerous newspaper references to Bellwood's involvement in carriage accidents and speculates that these may have acted as 'cover for an explosive private life'.[40] Bellwood also became an object of scandal because of a long-term affair with Viscount Mandeville (once known as Lord Kimbolton, and later to become the Duke of Manchester), a liaison which cut straight through the rigid class and sexual hierarchies of the period and served as peculiar kind of archetype for the (usually illicit) cockney female/aristocratic male sexual relationship that would subsequently become something of a cliché in British culture. Her last performance was at the London Pavilion in August 1896 and she died of heart disease – possibly induced by alcoholism – aged thirty-nine on 24 September in her flat in West Kensington. Like many of the first generation of music-hall performers, she died young. Bellwood's funeral was a grand affair, with many floral tributes including a 'magnificent Irish harp of very large dimensions' sent from Belfast.[41] The cortege departed from West Kensington and large crowds lined the streets as it passed through the East End. 'So great was the crush to catch a glimpse of the flower-laden coffin, as it was borne on the shoulders of stalwart bearers to the glass-panelled hearse, that it was with some difficulty that the police made a path for the mourners', reported the *Era*.[42] She was buried in St Patrick's Catholic cemetery, Leytonstone where a crowd of up to 3,000 gathered by the gates.[43] Despite the significant fees her performances commanded from the halls, the value of her estate was just £63.

By the time of her death, it was clear that Bellwood represented an era of the music hall that was receding. As the *Pall Mall Gazette* noted in its obituary, 'music-hall fashion has advanced and it left Bessie Bellwood behind it', while, according to Felstead, 'with Marie Lloyd just coming along nicely, Bessie found herself supplanted as a purveyor of cockney humour'.[44] In some ways this prediction was self-fulfilling, not least because, as Simon Featherstone observes, for some time Bellwood had been used by the popular press as the embodiment of 'nostalgia for an older loucheness and extravagance in an increasingly moderated variety theater'.[45] But nevertheless, it

---

[39] *Westminster Gazette* (26 September 1896), 7.

[40] Midge Gillies, *Marie Lloyd: The One and Only* (London: Victor Gollancz, 1999), 314.

[41] *Freeman's Journal and Daily Commercial Advertiser* (30 September 1896), 5.

[42] *Era* (3 October 1896), 19.

[43] *Illustrated Police News* (10 October 1896), 2.

[44] *Pall Mall Gazette* (25 September 1896), 7. Felstead, *Stars Who Made the Halls*, 68.

[45] Simon Featherstone, 'Vestal Flirtations: Performances of the Feminine in the late Nineteenth-Century British Music Hall', *Nineteenth Century Studies*, 19 (2005), 99–112, 101.

is clear that the kind of 'full-frontal carnivalesque' her act dealt in was increasingly unacceptable in the more regulated environment of the new halls.[46] However, it can also be argued that in other ways Bellwood was in fact in advance of contemporary cultural trends. As the humorous magazine *Pick Me Up* speculated at the time of her death: 'She suffered in being born before her time. Had she made her success half-a-dozen years later, syndicates would have been fighting to finance her in musical comedies. As it was she was at the height of her fame and health when this sort of piece was still undiscovered'.[47] Despite this, most music-hall cultural history has tended to estimate Bellwood's significance only in terms of her role as a precursor for more well-known performers such as Lloyd and Kate Carney. In this light, the fact that the *Era* reported in 1899 – just three years after her death – that her grave was badly neglected was somehow sadly appropriate.[48] But even within the context of her era, the case for Bellwood's centrality remains compelling. She was a cultural pioneer creating from the inheritance of an Irish diasporic musical culture a style of interactive, frequently confrontational, cockney chanteuse performance that spoke directly to urban audiences. Equally importantly, as Featherstone notes perceptively, 'Bellwood was a woman of her moment – a well-paid professional (on a salary of £40 per in 1890), sexually independent, socially mobile, verbally and physically forceful, and able to maintain a prominent public career despite a series of well-publicized scandals'.[49] Certainly Bellwood's massive – if ultimately fleeting – popularity helped propel music hall towards hegemonic dominance in the 1880s, driving the transition from tavern and public house to syndicated purpose-built theatre space. More than this, in Paul Matthew St. Pierre's words, Bellwood was a 'gender-subverting [...] *lionne comique*', a complex figure who seemed to embody many of music hall's most cherished myths about itself while simultaneously slyly undercutting many of its more complacent assumptions.[50]

Alongside her role in the growth of the halls, Bellwood is an emblematic figure in the history of Irish London. One of the best known of many Irish performers working in the city's popular entertainment venues at this time, unlike some, her popularity was not based on the suppression of her cultural inheritance but rather its overt celebration. As she claimed, 'I'm Irish in spite of my English accent, and I am just as proud of the old country as I would be if I had a brogue a foot and half thick'.[51] Such statements should be regarded with a little caution, but certainly there is evidence that she remained within Irish social networks during the period of her greatest success. Indeed Bellwood embodied the distinctively London-Irish attitude towards the city's host community that I describe in this book's introduction: her life was a constant process of cultural and social accommodation but the matter of Ireland remained as a marker of difference and a point of contestation. Her career took her to most of the venues that were

---

[46] Ibid.
[47] *Pick Me Up* (10 October 1896), 1.
[48] *Era* (15 July 1899), 17.
[49] Featherstone, 'Vestal Flirtations', 101.
[50] Paul Matthew St. Pierre, 'Music Hall Mimesis in *Those Were the Days* (1934), *Champagne Charlie* (1944), and *The Entertainer* (1960)', *Quarterly Review of Film and Video*, 18:4 (2001), 437–49, 444.
[51] *Westminster Gazette* (26 September 1896), 7.

significant for Irish performance in London from the Old Thatched House Tavern in Holborn to large halls such as the Oxford and the Tivoli, and her success at a time of rapid changes in popular entertainment in the city mirrors the general rise in the popularity of Irish music, comedy, and dance beyond areas of high Irish population. Alongside this, the fact that Bellwood's early success was recorded in close detail in various stage newspapers and journals allows the sometimes amorphous idea of 'Irish performance' in London to gain a clearer manifestation. This is valuable because, as Faulk warns in his own discussion of the 'message' of music-hall performance, 'art and culture are produced under impure conditions, and to profligate effect. Cultural messages get scrambled in the transmission; they face resistance, appropriation, and acclaim'.[52] In a similar manner, while the extensive variety of Irish performance at this time is remarkable, this very diversity can sometimes appear overwhelming and thus inhibits any historical understanding of the ways in which such activity connects to (and speaks of) the massive and often traumatic shifts in Irish diaspora life taking place in London during this time. As a result the performance of Ireland and Irishness in London can often appear as a series of isolated moments, a practice that emerges in a specific form and then either disappears or is absorbed into mainstream popular culture. What remains as a result is best described as a series of isolated 'Irish effects' removed from their material contexts. It is notable that performers such as Bellwood would manipulate these effects in sometimes dizzying (and sometimes politically ambivalent) ways as part of their stagecraft.

Although there were no performance spaces dedicated specifically to Irish entertainment in London – this was before the great Irish dance halls that would become such a distinctive feature of the city from the 1930s onwards – theatres and concert halls had long served as cultural and imaginative resources for the Irish community. The memoirs of Francis Fahy, who arrived in London from Galway in 1873, describe many nights at the theatre watching Irish actors and comedians, including 'Toole, the Cockney comedian, Shiel Barry as the miser in the *Cloches de Corneville*, Barry Sullivan in *Richard the Third*, and last but not least Dion Boucicault the Elder'.[53] Considering Boucicault 'the perfection of Irish acting and his plays flawless', Fahy and his group of Irish friends would attend his plays as 'an unasked for *claque*, whose boisterous enthusiasm must have been a nuisance to the rest of the audience'. As he recalls of one particularly memorable evening attending a performance of his *The O'Dowd*, 'Dion in the title-role of political prisoner makes a speech full of national feeling. This we cheered to the echo and insisted on a repetition of, to the detriment of all artistic illusion'.[54] Given the limited opportunities for the expression of Irish political sentiment in the city at this time, such moments were significant. As Fahy's experiences illustrate, popular entertainment was the most visible interface for Irish London's relationship with the rest of the city and the cultural form where stereotypes were introduced and modified, resistant counter-representations were projected and

[52] Faulk, *Music Hall and Modernity*, 2–3.
[53] Clare Hutton, 'Francis Fahy's "Ireland in London – Reminiscences" (1921)', in *Yeats's Collaborations. Yeats Annual, 15: A Special Number*, ed. Wayne K. Chapman and Warwick Gould (Basingstoke: Palgrave Macmillan, 2002), 233–80, 240.
[54] Ibid.

issues in Irish politics debated. As this suggests, the relationship of the stage to wider society was dynamic and heavily dependent on constantly evolving contexts. In the case of music hall, for instance, the performance of Irish songs, dance or comedy did not occur in isolation but rather functioned as an element of the overall evening's bill of acts. As such these turns were in constant dialogue with the performance of other national and ethnic identities. Indeed, because music hall played a foundational role in the creation of ideas of 'nationness' more broadly, 'Irishness' did not simply impose itself on a predetermined cultural landscape but rather played a role in establishing what a nascent 'national performance' (which included the performance of Britishness itself) might consist of. Performance was also highly venue specific; Irish performers would adjust their material according to the theatres in which they were appearing, toning up or down the 'Irish' content accordingly. For instance the indefatigable Irish comedian and singer Pat Rafferty chose to perform an overtly nationalistic song called 'The Land For the People' about agrarian reform at the Foresters music hall in Bethnal Green in March 1890 and because 'it was near the close of St. Patrick's Day the song was received with rapturous applause'.[55] On the other hand, according to John Bennion Booth's memoirs, a performance of Boucicault's *Arrah-na-Pogue* at the Princess's Theatre on Oxford Street on the night of the Fenian Clerkenwell explosion in December 1867 had to be adjusted for politically expedient reasons, with the song 'The Wearing of the Green' replaced with slightly less incendiary material.[56]

The meaning of these individual performances gains cultural resonance if they are understood as part of the wider landscape of Irish music and dance in London in the period. Beyond the formal concert venue and music hall spaces there were such diverse entertainments as church parades, Irish brass band competitions, Hibernian and United Irish League smoking concerts, street buskers and middle-class events such as the hugely popular concerts of the 'Irish Social Club' in High Holborn. Indeed before the period of music hall, the concept of the 'Irish song' in London was usually envisaged as a middle-class phenomenon circulated via private parlour recitals. Popular anthologies of Irish song, notably *The Harp of Erin: A Book of Ballad Poetry and Native Song* from 1869, played an important role in keeping this music alive and provided alternatives to what Ralph Varian, the book's editor, referred to as 'the low, disgusting caricatures which had been written and published in London as the songs of Ireland'.[57] These works would also be performed at Irish diorama shows, a multimedia form that became very popular during the second half of the nineteenth century and which appealed to both the middle and working class. The most well-known of these was 'Dr Corry's Diorama of Ireland' which toured London on many occasions through the 1870s and 1880s. The diorama was usually staged in theatres located in areas of significant Irish population (a four-month long residency at Shoreditch Town Hall in May 1870 with the show 'Ireland in Shade and Sunshine' was a typical example) and, as Booth observed,

---

[55] *Era* (22 March 1890), 14.
[56] John Bennion Booth, *Pink Parade* (London: Thornton Butterworth, 1933), 138.
[57] Ralph Varian, *The Harp of Erin: A Book of Ballad Poetry and Native Song* (Dublin: M. Glashan and Gill, 1869), 146.

the production was 'an active agent in familiarising London with Irish melodies'.[58] A considerable number of Irish performers took part in the diorama over the course of its long existence and would subsequently have successful music-hall careers as individual acts. For this reason Dr Corry's production did much to codify conventions about the performance of Irishness on stage, bringing decorum to previously derided stereotypes, and challenging negative representations. The Gaelic League was also alive to the use of music and dance as a means of contesting hostile national characterizations and offered tuition in Irish singing and step dancing alongside lessons in the Irish language. This was partly with the hope of broadening the organization's appeal among the Irish working class, especially in the East End of the city. Interestingly, as Reginald Hall notes, Polish and Lithuanian immigrant children would also take part in these classes 'not as Irish nationalists but as good Catholics'.[59] Other forms of cultural entertainment in London also had (sometimes obscured) Irish origins. As Hall observes, the cockney knees-up 'danced solo, in duet, four-handed and in groups and characterized by stepping, balancing, arming and reeling, derives from the jig and four-hand reel danced in pre-Famine rural Ireland'. Such dances would be performed 'in back streets and on Bank Holidays at Hampstead Heath to the street-piano [and represented] the survival of the transplanted Irish rural practice of outdoor dancing'.[60]

However, it is with the dramatic rise in popularity of the London music halls that the demand for Irish performance became something of a popular phenomenon. The origins of this are opaque, but it is clear that the 'penny gaffs', which provided stage time for poor Irish singers and dancers, and the more respectable 'workingmen's concerts', which frequently featured Irish turns, were important precursors.[61] Of greater significance again was the popularity of Irish dancing which, in turn, demanded the steady production of suitable music. These dance songs were designated Irish because they either adapted traditional Irish airs or were intended to be performed with lyrics of 'Irish' content, which meant in practice the deployment of a set of instantly recognizable (if limited) images and emotions. When the music-hall singer Nellie L'Estrange advertised in the *Era* in 1885 for 'a good Pathetic Irish song at once' her urgency indicated something of the form's popularity, as well as a recognition of the necessity of such songs in a balanced programme of turns for the night.[62] Such representations of Irish national character usually had their origins in long-established stereotypes prevalent in the host culture. These were modulated according to contemporary political events and became particularly negative in the cartoons and caricatures produced in the aftermath of the Fenian Rising and Clerkenwell explosion, a time when, as Paul O'Leary observes, 'Irish migrants to urban Britain were subject to an increasingly hostile public gaze that identified them as an intractable

[58] Booth, *Pink Parade*, 138. For more on Dr Corry's Diorama see Richard Kirkland, 'Dr. Corry's National Diorama of Ireland and Irish Performance in Nineteenth-Century Urban Popular Culture', *New Hibernia Review/Iris Éireannach Nua*, 19:4 (December 2015), 14–31, 25.
[59] Reginald Richard Hall, *Irish Music and Dance in London, 1890–1970: A Socio-Cultural History* (PhD Thesis, University of Sussex, 1994), 184.
[60] Ibid., 70.
[61] Ibid., 67.
[62] *Era* (26 September 1885), 24.

social problem'.[63] Such representations, which included presenting the Irish as being, in Dagmar Kift's words, 'lazy, slow, ridiculous and given to drink', were redolent of 'colonialist contempt', and yet the Irish performer was also a figure of identification who preserved the 'traditions and customs of his homeland and put them on public display'.[64] Perceived in this way Irish music-hall songs served a complex dual function and performances could be interpreted by audiences in radically diverse ways.

As this indicates, the performance of Irishness was more than just one element of the British music-hall programme; rather it was a crucial part of the halls' overall appeal and a way of referencing some of its vital emotions. Although music hall evoked Ireland through the articulation of predictable themes (typically the exile's lament, the yearning of the Celt, comedy based on Hiberno-English linguistic paradox and historical grievance), the emotional states which it conjured were intended to be universally recognizable and accessible to all. In this way Ireland was both a specific political/historical nexus and a state of mind. In many respects this corresponds to the Irish cultural critic Gerry Smyth's typology of Irish music which divides the genre into the two poles of 'Paddy sad' and 'Paddy mad'.[65] Smyth sets the nostalgic, wistful, residual Ireland expressive of loss and melancholy expressed in 'Paddy sad' against the desperate excesses of bacchanalian pleasure seeking embodied by 'Paddy mad'. As such, 'Paddy sad' 'connotes a history of dispossession and defeat [...] the tragic fall away from a Celtic Eden' while 'Paddy mad' is 'given to pleasure and excess as a quasi-religious response to the disappointments of everyday reality'.[66] This dichotomy can be found in many cultural forms other than just music; indeed, as Smyth observes, such is its ubiquity it can be considered as 'one of the principal means for the (mis)recognition and consequent reproduction of Irish identity in the modern era'.[67] Certainly in the London halls the 'Paddy sad/Paddy mad' opposition was deployed ruthlessly to create a vision of Ireland that was always in a state of perpetual excess and which existed at the limits of sentimentality, pathos, boisterousness, violence and drunkenness. As L'Estrange and others soon discovered, a well-aimed Irish song could instantaneously transport a music-hall audience to this emotional terrain and hold them there for its duration. Because of this Irish songs of lamentation and euphoria were positioned over the course of a programme to modulate the momentum of the evening. The titles of these songs tended to indicate their function, as a small example of the huge number performed on London stages categorized accordingly illustrates:

Paddy Sad:

'My Dear Old Irish Mother' (1898)
'The Little Irish Postman' (1904)

[63] J. M. Nelson, 'From Rory and Paddy to Boucicault's Myles, Shaun and Conn: The Irishman on the London Stage, 1830–60', *Eire-Ireland*, 13 (1978), 79–105, 82. Paul O'Leary, 'Mass commodity culture and identity: The "Morning Chronicle" and Irish migrants in a nineteenth-century Welsh industrial town', *Urban History*, 35:2 (August 2008), 237–54, 237.
[64] Dagmar Kift, *The Victorian Music Hall: Culture, Class and Conflict* (Cambridge: Cambridge University Press, 1996), 45–6.
[65] Gerry Smyth, *Music in Irish Cultural History* (Dublin: Irish Academic Press, 2009), 52.
[66] Ibid.
[67] Ibid., 53.

'He'll Never Forget Ould Ireland' (1906)
'Dear Ould Ireland's The Place For Me' (1908)
'Sing Me An Irish Song' (1911)
'Sing Something Irish To Me' (1911)
'I'm Coming Back To Old Kilkenny' (1913)
'If You're Irish, You'll Remember' (1916)
'Come Back To Ireland And Me' (1916)

Paddy Mad:

'He's Very, Very Ill Indeed!' (1890)
'It's Irish' (1891)
'The Floor Gave Way' (1893)
'There's An Irishman Up In The Moon' (1911)
'Be Sure He's Irish' (1912)
'We're Irish And Proud Of It, Too' (1914)
'It Takes An Irish Heart To Sing An Irish Song' (1914)
'Arrah! Go On, Now, Miss Emerald Isle' (1915)
'As Long As You're Irish You'll Do' (1916)
'You Can Have An Irish Name (But You Can't Wear The Shamrock)' (1916)
'There's A Little Bit Of Irish Everywhere' (1916)

Alongside (or perhaps within) this classification was a further distinctive element of Irish music-hall performance: songs that were written (or rewritten) to the moment in response to political events and shifts in public opinion. In these songs the Irish were always doing something, had just done something or were being asked to do something – and this something was usually to do with fighting on behalf of the British. As such their basic function was to assess, praise or condemn Ireland according to the enthusiasm with which it engaged with (or refused) the imperial project. One of the first examples of this tradition was 'No Irish Need Apply' by Mary Ann Dunn, a song about what some believed was a ban on Irish people working at the 1851 Great Exhibition site in Hyde Park despite their honourable record of military service:

At Balaclava, Inkerman and through the Russian War,
Did not the Irish bravely fight, as they've oft done before?
And, since that time in India, they made the rebels fly,
Our generals never hinted then 'No Irish Need Apply'.
If you want a second Wellington, I say it's all my eye.
You'll never get one while you write 'No Irish Need Apply'.[68]

---

[68] Richard Anthony Baker, *British Music Hall: An Illustrated History* (Stroud: Sutton Publishing, 2005), 16.

In its demand for a form of political and economic reparation, 'No Irish Need Apply' was also an early example of the 'special pleading' Irish song, a distinct subgenre sometimes referred to as 'suppliant' songs, that became increasingly common until the 1890s. The move from the kind of sympathetic recognition of discrimination found in such works to overt appeals for military support was often seamless. For instance Murray Ford's bloodthirsty 'Erin, Arouse Thee!' from 1886 (a song rewritten from an earlier version and dedicated to Lord Randolph Churchill) celebrated the role of the Irish in the British military and expressed the hope that the success of this violent union would continue into the future:

> Erin, arouse thee! Our war flags when flying
> Bear on them names we can both read with pride
> Battles they tell of where foemen lay dying,
> Vanquished by Saxon and Celt, side by side.

The song was very successful and provoked what *The Graphic* described as 'a somewhat violent reply' later in the year in the form of 'The Irish Marseillaise or Justice for Ireland' by A Moray St Patrick.[69] 'Both [songs] will command a certain attention at the present crisis, but for neither may lasting fame be anticipated', it observed sardonically. Another notable example of this form was 'What Do You Think Of The Irish Now?', sung by Rafferty about the role of the Dublin Fusiliers in the Battle of Talana Hill (also known as the Battle of Glencoe) in the Boer War in October 1899. The song's conclusion is of particular interest in that it indicated the extent to which music-hall composers used stories of Irish military heroism abroad to offset anti-Irish prejudice (and, more specifically, hostility to the Home Rule agenda) at home:

> What do you think of the Fusiliers,
> Who dashed o'er that fire-swept brow
> You used to call us traitors,
> Because of agitators,
> But you can't call us traitors now!

'What Do You Think Of The Irish Now?' soon became a phenomenon and its effect on public opinion was striking. As Dublin's *Freeman's Journal* reported, the song 'is howled in the London streets at present by a large proportion of the cockney population, male and female. With the London dialect it creates a raucous effect which haunts the hearer for hours'.[70] Rafferty (whose real name was Henry Browne) was born in Birmingham to Irish parents and was the single most important figure in the propagation of the Irish military/political song. Alongside 'What Do You Think Of The Irish Now?' he popularized many others including 'Bravo Dublin Fusiliers', 'Aren't We Loyal Now?', 'What Do We Want With Conscription?' and 'Why Do You Call them Hooligans?'

---

[69] *The Graphic* (25 September 1886), 22.
[70] *Freeman's Journal and Daily Commercial Advertiser* (13 March 1900), 5.

The last of these, from 1902, reflected on the bravery of Irish soldiers and contrasted this with what the press dubbed the 'hooligan' crime wave sweeping over London at the time: 'Do these Hooligans give Irish names when brought up in the courts?/No! They're just the scum of London slums, no Irishmen are they!' The final type of Irish political music-hall song was distinguished by a more satirical reflection on current events. These were essentially ephemeral comic pieces without the censoriousness occasionally found in other Irish songs. For instance, the *Era* reported on the success of Charles Bignell's performance of 'Charley Parney' at the Oxford in December 1890: a song about the Parnell crisis and 'the naughty boy who wants Home Rule for Ireland but can't Home Rule himself'.[71]

These examples are illustrative of the liberal unionism that was the dominant political world view of most Irish music-hall songs during this time. Such material was prone to reflecting on the glories of British imperialism and Ireland's role in enabling this, but there were also significant, if infrequent, diversions from this agenda. A striking example of this was Nelly Farrell, 'the glittering star of Erin', whose brief career was typified by the performance of more overtly political material such as 'Home Rule for Ireland', 'They'd do as the Irish do' and 'There's as good men in Ireland as in England Today'. Like Bellwood – whom she resembled in many ways – Farrell combined this stance with what Paul Maloney has termed 'a formidably assertive femininity which enabled her to win over disruptive male audiences'.[72] Her most well-known and politically resonant song was 'An Irish Girl's Opinion', which she first performed across London's music halls in 1886. This was markedly uncompromising in its argument:

> An Irish girl, and proud of it, a word I'd like to say
> About the state of Erin's isle, my native place, to-day;
> And those with Irish blood in them will understand me best,
> And feel for those poor peasants who are starving in the west
> Rack-rented, oft evicted, and turned out in the snow;
> The sky their only shelter, not knowing where to go.
> 'Tis scenes like these that shake our faith in England and its throne;
> Oh! is the good time coming when the land shall be our own?[73]

Farrell died of typhoid in Belfast in 1889 aged just thirty, and was buried with (what was regarded at the time as) unseemly haste.[74] Younger artistes jostled to replace her as, to use Barry Anthony's term, 'the premier Irish female performer', but those that followed in her wake were (on stage at least) less bold in their political views.[75] That said, the later music hall did not entirely neglect pressing Irish social concerns such as the land issue and agrarian poverty. A striking feature of the 1890's music-hall programme was

[71] *Era* (27 December 1890), 14.
[72] Paul Maloney, '"Flying down the Saltmarket": The Irish on the Glasgow Music Hall Stage', *Nineteenth Century Theatre and Film*, 36:1 (2009), 11–36, 32.
[73] Manus O'Conor, ed., *Old Time Songs and Ballads of Ireland* (New York: Popular Publishing Company, 1901), 66.
[74] *Era* (16 February 1889), 17.

the rise of what Dave Russell calls 'lachrymose ballads with fairytale endings', such as Tom Maguire's 'Don't Burn the Cabin Down' from 1894.[76] This was about a family due 'to be evicted into the snow on Christmas Eve, because they had defaulted on one rent payment while the father was away fishing, unaware of his family's plight'. At the song's climax, 'a young priest rushes in to tell them the father has returned to pay his debt'. Of perhaps greater relevance to a London-Irish audience were songs of exile such as 'Only a Few Miles of Water' by Harry Wright and J. M. Harrison, which expressed a yearning to return to 'the old cabin [...] in Ireland my own native home'.[77] The song was performed by Nellie Gannon (who was married to Wright) through the 1895 London winter season and was powerfully effective in its description of physical displacement and the yearnings of exile. Crucially, however, if there was a sense of political injustice represented in these songs, it was located at a local level and was not seen to reflect any kind of structural problem with the Union itself.

Generally these ballads would be performed by a manifestation of the 'stage Irishman' (or woman), dressed in what Booth described as 'the regulation music-hall Irish national costume'.[78] In fact, as R. A. Cave observes, by this stage 'the stereotype of the stage Irishman was so hardened, resilient and prevalent on the British stage that it was difficult to dramatize an Irish subject without one's artistry being suspected in some quarters, especially if one were of Irish descent'.[79] Bessie Bellwood in her early years was a raucous version of this figure, but by the late nineteenth century singers and comedians such as Rafferty and Michael Nolan had refined the performance so that it expressed a particularly intense and self-reflexive sentimentality. This was a figure with few rough edges or moments of political antipathy. Of this revised stage Irishman Jerome K. Jerome observed in 1890:

> He is very poor, but scrupulously honest. His great ambition is to pay his rent, and he is devoted to his landlord. He is always cheerful, and always good. We never knew a bad Irishman, on the stage. Sometimes a Stage Irishman *seems* to be a bad man – such as the 'agent', or the 'informer' – but, in these cases, it invariably turns out, in the end, that this man was all along a Scotchman, and thus what had been a mystery becomes clear and explicable.[80]

The rise of this particular form of Irish performance accorded with the general *embourgeoisment* of the Halls and melodramatic theatre during this period – this was certainly an Irish figure fit for British middle-class consumption – although the fact that his (and sometimes, although less frequently, her) emergence also coincided

---

[75] Barry Anthony, *Chaplin's Music Hall: The Chaplins and Their Circle in the Limelight* (London: Bloomsbury, 2012), 169.

[76] Dave Russell, *Popular Music in England* (Manchester: Manchester University Press, 1987), 102.

[77] *Music Hall and Theatre Review* (3 May 1895), 24.

[78] Booth, *Pink Parade*, 138.

[79] R. A. Cave, 'Staging the Irishman', in *Acts of Supremacy: The British Empire and the Stage, 1790–1930*, eds. J. S. Bratton, et al. (Manchester: Manchester University Press, 1991), 62–128, 64.

[80] Jerome K. Jerome, *Stageland: Curious Manners and Customs of Its Inhabitants* (London: Chatto and Windus, 1890), 69.

with an increased sympathy for the Home Rule agenda among much of the British population was not a coincidence. In this context the stage Irishman embodied a cause and a mode of popular appeal, but, more importantly, he was also a character to whom aid could be offered with the expectation that it would be gratefully received. This was Ireland imagined as a suitable case for treatment, not a recalcitrant political problem. With the rise in revolutionary politics in Ireland during the first quarter of the twentieth century, this kind of figure would soon appear to be a hopelessly ironic projection – in 1913 the revolutionary nationalist Roger Casement located it within a crude version of Irish history 'written by buffoons and English music hall artistes' – and the collapse of the Home Rule agenda almost instantaneously killed it off as a plausible stage character.[81] As such it can now appear to be little more than a trace of one of the many lost futures embedded in Irish history.

Within Ireland the greatest opposition to the music hall and the stereotypes that it promoted came from the Irish cultural revival which, from its inception, regarded it as nothing less than the pre-eminent symptom of industrialized decadence and thus its natural enemy. In these terms, music hall was 'an Anglo-Saxon phenomenon, born in the world of abrupt urban concentrations and the great Protestant myths of labour', as Roland Barthes described it.[82] It is unsurprising, then, that for revivalists keen to give material form to what could appear an abstract series of ideological rejections the assumed moral and artistic degeneracy of music hall became a key element of the movement's propaganda, and a shorthand way of referring to everything that was most corrupted and corrupting about Britishness more generally. For instance, one of the foundational statements of revivalism, Douglas Hyde's 'The Necessity for De-Anglicising Ireland' from 1892, attacked what it saw as the mindlessness and spiritual impoverishment of English music-hall ballads and the manner in which they 'have gained an enormous place in the repertoire of the wandering minstrel'.[83] Such was their sentimental power that Hyde fretted as to how Irish people 'may be brought to love the purity of *Siúbhail Siúbhail*, or the fun of the *Moddereen Ruadh* in preference to "Get your hair cut", or "Over the Garden Wall", or, even if it is not asking too much, of "Ta-ra-ra-boom-de-ay"'. Expressing a similar fear in 1900, David Patrick (D. P.) Moran's ferocious nationalist paper *The Leader* complained that the music halls acted as 'regular night-schools for Anglicisation [and] a powerful propaganda for the lowest and grossest moral standards', while in the same year the inaugural meeting of Maud Gonne's national women's movement Inghinidhe na hÉireann (Daughters of Erin) sought, as a matter of urgency, to discourage women from 'the attending of vulgar

[81] *Ulster Guardian* (14 May 1913), 5.

[82] Roland Barthes, 'At the Music Hall', *The Eiffel Tower and Other Mythologies*, trans. Richard Howard (New York: Noonday Press, 1979), 123. Interestingly, this was by no means the default contemporary perspective: indeed for many middle and upper class aficionados of music hall, such as George Moore, the opposite was true as, in Faulk's words, it 'came to signify the possibility that an expressive practice outside the levelling impulses of capitalism, urbanism, and modernism could exist and would be desirable' (Faulk, *Music Hall and Modernity*, 28).

[83] Douglas Hyde, 'The Necessity for De-Anglicizing Ireland' (1892), in *Language, Lore, and Lyrics*, ed. Breandán Ó Conaire (Dublin: Irish Academic Press, 1986), 167.

English entertainments at the theatres and music hall'.[84] Also in 1900 George Russell (*AE*) lamented in his 'Nationality and Imperialism':

> The music that breathed Tir-nan-og and overcame men's hearts with all gentle and soft emotions is heard more faintly, and the songs of the London music halls may be heard in places where the music of fairy enchanted the elder generations. The shout of the cockney tourist sounds in the cyclopean crypts and mounds once sanctified by druid mysteries, and divine visitations, and passings from the mortal to the immortal. Ireland Limited is being run by English syndicates.[85]

That *AE* was obsessive about the potential dangers of music hall was well known; James Joyce clearly knew as much, as the lightly fictionalized version of him that is depicted in *Ulysses* also articulates anti-music hall sentiments as part of his low-level chatter.[86]

W. B. Yeats spent much of his time shuttling between London and Ireland during this period and thus was particularly well qualified to observe the emergence of music hall in the city as well as the manner in which it spread to Ireland. Moreover, some of his close London associates, including Arthur Symons, John Davidson and George Moore, were to a lesser or greater degree immersed in the 'cult of the halls', a distinctive feature of London elite culture in the early 1890s which fetishized the experience of attending music hall as a means of exploring sometimes esoteric aesthetic theories. Symons, especially, was energized by its potential; described by Yeats as a 'scholar in music hall as another man might be a Greek scholar', as Faulk notes, 'he imagined his music-hall accounts as a form of collaborative effort'.[87] Although Yeats himself was never as entranced by the halls' charms, he remained intrigued if ambivalent about the phenomenon. In 1892 he regarded the fact that Symons and Davidson were so fascinated by music hall as 'a reaction from the super-refinement of much recent life and poetry', observing (slightly sarcastically) that 'the cultivated man has begun a somewhat hectic search for the common pleasures of common men and for the rough accidents of life'.[88] This search was driven – in part at least – by a weariness with the assumed hypocrisy of Victorian middle-class culture, but it still required the ability to indulge (or at least tolerate) the enthusiastic endorsement of Britishness that the halls promoted. For Yeats, whose commitment to revivalism was becoming more profound, such a stance was not possible and, predictably perhaps, it would be during his periods in Ireland that his growing dislike of music hall would be expressed most vividly. In 1899 the Gaelic League magazine *An Claidheamh Soluis* reported on a League meeting at Kiltartan at which Yeats complained about hearing 'people singing London music

[84] Cheryl Herr, *Joyce's Anatomy of Culture* (Urbana: University of Illinois Press, 1986), 203–4. Margaret Ward, *Unmanageable Revolutionaries: Women and Irish Nationalism* (London: Pluto Press, 1983), 51.

[85] AE, 'Nationality and Imperialism' (1900), in *Poetry and Ireland since 1800: A Source Book*, ed. Mark Storey (London: Routledge, 1988), 142.

[86] James Joyce, *Ulysses* (London: Bodley Head, [1922] 2008), 9, 107–8.

[87] W. B. Yeats, 'The Rhymers' Club', in *Letters to the New Island* (Cambridge, MA: Harvard University Press, 1970 [1934]), 144. Faulk, *Music Hall and Modernity*, 48.

[88] Yeats, 'The Rhymers' Club', 59.

hall songs of the vulgarest kind in a Connacht fishing village'.[89] Similarly, in the Abbey Theatre's journal *Samhain* in 1906, he recalled a visit to Galway and the sight of 'some young men marching down the middle of a street singing an already outworn London music-hall song, that filled the memory, long after they had gone by, with a rhythm as pronounced and as impersonal as the noise of a machine'.[90] Yeats articulated the precise threat that these incursions posed in a lecture in New York in 1904:

> Ireland will always be a country where men plough and sow and reap [...] and Ireland, too, as we think, will be a country where not only will the wealth be well distributed but where there will be an imaginative and spiritual culture among the people. We wish to preserve an ancient kind of life. Wherever its customs prevail, there you will find the folk song, the folk tale, the proverb and the charming manners that come from ancient culture. In England you will find a few thousands of perfectly cultivated people, but you find the mass of the people singing songs of the music hall.[91]

Such comparisons raised the stakes of the revival's culture war to a startling degree, with English music hall standing symbolically for the entire process of spiritual impoverishment wrought by industrialization. Yeats's horrified realization revealed not only what Ireland stood to lose – if it had not lost it already – but also how much his dislike of music hall drew on more banal attitudes including class snobbery, a tendency he shared with some of his fellow revivalists. From this perspective music hall was disliked (at least in part) because of its regimented nature – the vision of an undifferentiated mass singing the same songs at the same time – and its denial of an idea of middle-class individuated 'taste'.

Another distinct element of the revival's attacks on music hall was based on a recognition that it could be addictive: in other words, that its sentimental pull was so seductive that it would spread inevitably and inexorably beyond the confines of the hall itself, disseminating Anglicization as went. As Joyce's fictional *AE* bemoans in *Ulysses*, 'people do not know how dangerous lovesongs can be'.[92] For this reason, while revivalists despised music hall as both a symbol of all that was most debased about Anglo-Saxon capitalist industrialism and as a cultural form that repeatedly displayed and made a fetish of the most fraudulent and often offensive forms of Irishness, it was also something to be slightly feared, exasperated by, and even, perhaps, grudgingly admired in that its mass audiences cast in sharp relief the limits of the revival's own appeal. As a result the revival's criticism of music hall was also a means of indirectly discussing one of its own major challenges: how a self-proclaimed (and frequently elitist) cultural movement might deploy a message of cultural renewal to transform

---

[89] 'Public Meeting at Kiltartan', *An Claidheamh Soluis* (29 July 1899), 314.
[90] W. B. Yeats, *The Collected Works of W. B. Yeats Volume VIII: The Irish Dramatic Movement*, ed. Mary FitzGerald and Richard J. Finneran (New York: Scribner, 2003), 95.
[91] Richard Ellmann, *Yeats: The Man and the Mask* (London: Faber, 1948), 116–17.
[92] Joyce, *Ulysses*, 9.103.

mass consciousness. Revivalists rarely articulated an explicit plan as to how this transformation would occur, but it was generally assumed to be a cumulative process involving language, culture, political education and social combination. Through this slow accretion of associations it was assumed a politics of national identity would emerge. Described as such, it is hard to imagine a greater contrast with the version of Irish identity offered on the music-hall stage, where the typical Irish ballad's sugar-rush of sentimentality provided a momentary hit that was not dependent on any such personal experience. Indeed, one did not even have to come from Ireland to feel the yearning of a song such as 'Only a Few Miles of Water'. Understood in this way music hall's vision of Ireland was as a purely abstract space of emotional projection, a feature it shared with the American Deep South in the British music hall's collective imagination. The idea of national identity that it proclaimed was envisaged as little more than a series of external markers that were not predicated on psychological depth or interior consciousness. By comparison, revivalism was built on a frequently stern sense that such external identifiers aligned with a coherent emotional and ideological psychic landscape and it was with this self-assured sense of identity that the movement urged the Gael to face the world. Viewed from the outside this process could appear exhausting in its self-discipline and it is no coincidence that a spate of music-hall songs such as Charles William Murphy's 'How Can They Tell That Oi'm Oirish?' from 1898 offered their own implicit comment on what were often-agonizing processes of national overidentification.

This collision of competing visions of national identity was felt especially keenly among London's Irish community and, as a result, the subject of music hall was invariably a flashpoint for political argument. Even the success of a small fundraising concert in Bermondsey for a local (predominantly Irish) school in 1882 was assessed according to the extent to which the performers countered the 'hideous burlesques' of Irish identity provided by the city's halls.[93] More profoundly, a letter by South Islington Irish National League member Thomas Glynn to the *United Ireland* in 1897 described a twenty-year history of London-Irish nationalist opposition to the 'practice of caricaturing Irishmen and women on the music hall stage', as well as 'Catholic entertainments [which] produced for the edification of their supporters, no doubt unintentionally, ludicrous figures representing Irish country life'.[94] This 'crusade', undertaken 'by that popular and representative body of Irishmen which made the old Surrey Rooms, in the Blackfriars Road, their headquarters' was, he claimed, 'a complete success':

> At all events, the slanderous so-called comic song disappeared from the programme of every concert organised by members of the various Catholic societies; and it is almost needless to add that branches of the Irish National organisation rigorously expunged every item of an objectionable nature from their list of songs also.
>
> I was a witness many years ago, in the Bermondsey Town Hall, to a demonstration against songs that were anything but complimentary to the fair fame of Ireland. A

---

[93] *Dublin Weekly Nation* (25 February 1882), 4.
[94] 'Music Hall Songs at Irish Concerts', *United Ireland* (27 February 1897), 3.

very popular Irish music hall artist was the objectionable person. A forcible protest was made without creating anything like confusion, or bringing discredit on the evening's proceedings. It acted like magic. To this day no person dare insult the susceptibilities of the Irish people in the district.

Given the date and the reference to the Surrey Rooms, it is likely that the organization Glynn is referring to here was either the Southwark Irish Literary Club (founded in 1883) or the Irish National League (which established its Southwark branch in 1883), although there is little to corroborate either suspicion. That said, Fahy, the Southwark Literary Club's first president and guiding force, was certainly no fan of music hall, once describing 'the songs now sung, in public and in private in Ireland' as 'the lowest music hall trash, which no decent person or people would demean themselves to listen to' at a Gaelic League meeting in Co. Clare.[95] He also used the Southwark Club as a forum for lecturing on 'the number of good Irish humorous songs which were practically unknown, while the music-hall productions of the stage Irishman type were in high favour'.[96] But regardless of the campaign's success (if campaign it was) Glynn's letter does at least indicate that the representation of Irish caricature on London stages was a live issue and one that provoked a particularly sensitive response in nationalist circles. Indeed his point in writing was not to recall an insult from many years before but to draw attention to an incident that had occurred at a Gaelic Athletic Association (GAA) concert at the Clown Public House in Clerkenwell the previous week, when a 'young man "rendered" a song' while 'decked up with a caubeen resembling those seen now and again in the pages of the ignorant comic papers of this city, when representing an Irishman, probably accompanied by a pig'. The brimless felt caubeen hat was the key accoutrement of the stage Irishman at this time – Walter MacQueen-Pope describes Sam Collins, one of the earliest stage Irish performers in the London halls, performing in a caubeen, with a 'green coat cut like a dress-coat of today, drab whipcord knee breeches, worsted stockings and brogues, and [...] a shillelagh' – and the nature of the insult would have been obvious.[97] As ever the production of offensive stereotypes from within the London-Irish community was judged much more severely than representations of the Irish that derived from elsewhere.

The *United Ireland*, the place of publication for Glynn's letter, was a Dublin nationalist newspaper that kept a close eye on the fortunes of the Irish in London. It was also notably hostile to what a correspondent termed 'trashy music-hall ballads' and thus was a focal point for those in London that wished to contest prevailing stage-Irish representations.[98] Despite the revival's attempts at cultural renewal, the scale of this task was considerable: 'We are fast losing our taste. It is no uncommon thing to hear vulgar London songs from the boatmen on the Lakes of Killarney, and to have to sit by,

---

[95] *Freeman's Journal* (29 August 1899), 6.

[96] *Dublin Weekly Nation* (24 November 1888), 10.

[97] Walter MacQueen-Pope, *The Melodies Linger On: The Story of Music Hall* (London: W. H. Allen, 1950), 82.

[98] *United Ireland* (24 April 1897), 5.

helpless, while that heaven earth is desecrated by horrid ditties from the music halls', it recorded despairingly in 1896.[99] In London itself matters were more serious again:

> We have before us a report of an Irish (sic) night which was given recently in London, and the only thing Irish about it was that two Gaelic songs were sandwiched into a programme containing the most inane and rubbishy emanations of the London music halls. The promoters of this West British night referred to it in their report as being an example for Irishmen in other parts of England to follow; but we strongly hope, for the sake of the Irish language movement, that no Irishmen will so far degrade the language of their country as to introduce it into a programme of Coster songs of the 'Old Kent Road' type.[100]

Such events clearly demanded (and received) a response. Noting the prevalence of 'low, vulgar music hall songs' at Irish social events, the London GAA attempted to ban all music-hall numbers from its St Patrick's night concert programme of 1897 and strove to engage only Irish performers.[101] But, as Glynn's encounter with the caubeen-wearing stage Irishman at the Clown pub that very night proved, such aspirations were difficult to police. As the *United Ireland* observed glumly, 'at many an Irish gathering in London, [...] Irishmen and women will not only tolerate, but actually enjoy "caricature songs" of themselves and their country'.[102] Perhaps this was a battle the League could not win, although it remained a matter of great sensitivity. In 1902 the nationalist journalist and politician Stephen Gwynn reported on the London Gaelic League's 'vehement protest against the Irish peasant of English tradition – the "stage Irishman"', and noted that 'even Mr. Denis O'Sullivan, most popular of singers at an Irish concert, excites the suspicion of purists when he sings and acts the song of the Irish fiddler, written by an ornament of the Irish revival, Mr. Fahy'.[103] O'Sullivan, an Irish American from San Francisco, was a Feis Ceoil adjudicator and arguably the leading performer of traditional Irish song in the world at this time, while Fahy's status as the father of the revival in London was unassailable. That even this combination elicited murmurs of disapproval indicates the degree to which an ideal of cultural authenticity underpinned the League's popular appeal. More problematically, it also revealed the impossibility of ever quite attaining that ideal.

Although it too had a limited timeframe, the Irish cultural revival outlasted the high period of London music hall and its craze for Irish performance. As Russell notes, by 1900 music halls in England were so 'saturated' with American material that 'the old Victorian language and feel of the songs was disappearing'. Ten years later this, in turn, triggered a nostalgic return to the earlier material, which was consumed in an ironic mode for 'older members of the audience'.[104] As this indicates, by 1910 there

---

[99] *United Ireland* (13 June 1896), 15.
[100] *United Ireland* (20 November 1897), 1.
[101] *United Ireland* (13 February 1897), 13.
[102] Ibid.
[103] Stephen Gwynn, 'Gaels in London', *Westminster Gazette* (3 June 1902), 3.
[104] Russell, *Popular Music in England*, 108.

were signs that music hall was beginning to eat itself. Music hall's gradual decline provoked an extended period of mourning that was typically expressed through a mode of whimsical nostalgia articulated by a host of self-appointed cognoscenti or 'nostalgic apologists from within "the Profession"', as Bratton calls them.[105] However, throughout this time, and despite the pessimism voiced by publications such as the *United Ireland*, Irish music in the city remained a more diverse affair than the stern anti-music hall revivalists depicted it and it continued to have a vigorous life beyond the halls. Alongside the work of revival organizations such as the Gaelic League, there was always a broad range of Irish cultural events taking place in the city. These contested the worst of the stage-Irish stereotype and usually expressed pro-Irish attitudes. Many (perhaps most) concert halls had occasional 'Irish nights', where solely Irish-themed music was performed. One such example was the St James Hall in Piccadilly which promoted an annual Irish ballad evening.[106] The 'Irish Folk Song Society', an organization essentially for elite Irish London which sought to collect, publish and perform Irish music, held its inaugural meeting at Londonderry House on Park Lane in 1904 and flourished for some time.[107] For a similar audience, the Irish Literary Society promoted regular concerts of Irish music throughout this period. There were also organizations such as the 'Popular Musical Union', a benevolent body 'intended for the musical training and recreation of the industrial classes', which provided free or cheap concerts across the East End of the city and often performed Irish music.[108] Indeed any view of the full range of Irish performance in the city is distorted by the dominating effects of the music hall/revival binary and the constrained images of Ireland both advanced. Most importantly, music continued to be performed across London as an expression of Irish emigrant memory. Musical instruments such as fiddles were often regarded as heirlooms in London Irish families and would be passed on to succeeding generations. These would be augmented by cheap tin-whistles, and recitals would happen in kitchens, on the streets, and by groups of itinerant musicians who would earn small amounts of money by performing in public houses. Unlike Irish performance in the halls or the music performed by the Gaelic League, such activity escaped the gaze of the professional aficionado and it would not be until considerably later in the twentieth century that it would be recorded, archived and cherished. For this reason the vast majority of Irish music performed in London though this period is lost almost without trace. This absence is a considerable cultural loss and means that any picture of the London Irish will necessarily remain incomplete. More poignantly again, it also represents in microcosm the greater historical silence that envelops the vast number of London-Irish poor, the near-countless individuals who passed through the city living lives that were either elusive or little regarded.

---

[105] Bratton, *Music Hall: Performance and Style*, X.
[106] *Daily Telegraph & Courier* (10 March 1890), 1.
[107] *Morning Post* (21 May 1904), 4.
[108] *The Graphic* (11 October 1890), 18.

6

'An Irish colony in the midst of the strangers':
The road to 1916

In July 1901 an anonymous *Blackwood's Edinburgh Magazine* article titled 'The London Irish' attempted an overall assessment of the state of the Irish community in the capital, concentrating on its locations, work patterns, cultural practices and politics. At best a supercilious piece and at its worst deeply prejudiced, it concluded with an evaluation of Irish London's potential for revolutionary violence:

> And so it comes to this, that despite numbers, powers of combination, and identity of belief, the London Irish element among the working classes will not, so far as sane prediction goes, become actively anti-British, or be persuaded, indeed, to take more than a languid interest in politics. They will live apart, believing their country to be deeply wronged, but perceiving that schemes of vengeance had best remain unrealised. They even revisit Ireland but rarely, unlike the emigrants to the United States, and regularly drift back to London again. Theirs is a most voluntary exile; and in justice to them it must be admitted that they often dismiss the topic of Saxon tyranny with a most good-natured grin. No, they are not a White Peril.[1]

Although the tone of this conclusion is complacent, painting a picture of the London Irish as culturally active but politically quiescent, given the extent of integration and the emergence of the 'London cockney' as a significant social presence, it was a reasonable judgement to pass at the time. Although many London Irish at the turn of the century exhibited what Jonathan Schneer has called a 'profound if slightly amorphous anti-imperialism', this did not naturally translate into political activity on behalf of Irish nationalism despite the energetic work of the many revival organizations I discussed in Chapter 4.[2] However, this situation would soon change dramatically. In the years leading up to 1916 Irish London would become markedly more radicalized, with significant elements of it attracted to the 'military posturing, and the cult of guns', which R. F. Foster has argued typified much of Irish political life during this period.[3]

---

[1] 'The London Irish', *Blackwood's Edinburgh Magazine*, 170 (July 1901), 124–34, 134.
[2] Jonathan Schneer, *London 1900: The Imperial Metropolis* (London: Yale University Press, 1999), 174.
[3] R. F. Foster, *Vivid Faces: The Revolutionary Generation in Ireland, 1890–1923* (London: Allen Lane, 2014), 180.

Irish people living in London would play an important role in the Easter Rising and the subsequent revolutionary war, while the city itself would also be the stage for many of the most momentous events of the time, including the planning for the Howth gun running in the summer of 1914, the trial and execution of the 1916 revolutionary Roger Casement, the hunger strike and death of Terence James MacSwiney in Brixton Prison in October 1920, the location of the Anglo-Irish Treaty negotiations and agreement from June to December 1921 and the assassination of Field Marshal Sir Henry Wilson by two London-based Irish Republican Army (IRA) men outside his house at 36 Eaton Place in Belgravia in June 1922.

As these events indicate, during this period it becomes more difficult to separate the specific activities of the Irish in London from the general swirl of Irish politics taking place elsewhere as the crisis which engulfed Ireland from 1914 onwards threw previously disconnected individuals and organizations into shared ideological orbits, rendered old alliances and affiliations obsolete and generally hastened the momentum and urgency of political life. In this regard many of the Irish in London were clearly part of the wider 'revolutionary generation' of Irish radicals as identified by Foster's *Vivid Faces*, a generation committed to Irish independence but who were also motivated by the possibility of attaining other freedoms, be they political, cultural or sexual. Indeed, such radicalism was intensified by the experience of living in London itself, a city where it was easier to encounter alternative (or, perhaps more importantly, comparative) international political movements and radical countercultural texts and organizations than it was in Ireland itself. Alongside this was the simple and inescapable fact that in London the primary enemy of Irish freedom – whether this was understood in cultural terms, as a system of values or as embodied in specific individuals – was ubiquitous; the British were workmates, neighbours and sometimes friends and as such had to be engaged with and accounted for. It is this proximity above all else that gives Irish political activism in the city its distinctive nuance. As Joe Good, Michael Collins's friend in London and fellow combatant in the GPO, recalled, as an adolescent he would carry a copy of the Gaelic League newspaper *An Claidheamh Soluis* around the city 'feeling somewhat like a small Guy Fawkes'.[4]

This shift in the nature of political activism changed the ways in which the London Irish engaged with the city itself. While radical Irish politics remained focused on activities in the old Fenian headquarters at 55 Chancery Lane, elsewhere there was evidence of a greater mobility as traditional areas of high Irish population faded in significance and organizations such as the Gaelic Athletic Association (GAA) moved out to the peripheries of the city in search of suitable playing spaces. As a result what constitutes an 'Irish area' in London during this time is no longer as clearly defined. For instance, while the docks of the East End remained a district where many skilled working-class Irish resided, the emergence of the Post Office as a major employer of Irish immigrants meant that many newly posted to the city lived near to its major headquarters in Kensington (such as Collins and his sister Johanna) and Mount Pleasant in Islington (such as Patrick Sarsfield (P. S.) O'Hegarty and Sam Maguire). As

---

[4] Joe Good, *Enchanted by Dreams: The Journal of a Revolutionary*, ed. Maurice Good (Dingle: Kerry, 1996), 8.

Tony Murray has noted, the Post Office Savings Bank in West Kensington 'employed approximately 2000 workers, mainly women, a large proportion of whom were Irish and committed nationalists'.[5] Meanwhile those of greater economic means followed the Yeats family a generation previously and moved to the new suburbs further from the city centre. These relocations could sometimes appear slightly incongruous, such as when the future revolutionary and gunrunner Darrell Figgis moved to the prim surroundings of Asmuns Hill in the newly built suburb of Hampstead Garden Suburb in 1910.

It is also important to account for the significant number of future revolutionaries who were second (or even third) generation London Irish. While much of the transformation of Irish life in London – and certainly its militarization – was driven by politicized and sometimes militant figures newly arrived from Ireland, there were clearly many of Irish descent already established in the city eager to hear their message. The Easter Rising combatant Jeremiah J. (Diarmuid) O'Leary, for instance, was born in Colchester of Irish parents in 1889 and grew up in Clapham. His radicalization followed what would become a typical path for an Irish revolutionary in London: he was a member of the Clapham branch of the Gaelic League and the Thomas Davis GAA club at Mitcham from an early age, joined the Irish Republican Brotherhood (IRB) in 1908, organized the 'United Irish Associations in London' to provide relief funds for the Dublin lock-out of 1913, and in 1914 became chief organizer of the South London Company of the Irish Volunteers, drilling his recruits in St George's Hall on Westminster Bridge Road.[6] As such, and despite only sporadic visits to Ireland itself, it is no exaggeration to suggest that his entire early life took the form of preparation for the events that would later unfold in Dublin's General Post Office. Equally remarkable was Mary 'Cis' Sheehan's life of energetic political activism among the London Irish, which she described in vivid detail in her Irish Bureau of Military History Witness Statement in 1954. Born in London with parents from Tipperary and Wexford, Sheehan was the archetypal London Irish political radical and a figure deeply immersed the cultural principles of Irish Ireland. As a child she attended classes at the Irish National Club in Chancery Lane, one of the myriad Irish organizations that occupied the building through this period, and attended different branches of the Gaelic League across the city, eventually becoming Secretary of the League's central branch in Holborn. For young enthusiasts such as Sheehan, the League, along with its partner organization the GAA, provided a complete (and enclosed) social life, and also acted as a vehicle of radicalization that enabled the transition from cultural to political (or even military) activity. This process was encouraged by her contacts with such energetic mobilizers as O'Hegarty and Robert Lynd. As she recalled, 'we used to have Gaelic League outings that took us to the outskirts of London. We played camogie in Hampstead Heath and attended the boys' football matches at Leebridge Road [*sic*] and elsewhere. On Sunday nights we had céilís or parties in houses which were attended by some of the boys

---

[5] Tony Murray, 'Winifred M. Patton and the Irish Revival in London', *Irish Studies Review*, 22:1 (February 2014), 22–33, 25.

[6] Jeremiah J. (Diarmuid) O'Leary, BMH Witness Statement: 1108 (2 March 1955).

and girls who were members of the Gaelic League or GAA.[7] As this suggests, even in London it was possible to entirely immerse oneself into an Irish cultural life and thus be a member of what the London Gaelic League journal *Guth na nGaedheal* termed 'the mental and spiritual kingdom of Eire'.[8] This experience could become extremely intense; Sheehan describes being inspired by a 'wonderful speech' delivered by Patrick Pearse – at this point at the peak of his recently discovered rhetorical powers – to the London Gaelic League in October 1915: 'We listened to him breathless and spellbound and when he had finished we remained silent in the hope that he would go on. He spoke like an inspired man and practically without a gesture. You could nearly feel the people becoming Irish as well as Gaelic under his influence that night. It was great to have seen him.'[9]

Alongside notable figures including Alice Stopford Green and Sorcha Nic Diarmada (aka Sarah McDermott: a teacher from West Yorkshire of Irish descent, self-professed 'Irish feminist', and another indefatigable activist in the circles of Irish London), Sheehan was one of the founders of the London branch of Cumann na mBan ('The Irishwomen's Council') in the spring of 1914.[10] Although the organization was envisaged as working in conjunction with the recently formed Irish Volunteers, its role in London was always more complex than this brief indicated, not least because of the difficulties inherent in organizing what sometimes appeared to be overt displays of Irish nationalist militarism in the British capital. As Sheehan recalled:

> There was a priest, Father McKenna, in the East of London who loaned us a room where we members of Cumann na mBan, which was founded some time after the Volunteers, drilled. We got some drill books from the Volunteers we knew and practiced the movements. There would be 20 to 30 girls present. We only drilled for a short time and then took up the social side of Cumann na mBan work, running céilís and concerts. We did First Aid in a Council School which we were able to rent and a doctor, whose name was McDonnell, gave us instruction free, when he heard what we wanted it for, as he was a Republican. This lasted for one winter and we got no certificates.
>
> It was probably early in 1914 – it was definitely before the war – that we used to attend lectures at a place called the Bijou Theatre, somewhere off the Strand and members of the Volunteers and Cumann na mBan were present. Word went round that money was needed for arms, the strictest secrecy was observed but the money flowed in. We understood that Mrs. Stopford Green had guaranteed to provide a certain amount of money for the purchase of arms and we all subscribed a monthly sum to reimburse her.[11]

---

[7]   Mrs. Michael Cremin ('Cis Sheehan'), BMH Witness Statement: 924 (25 February 1954).

[8]   *Guth na nGaedheal* (March 1917), 10.

[9]   Cremin, BMH Statement: 924. The date for this event is confirmed in *The Letters of P. H. Pearse*, ed. Séamus Ó Buachalla with a foreword by F. S. L. Lyons (Gerrards Cross: Colin Smythe, 1980), 348.

[10]   *The Irishman* (January 1913), 5.

[11]   Cremin, BMH Statement: 924.

The range of London Cumann na mBan's diverse activity was both its strength and weakness. Engaged in matters as varied as military training, running social and educational events, fund raising and providing medical care, the organization sought to anticipate all eventualities. Later in its existence and when appropriate (usually when it was fund-raising or collecting relief supplies) it would masquerade under the name of 'the Irish Ladies Distress Committee', although according to Nic Diarmada this was not without controversy as some members 'wanted us to do what the Cumann na mBan did here [in Ireland] openly such as marching in uniforms openly in military formation. It was ridiculous in a foreign country'.[12] Eventually these tensions would lead to an acrimonious split in the organization in September 1921. That said, it was as a covert organization rather than an overt paramilitary unit that the London branch was able to make its most effective contributions in the revolutionary war. Many of its members, including Sheehan, were resourceful in helping English-based Irish republicans evade conscription into the British army following the Military Service Act of January 1916, and, as Sharon Furlong notes, the organization would become 'particularly efficient in the intelligence war during 1918–1921'.[13] This activity included spying, moving and storing weapons and ammunition across London prior to their transport to Ireland, and communicating secret messages between the two islands. As Nic Diarmada recalled:

We were all very cautious and never confided our activities to each other. For instance, Mrs. Cremin, then Miss Sheehan, would not know what I was doing and I would not know what she was doing but I knew generally that she was very active and came to Ireland very frequently where she deposited money and guns very often at various places.[14]

Alongside this clandestine activity, Sheehan would also take part in acts of intimidation across London. These included visiting relatives of Black and Tan soldiers fighting in Ireland and threatening to burn their homes should they not persuade their relations to return home. As her witness statement recounts:

It was arranged that I would meet an IRA boy at Notting Hill. He carried a gun and visited the house of a sister of a Black & Tan, who lived in that area to warn her to get her brother to leave Ireland or else she would have to suffer reprisals. I waited a little distance away while he went to the door. I watched the door being opened and he went in. He did not stay long as the lady made no fuss, but quietly promised to do what she was asked. My function was to act as a cover and make it appear that we were just a boy and girl out for a walk and if he were attacked to help in his escape by taking his gun.[15]

---

[12] Sorcha Nic Diarmada, BMH Witness Statement: 945 (13 May 1954).
[13] Sharon Furlong, '"Herstory" Recovered: Assessing the Contribution of Cumann na mBan 1914–1923', *The Past: The Organ of the Uí Cinsealaigh Historical Society*, 30 (2009–2010), 70–93, 84.
[14] Nic Diarmada, BMH Statement: 945.
[15] Cremin, BMH Statement: 924.

Although in many ways the respective London branches of Cumann na mBan and the IRA had a fraught relationship characterized by a considerable degree of mutual mistrust, it was with joint operations such as this that they were able to extend the conflict in Ireland to the British capital, a tactic that Irish republicanism would continue to deploy through the century.[16] Sheehan herself would remain an active combatant for a considerable period. Like nearly all the other members of the London Cumann na mBan branch, she rejected the terms of the 1921 Anglo-Irish Treaty and in the spring of 1923, alongside a number of other London-Irish republican activists including Nic Diarmada, she was arrested on charges of conspiracy, deported to Ireland and imprisoned in Mountjoy Gaol in Dublin by the Irish Free State government. It was only after a successful legal challenge that they were released and indemnified.

This focus on Sheehan, Nic Diarmada and O'Leary – revolutionaries who were born and raised in England – should not underplay the extent to which Irish political life in London was galvanized from around 1900 onwards by a generation of radical nationalists who arrived from Ireland seeking educational and professional advancement. Typically consisting of teachers, civil servants, clerks and priests, one of the most significant of this group was P. S. O'Hegarty, a historian, editor, book collector and (from 1908 to 1914) a member of the IRB's Supreme Council. A complex and talented figure with considerable academic ability, O'Hegarty had been transferred to London's Mount Pleasant Sorting Office from Cork in 1902 and, in the words of his biographer Keiron Curtis, he 'quickly placed himself at the heart of the émigré separatist movement'.[17] He would stay in London until 1913 and during that time was a tireless organizer on behalf of Irish nationalism, a keen builder of networks of influence, a prolific writer for a number of Irish journals and a sometimes sardonic recorder of Irish political and cultural life in the city (indeed his critical reviews of the London Gaelic League's St Patrick's Night concerts became known as 'Hegarty's Annual Growl').[18] He was at various times a very active member of the Gaelic League, treasurer for the London GAA and an enthusiastic figure in the Irish Literary Society (ILS); as he recalls: 'there was a period during which I was secretary to one club, treasurer of a second, chairman of a third and a member of the committee of a fourth'.[19] Alongside his talents for administration, O'Hegarty was impeccably connected, with associates and confidants across the range of nationalist Ireland; he was a close friend of Terence MacSwiney from his Cork days and while in London became the ally and mentor of Collins (who was eleven years his junior). He was also on good terms with W. B. Yeats; indeed his daughter Grainne would eventually marry Yeats's son Michael in 1949. It is for these reasons that O'Hegarty is a particularly important figure in the history of Irish London as he constitutes a point of continuity between a previous wave of Irish cultural revivalists (including figures such as Yeats, Frank Fahy and W. P. Ryan), and a later more radical generation of revolutionary activists (typified by Collins and

[16] For a good account of this mistrust see Gerard Noonan's *The IRA in Britain, 1919–1923: 'In the Heart of Enemy Lines'* (Liverpool: Liverpool University Press, 2014), 189–90.

[17] Keiron Curtis, *P. S. O'Hegarty (1879–1955): Sinn Féin Fenian* (London: Anthem Press, 2010), 3.

[18] *The Irishman* (April 1913), 3.

[19] P. S. O'Hegarty, 'Personal Recollections', *Sunday Independent* (26 August 1945), 7.

Lynd). Alongside this, his memoirs, correspondence and (perhaps most vividly) his Bureau of Military History Witness Statement provide us with much of our sense of the fine texture of Irish radical politics in London at this time, as well as a nuanced understanding of his own tastes, prejudices, and habits of mind.[20] As a Gaelic League tribute to him at the time of his departure from London recalled 'where Padraig was so also were life and activity in a truly decisive sense. He has been an athlete in the national and intellectual as well as the social order'.[21]

O'Hegarty was first engaged by the politics of Irish London in 1903 when he became chairman of the North London Branch of Cumann na nGaedheal ('Society of Gaels'), although this outcome was far from his initial intention:

> Early in August 1903, a notice appeared in *The United Irishman* of a forthcoming meeting to be held in premises somewhere near Highbury Station for the purposes of starting in North London a Branch of Cumann na nGaedheal. I was living in Highbury, and on the evening of the meeting I walked down to the place named with the intention of paying whatever modest subscription was necessary to get the club started. I knew nobody in the room, and I was under the impression that there was nobody there who knew me. I remember little now of who were the speakers, of what any of them said, but something which was said roused me to get up and say a couple of dozen words in a very halting and stumbling voice – it was my first attempt at speaking. It then appeared that there was somebody there who knew my name, for when the time came to elect officers to the newly established club, I was proposed as Chairman, and despite several attempts to refuse, and the repeated assurance that I was an entirely unsuitable person, I found myself at the end of the meeting elected Chairman with the members thinking they had done a good night's work. They knew not what they did. If I had to be Chairman I would be Chairman and for the ten years after that that I remained in London that Club was run on severely puritanical lines. No smoking, no dancing, very little sing-song, nothing but work. We began with a language class, which I had to teach, a couple of lessons in front of the others, followed by a lecture, a set debate, or a manuscript journal, which were debated at length and with great seriousness. And we finished always with *A Nation Once Again*. The same sort of thing was being done in Clubs in East, West, South, and Central London, and at home.[22]

'The severely puritanical lines' that O'Hegarty refers to were a distinctive feature of Irish nationalist circles at this time. Inspired by the Ulster Quaker and Republican, Bulmer Hobson and his colleague Denis McCullough in their reform of Irish political organizations in Belfast, many younger activists exhibited a markedly austere dedication to the cause which it was hoped would distinguish them from the previous generation of nationalists, many of whom they regarded with something near to

---

[20] P. S. O'Hegarty, BMH Witness Statement: 839 (17–31 December 1952).
[21] *The Irishman* (October 1913), 4.
[22] O'Hegarty, BMH Statement: 839.

contempt. Most notoriously, McCullough would go so far as to remove his father from the ranks of the Belfast IRB because of his alcoholism. Conveniently for O'Hegarty, this stance accorded with his natural instincts. As Frances Flanagan observes, he 'lived a highly disciplined, almost ascetic lifestyle [...] He compressed a day's worth of work at the Post Office into three hours in order to keep up with a hectic schedule of meetings, reading, and writing obligations, did not drink, and rarely went to bed before one or two in the morning.'[23] His activities on behalf of Ireland were also aided considerably by the attitude of his Post Office employers, who appear to have asked remarkably little of their talented young clerk in return for his salary. As he recalled in 1929, 'when I think of it now in cold blood it astonishes me what generous treatment the English always give the Irish individually. I spent 11 years in the London GPO and never experienced anything but kindness, almost indulgence.'[24] Despite his hard-line political instincts, O'Hegarty's acknowledgement of this kindness was not as unusual as it might first appear; in activist circles in London there was often a marked contrast between public declarations of Anglophobia and private expressions of regard, or even affection, for English work colleagues and social associates. However, even with the benefit of his employer's lenience and his own considerable resilience, O'Hegarty's workload would sometimes prove overwhelming. The London Gaelic League journal *Inis Fáil* reported in April 1909 that he had been struck down with an illness related to overwork. 'We had ourselves besought "Sarsfield" more than once to take things easier, but to try to stop him working was like trying to sweep back the ocean with a broom. [...] To put too much work on one man's shoulders is immoral,' it grumbled.[25]

Alongside his work for Cumann na nGaedheal, O'Hegarty also founded and acted as secretary of the London Branch of the Dungannon Clubs, a separatist organization initiated by Hobson and McCullough in 1905 that played an important role in prefiguring the emergence of Sinn Féin. The Dungannon Clubs were, in the words of their associate Patrick McCartan, 'semi-literary, semi-political and patriotic', and the London branch brought together the more radical elements in the national movement in the capital such as Lynd and George Gavan Duffy (Sir Charles Gavan Duffy's son).[26] Although McCullough regarded the organization as not much more than 'a cover for the IRB', it played a significant, if brief, role in mobilizing new activists and would eventually merge with Cumann na nGaedheal in April 1907 to form the 'Sinn Féin League'.[27] In conjunction with its political activities, the London branch produced its own plays, staging Padraic Colum's *The Saxon Shilling* and Lewis Purcell's comedy *The Enthusiast* at Hampstead in 1905. Key to this venture was the involvement of the illustrator Norman Morrow as both set designer and actor.[28] One of the eight Morrow

[23] Frances Flanagan, *Remembering the Revolution: Dissent, Culture, and Nationalism in the Irish Free State* (Oxford: Oxford University Press, 2015), 86.

[24] Foster, *Vivid Faces*, 55.

[25] *Inis Fáil: A Magazine for the Irish in London* (April 1909), 4.

[26] Gerard MacAtasney, *Seán MacDiarmada: The Mind of the Revolution* (Manorhamilton: Drumlin Publications, 2004), 15.

[27] Denis McCullough, BMH Witness Statement: 915 (11 December 1953).

[28] 'The Propagandist Players', *Inis Fáil: A Magazine for the Irish in London* (January 1906), 2.

brothers who had done much to establish the pioneering Ulster Literary Theatre as a Belfast-based version of Yeats's Irish literary Theatre in 1904, he had recently relocated to London to live with his brother Eddie. The London Dungannon Club used his studio in Chelsea for its meetings.

O'Hegarty combined his work reforming the political structures of Irish London with obsessive book collecting (according to Colm Ó Lochlainn he 'amassed an enormous library' while in the city), and cultural and literary journalism, writing for notable journals and newspapers across a range of nationalist opinion including *Inis Fáil, United Irishman,* and *The Peasant.*[29] According to fellow London IRB member Brian Cusack, he 'tightened up on the [IRB's] organisation and brought things up to a high standard' and was sporadically engaged by other social struggles beyond the matter of Ireland.[30] He married the suffragist and 'ex-Protestant agnostic' Wilhelmina (Mina) Smyth in 1915 and was a supporter of the suffragette movement for a period, although in his later years he developed a tendency to blame female activists and politicians for what he saw as the failings of the revolutionary project.[31] Unusually among his generation of activists, his literary tastes extended to the avant-garde and the proto-modernist and, unlike many of his colleagues in the Gaelic League, he was comfortable in acknowledging the inherent Irishness of literary works written by Irish writers in the English language. More specifically, he praised the work of the Abbey Theatre and especially Yeats's *Cathleen Ni Houlihan,* though he could find little of value in Augusta Gregory's work, condemning an Abbey production of her short play *Coats* in London in 1911 as 'the most absolute piffle ever produced on any stage. It is as dull as ditchwater and has not a redeeming feature.'[32] In later life he would be a prominent defender of James Joyce's *Ulysses,* describing it as 'the biggest book that has ever been done in English [...] in which the language is used as it never was used, and used triumphantly'. 'It is not a story merely but an epoch, and an Irish one,' he continued.[33] As this suggests, O'Hegarty's literary criticism was frequently perceptive. His reviews displayed a natural instinct for comparative cultural analysis and an understanding of how a modernist aesthetic sensibility could enter into a dialectical relationship with a Gaelic past, a possibility which mystified many of his contemporaries. Indeed, O'Hegarty was not alone among London revivalists in taking a more inclusive view of Irish literary achievement than could often be found in Ireland itself. The reasons for this might include, as Philip O'Leary has suggested, 'the polyglot literary scene of the imperial capital, the exile's sharpened appreciation of the distinctively Irish quality of much Irish writing whatever its linguistic medium, and a simple national pride in the recognition accorded their countrymen by the English literary establishment'.[34]

---

[29] Wayne K. Chapman and James Helyar, 'P. S. O'Hegarty and the Yeats Collection at the University of Kansas', in *Yeats Annual No. 10* (Basingstoke: Macmillan, 1993), 221–38, 234.

[30] Brian Cusack, BMH Witness Statement: 736 (9 October 1952).

[31] Flanagan, *Remembering the Revolution,* 87.

[32] *The Irishman* (August 1911), 11.

[33] Donagh MacDonagh, 'The Reputation of James Joyce: From Notoriety to Fame', *University Review,* 3:2 (Summer 1963), 12–20, 17.

[34] Philip O'Leary, *The Prose Literature of the Gaelic Revival, 1881–1921: Ideology and Innovation* (Pennsylvania: Penn State University Press, 1994), 289.

O'Hegarty left London and returned briefly to Ireland in 1913 but he would find himself back in England at the outbreak of the Great War. His refusal to swear an oath of loyalty to the Crown in 1918 meant that he could no longer remain an employee of the Post Office and he returned to Ireland on a permanent basis becoming the manager of an Irish book shop in Dublin. He eventually became Secretary of the Department of Posts and Telegraphs in 1922. A supporter of the Treaty in the Civil War, from this point on O'Hegarty's life would be marked by his continued preoccupation with the national question. This took the form of a long-standing uneasiness about the manner in which the events of Easter 1916 had been transformed into a narrative of martyrdom, his absolute adherence to the principles of Fenian separatism and a consistent opposition to any form of what he saw as clerical interference in the national movement. His influential polemic *The Victory of Sinn Féin: How It Won It, and How It Used It* (1924) despaired of the violence of the Civil War and the activities of the Irregulars in particular, which, he argued, demonstrated that 'our deep-rooted belief that there was something in us finer than, more spiritual than, anything in any other people was sheer illusion, and that we were really an uncivilised people with savage instincts'.[35]

As the stark terms of this condemnation indicate, O'Hegarty's politics were always markedly uncompromising. In 1907, a point when his immersion into the cultural world of Irish London was at its deepest, his reflections in the short-lived Dungannon Clubs newspaper *The Republic* on the relationship of revivalism to physical force nationalism concluded that ultimately the threat of violence had to underwrite all other activity on behalf of the nation. As he asserted, 'Revivalists for whom the "extreme" Nationalist or physical force man remained somewhat of a "bogey" must get over their puerile view, and recognize the physical force man is just as severe, as honest, and as practical as themselves; and that physical force is the moving weapon behind the whole Revival.'[36] In the context of O'Hegarty's London life, his amiable relationships with the founders of the Southwark Literary Club, and the manner in which he could move with ease among the Anglo-Irish members of the ILS, this statement comes as something of a jolt. But when considering O'Hegarty's opinions in the context of London's metropolitan culture, it is easy to disregard the peculiarly compressed nature of Irish experience at this time and, more significantly, the fact that two of his great uncles died in the potato famine while other members of his family were forced to emigrate, and that in 1888 his father died of tuberculosis aged forty-two leaving a trail of family poverty in his wake. As this suggests, his early exposure to the violence of Irish history never left him, and it is in this context that his view of the function of physical force republicanism as ultimately 'severe', 'honest' and 'practical' becomes more explicable.

O'Hegarty was clearly a luminary figure in London's Irish circles. Articulate, charismatic and absolutely dedicated to the cause, it is no surprise that he exerted

---

[35] P. S. O'Hegarty, *The Victory of Sinn Féin: How It Won It, and How It Used It* (Dublin: Talbot Press Ltd., 1924), 126.

[36] Curtis, *P. S. O'Hegarty*, 26.

considerable influence over the young Michael Collins, who had arrived in the city from Clonakilty, West Cork, in 1906, aged fifteen. As an intelligent boy from rural Ireland, educated in the national school system and provided with what appeared to be a viable career path in the vast networks of British imperial administration, he was an archetypal product of his time – a version of what Foster has termed a 'supermick on the make'.[37] Indeed, as Collins himself reflected, he was 'like thousands of other Irish lads of my station'.[38] In total, he would spend nine years in London (almost a third of his life) and the experience was profound if not always positive. On his arrival Collins moved in with his sister and fellow Post Office employee, Johanna, and they would continue to share accommodation during his time in the city, living in various properties in Shepherd's Bush, South Kensington, Notting Hill and (from 1909 onwards) back in Shepherd's Bush in a relatively spacious flat on Netherwood Road. This residence would become something of a social hub for young Irish people living in the area. His first role in London was as an 'Irish Boy cop'. As Cis Sheehan recalled, these were:

> the boy clerks in the Post Office Savings Bank, earning very little money [...] they had no amusements such as the cinema as they have nowadays, so they were welcomed in many Irish homes like ours in the evenings, and we got to know many of them intimately. They were members of the GAA and the Gaelic League and were to be found in all the branches of those organizations throughout London.[39]

Collins was soon deeply integrated into the city's Irish world and his ability to create and nurture strong friendship groups and coteries is a defining aspect of his time in the city. Although, as Frank O'Connor put it, Collins 'behaved as though he owned the post office', he would eventually find the job tedious and demeaning and in April 1910 he moved to a position at the stockbroking firm Horne and Company in Moorgate.[40] In 1914 he would move back to the civil service as a labour exchange clerk in the Board of Trade based in Whitehall. His final London position was a clerkship at the London branch of the Guarantee Trust Company of New York. This post came with the option to relocate to New York – a possibility he considered seriously until the senior Fenian Thomas Clarke informed him that 'there was going to be something doing in Ireland within a year'. As Collins recalls, 'that was good enough for me', and he left London for Ireland in January 1916.[41] He would return to the city as an uneasy plenipotentiary for the Anglo-Irish Treaty negotiations in June 1921.

Aside from the generally unsatisfactory progress of his professional life, other aspects of Collins's time in London were more dynamic. Although his talents and

---

[37] R. F. Foster, 'Marginal Men and Micks on the Make: The Uses of Irish Exile, c. 1840–1922', in *Paddy and Mr Punch: Connections in Irish and English History* (London: Penguin, 1993), 300.

[38] Hayden Talbot, *Michael Collins' Own Story* (London: Hutchinson & Co., 1923), 25.

[39] Cremin, BMH Statement: 924.

[40] Frank O'Connor, *The Big Fellow: A Life of Michael Collins* (London: Thomas Nelson and Sons, 1937), 26.

[41] Talbot, *Michael Collins' Own Story*, 26.

energy were frustrated by the grinding cogs of the British civil service, he became increasingly radicalized to the cause of Irish Ireland and more inclined to move in solely Irish social circles. He joined the Gaelic League, the Sinn Féin Club in Chancery Lane and, in 1907, the Geraldine Athletic Club in west London, the favoured GAA club of many Irish workers in the Savings Bank. He would play for the Geraldine's hurling team to the best of his (somewhat limited) ability and would occasionally turn out for the all-London side against other British provincial clubs. In January 1909 he was elected club secretary, a position he would hold until his return to Ireland. His period of office was distinguished by an unusual degree of success on the field and by his often acerbic twice-yearly reports. As was the case with many young activists in London at this time, the cultural institutions of Gaelic Ireland acted as a gateway to an ideological commitment to militarism and in November 1909 Collins was sworn into the IRB in the Barnsbury Hall in Islington, probably by either Sam Maguire (a fellow Cork man and colleague in the Savings Bank) or Pat Belton (a fellow member of the Geraldines and yet another young Irish man working in the civil service). Collins became an IRB Section Master in 1913 and, a year later, treasurer of the organization's South of England district. Although IRB numbers in England were tiny (estimated to be around just 117 at this point), this was still an impressive achievement. However, despite this advancement and the obvious energy he brought to all that he attempted, ultimately Collins's time in London was marked by a process of disillusionment as the excited new immigrant who wanted 'to live in the world's biggest city' realized 'with each passing year [...] that London for me held as little real opportunity as did Ireland'.[42] Indeed by the end of his time in London he wrote to his close confidant (and possible early girlfriend) Susan Killeen of his loneliness and despondency, complaining 'London is a terrible place, worse than ever now – I'll never be happy until I'm out of it and then mightn't either'.[43] Collins was not unusual among Irish exiles in the city in expressing such bitter sentiments.

Such is the ongoing fascination with Collins and his complex if foreshortened life of revolutionary struggle that it is unsurprising that the minutia of his time in London has been investigated in great detail by many biographers.[44] Often this task has been undertaken with the expectation that it will explain precisely how and where he gained his remarkable talent for the management of insurrectionary violence, and yet the overall sense of his London life that tends to emerge is more mundane, and one that, in actuality, was shared by many other young Irish immigrants at this time. In short, most of his experiences were typical rather than exceptional. Alongside this, earlier (and frequently more hagiographical) accounts of his life, such as Piaras Béaslaí's monumental two-volume *Michael Collins and the Making of a New Ireland* from 1922, emphasize the corrupting nature of London life and praise his steely refusal to yield to the temptations

[42] Talbot, *Michael Collins' Own Story*, 25.

[43] Letter from Collins to Susan Killeen (19 October 1915), reproduced in Tim Pat Coogan's *Michael Collins* (London: Arrow Books, 1990), p. 21.

[44] Of more recent biographies, the best are Anne Dolan and William Murphy's *Michael Collins: The Man and the Revolution* (Cork: Collins Press, 2018), Peter Hart's *Mick: The Real Michael Collins* (London: Macmillan, 2005) and James Mackay's *Michael Collins: A Life* (Edinburgh: Mainstream, 1996).

of the 'big Babylon'.[45] In this interpretation, as Béaslaí asserts, London was little more than an 'environment' to be 'resisted'.[46] In fact, Collins fell a little short of this idealized image. O'Hegarty, who knew him throughout this period, observes that 'when he came to London as a mere boy, he fell into spasmodic association with a hard-drinking, hard-living crowd from his own place and their influence was not good. During most of his years in London he was in the "blast and bloody" stage of adolescent evolution, and was regarded as a wild youth'.[47] This judgement may be excessively stern; as we have observed, O'Hegarty was especially abstemious in the conduct of his private life and was quick to judge those who fell beneath his standards. Indeed, according to Cusack, it is even possible that O'Hegarty delayed Collins's entry into the IRB as he was concerned about his excessive drinking.[48] Alongside this weakness, as O'Hegarty's reference to a 'hard-living crowd from his own place' indicates, Collins's social habits were, by any measure, extremely clannish. He sought only the company of Irish people (preferably men from Cork) and was wary of fraternizing with the British. As he reflected:

> of course, I had Irish friends in London before I arrived, and in the intervening years I had made many more friends among Irishmen resident in London. For the most part we lived lives apart. We chose to consider ourselves outposts of our nation. We were a distinct community a tiny eddy, if you like, in the great metropolis. But we were proud of our isolation, and we maintained it to the end.[49]

One probably unanticipated side-effect of this deliberate removal from wider London society, as Collins himself later speculated, was that despite his long period in the city he remained so 'little known that 120,000 British troops and Black and Tans could not find me in four years of hunting me in Ireland'. As he further explained, 'I can only attribute it to that policy of voluntary isolation we all observed in London. And, after all, Michael Collins, junior clerk, could hardly be expected to have attracted any notice especially in an English business house.'[50]

Despite this, there is some evidence that Collins's life was not quite as hermetically sealed from English influence as these assertions insist. He did, for instance, form a deep affection for Albert Lawrence, his and his sister's landlord in Shepherds Bush and South Kensington. He was also an enthusiastic theatre goer, frequently attending the Royal Court in Sloane Square and the Coronet in Notting Hill, and, thanks to the guidance of his sister, he was deeply read in English literature. However, these were unusual elements in a life that was generally lived in solely Irish circles.[51] As Béaslaí puts it, he existed – and to some extent thrived – in 'an Irish colony in the midst of the strangers'.[52] Indeed his isolationist instincts would become more pronounced over

[45] Piaras Béaslaí, *Michael Collins and the Making of a New Ireland* (Dublin: Talbot Press, 1922), 12.
[46] Béaslaí, *Michael Collins*, 24.
[47] O'Hegarty, *The Victory of Sinn Féin*, 23.
[48] Cusack, BMH Statement: 736.
[49] Talbot, *Michael Collins' Own Story*, 25.
[50] Ibid., 25–6.
[51] Mackay, *Michael Collins: A Life*, 27.
[52] Béaslaí, *Michael Collins*, 24.

time; in July 1909 he wrote to *Inis Fáil* in his role as Secretary of the Geraldines in order to 'record its indignant protest against the action of the County Board in readmitting to the GAA Messr's Brown, Collins, Dineen and Minogue – who competed for England at the Olympic Games last year, after the said Board has warned all members of the GAA that such competition meant expulsion from the GAA'.[53] In this Collins was eagerly enforcing the GAA rulebook at the time, which stated that its members were forbidden from participating in 'foreign' sports and would be expelled from the organization if they did. Even in ideal circumstances the rule was never easy to enforce, but in the context of Irish London, where many of the best GAA athletes were also enthusiastic about other sports, it became a highly volatile point of conflict. The crisis would rumble on for a few years and the manner in which it forced both clubs and individual members to take an unambiguous and frequently divisive position on the issue did long-term damage to the overall fortunes of the GAA in the city.

Such episodes illustrate the extent to which the refusal to assimilate was always a dynamic (and sometimes exhausting) activity, which required a process of constant self-examination and policing. It also provoked a distinctive self-consciousness about Irish identity and the values that it embodied. O'Hegarty's *The Victory of Sinn Féin* transcribes an older Collins reflecting on his time in London in precisely these terms:

> I stand for an Irish civilisation based on the people and embodying and maintaining the things – their habits, ways of thought, customs – that make them different – the sort of life I was brought up in. That is what I mean by Irish Ireland, and if Irish Ireland means anything else, I don't want it. Once, years ago, a crowd of us were going along the Shepherd's Bush Road when out of a lane came a chap with a donkey – just the sort of donkey and just the sort of cart they have at home. He came out quite suddenly and abruptly and we all cheered him. Nobody who has not been an exile will understand me, but I stand for that.[54]

O'Hegarty's recollection of the detail of this anecdote may not have been exact, but Collins's emphasis on exile as the foundation stone of his sense of Irishness is arresting. The life of London Irish revivalists was often viewed (not least by themselves as expressed in the pages of *Inis Fáil*) as typified by a state of loss or absence when compared to the happy state of activists living back in Ireland, individuals for whom territory, belonging and language were presumed to be in alignment. However, Collins's anecdote is a powerful reminder of the vivid nature of emigrant political consciousness and the manner in which it could create startlingly intense parables of self-determination, often when least expected. It is at such moments that the particular and distinctive contours of national identity as it developed among the London Irish are revealed most clearly, and in light of future events, it is telling that Collins adds

---

[53] 'Protest of the Geraldines', *Inis Fáil: A Magazine for the Irish in London* (August 1909), 10.
[54] O'Hegarty, *The Victory of Sinn Féin*, 139.

the caveat that 'nobody who has not been an exile will understand me'. The fact that many of those who were closest to him during his time in London remained his most trusted confidants through the subsequent revolutionary period tells its own story. More prosaically, his exile gave him other notable benefits. As Joe Good observed, he 'had one great advantage over his contemporaries; he knew the English and their art of dissimulation, and he had the common touch'.[55]

The examples of O'Leary, O'Hegarty, Sheehan and Collins indicate the overall success of the Irish organizations I discussed in Chapter 4 in producing dedicated political agents who were willing and able to commit acts of violence should it be necessary. Certainly if any of them were ever tempted from their chosen path of political commitment by the attractions of Anglicized London life they never mention it – although as the major source of information we have for the London lives of O'Leary, O'Hegarty and Sheehan is from their testimony in Irish Military Witness Statements, this is perhaps not entirely unsurprising. Collins, too, had reason to underplay the extent to which he integrated into London life given the readiness of his enemies in the republican movement to accuse him of compromise in the years after the Treaty. But it is also notable that these accounts of their formative years all describe another crucial, if slightly nebulous, element of radical Irish political life in London during this time: the manner in which social, political and cultural experience became markedly more intense as the political crisis developed. This would take different forms. For instance, Sheehan's early life was illuminated by a series of cultural revelations and epiphanies; O'Hegarty exhausted himself by the overwhelming amount of committee work he undertook, while Collins's time in the capital was defined by what appears to be a sometimes dizzying mobility. Although he chose to live in a small area of west London, he was ever restless and would range across the city at will, touching base with its various scattered pockets of Irish activism. Collins was not alone in exhibiting this dynamism. Although figures such as Lynd and Stopford Green often had quite different priorities, they resembled each other in the extraordinary dedication with which they pursued their plans and the impatience they expressed when these plans encountered obstacles. Within the limited circles of Irish London much of what occurred was dependent on little more than the determination of a small number of charismatic individuals.

However, acknowledging the intensity of these individual lives is not to imply that every part of Irish London was aflame with nationalist feeling. Certain areas, despite having a high proportion of first- and second-generation Irish, remained stubbornly uninterested in the national question. For instance, O'Hegarty's Witness Statement describes an attempt 'to do some propaganda in Battersea where there was a large Irish population but no branch of the [Gaelic] League'. After much deliberation about choosing the right speaker for an area identified as a United Irish League (UIL) stronghold, eventually the Gaelic scholar and activist P. J. (Padraic) O'Shea (who used the pen name 'Conán Maol') was selected and 'the great night came':

---

[55] Joseph Good, BMH Witness Statement: 388 (19 May 1950).

Battersea Town Hall was a large one, and it was all ready, with rows of chairs and benches. About ten minutes to eight Robert Lynd, George Gavan Duffy, Mrs. Dryhurst, Seaghan O Siothcan, Caitlin Nich Gabhain, and myself, went in, and sat in the back row so as not to be conspicuous. Just before 8 a group of about half-a-dozen people came in, of whom the only one I knew was Councillor Brogan, the United Irish League leader in South London. Nobody else came in. Conan had to speak to empty benches.[56]

As O'Hegarty noted, dryly, 'we did not get a branch started at Battersea'. Anecdotes such as this serve as a salutary reminder not to mistake the determined energy of an active minority for the general attitude of Irish London as a whole and illustrate the manner in which the fortunes of the League in London fluctuated considerably over this period in ways that reflected (if not always straightforwardly) the wider political landscape. As League member Mairtin MacDonagh reflected glumly, 'out of at least 70,000 Irish-born people in London there are not 5000 consistent supporters of nationalism, chiefly for the reason that they are under process of assimilation by the circumstances of exile and environment'.[57] Despite the seemingly tireless work of figures such as O'Hegarty, the Irish Parliamentary Party (IPP) remained the dominant political vehicle for Irish nationalists in London and, alongside the UIL, it promoted a Home Rule agenda which attracted and retained a broad spectrum of Irish political views. Significantly, this included many members of the Catholic Church and much of London's more established and propertied Irish middle class. It was in this way that moderate nationalist opinion and British liberalism maintained an uneasy alliance through the early years of the century.

Such were the London Gaelic League's travails through this period it is possibly only because of what Arthur O'Brien (Art Ó Bríain), the President of the branch from 1914 to 1935, refers to as the 'elastic character of its scheme of organisation' that it managed to survive in any kind of continuous form.[58] As I discussed in Chapter 4, the high point of the organization's success was probably in 1906 when, alongside its central operation in St Andrews Hall on Oxford Street, it ran around twenty-two schools teaching Irish across the city and twice filled the Royal Opera House in Covent Garden for its St Patrick's Day concerts. Although it is difficult to give a precise figure, it is likely that overall membership at this time was over 2,000.[59] However, the election of Henry Campbell-Bannerman's Liberal Government in the general election of that year raised the prospects for achieving Home Rule through parliamentary nationalism and this, in turn, dramatically reduced enthusiasm for the League's 'Irish-Ireland' project.

[56] O'Hegarty, BMH Statement: 839.

[57] M. MacDonagh, 'GAA in London and the Question of National Principle', *The Irishman* (April 1911), 4.

[58] Art Ó Bríain, 'Gaedhil thar sáile: Some Notes on the History of the Gaelic League of London', *The Capuchin Annual* (1944), 116–26, 120.

[59] W. P. Ryan asserts that even before this – at the end of 1903 – the London Gaelic League had over 2,000 members. Even accounting for any over-estimation fired by his habitual enthusiasm, the number of functioning regional schools across the city suggests this is possible ('Twenty-Five Years of the London Gaelic League', *Guth na nGaedheal* (March 1924), 7–11, 10).

The Kensington Branch reported in March 1911 that 'we have a few of the sturdiest of the old-time campaigners with us still. But alas! They are all too few and for ever dwindling', while the Clapham branch complained about the 'defection of old members, which makes work in the League seem like ploughing the sands'.[60] The organization's membership would continue to decline to the extent that, according to O'Brien, by 1914 'all activities of the London League were on the wane'.[61] By this point there were only four functioning schools and, as he continued, 'even these only maintained a more or less, symbolic existence, with perhaps only one class and few pupils'. Despite the determined efforts of its office holders to rally enthusiasm among its remaining members, at this point the organization appeared to be in a terminal condition and it was only the unforeseen events of Easter 1916 that prompted a startling revitalization of its fortunes. Members, new and lapsed, flocked back and, as O'Brien notes, 'embarrassed our reduced resources of organisation'. As a result, 'classes which had closed for the summer had to be re-opened. Local schools, which had become extinct, were now re-started, and by 1921 their number had again risen to fourteen. The national spirit was once more in the ascendant, and all phases of national effort were increased and strengthened thereby'.[62] The momentum of this renaissance would endure for a decade, yet the League would continue to face further challenges through this time: during the wartime years male membership was badly affected by conscription and by the number of men returning to Ireland either to avoid joining the army or to take part in revolutionary activity, while its classes always suffered from a shortage of competent language teachers. However, the London League's biggest difficulty remained fundamental to its very existence: the fact that it was not in Ireland. As such, and despite the considerable energy it expended on nurturing a Gaelic life in the city, it always deemed its achievements less worthy than the activities of the League back in Ireland. As a result, it was inevitable that many of its more committed members would leave London and return, a debilitating process of loss which it was obliged to glumly celebrate. As 'Mnemosyne' lamented in the pages of the London Gaelic League newspaper, *The Irishman*, in 1913:

> the Gaelic League of London was fortunate in attracting men of fine intellect, strong will, and pure-souled patriotism while yet in its infancy [...] under their fostering care it throve amazingly, and, as Kathleen Ni Houlahan [*sic*] attracted each in turn, the loss to London Gaeldom has been but the gain to Ireland. The return to the fount of their enthusiasm was surely inevitable.[63]

The Irishman, a monthly supplement for *Inis Fáil*, described itself on its masthead as 'devoted to the advancement of the *Irish-Ireland* movement' and was designed to appeal to 'quarters where the present organ, with its relative limitations, could not have been expected to reach'.[64] It recorded the activities of the League during the

---

[60] *The Irishman* (March 1911), 5.
[61] Ó Bríain, 'Gaedhil thar sáile', 123.
[62] Ibid., 123.
[63] 'Reminiscences of the London Gaelic League', *The Irishman* (March 1913), 4.
[64] *Inis Fáil* (June 1910), 14.

period of its greatest difficulties and, despite the generally unfavourable political conditions, managed to convey a remarkable vibrancy in its engagement with the various aspects of London's Irish life. Much of this was doubtless due to the restless energy of O'Hegarty, who served as editor, contributed reams of copy (including a long-running series 'Lectures on Irish history') and constantly chivvied its readers to make greater commitment to the League and to the cause of Irish Ireland more generally. He would, for instance, encourage the shy or inexperienced to make a more vocal contribution to the regular Seanchus (a formal storytelling and discussion group) held at the League's headquarters at 77 Fleet Street, criticize male League members for 'sheepishly hanging about the door and sides' rather than taking part in Irish dancing at the New Year Festival in St Andrew's Hall and demand contributions in order to improve the annual Aonach (an exhibition and sale of Irish goods and one of the League's traditional showpieces).[65] The paper offset some of this sternness with a wry humour often directed at the sheer unlikeliness of the task the London branch had set itself in seeking to develop the language in what were deemed such inhospitable conditions. Reporting on an Irish-language production of Yeats's *Cathleen ni Houlihan* by the League's Clapham branch in 1913, *The Irishman*'s Aodh de Blácam attended with some trepidation, admitting with perhaps unwise candour, that he was 'fully expecting a fiasco. Everyone, probably, dreaded that Clapham was too ambitious'.[66] As it transpired, he reported that his 'fears were wasted' and 'the play was a tremendous success', but what is significant (and what was less frequently found in the League's assessments of its sombre activities elsewhere) was the willingness to contemplate the possibility of imminent ridicule. Such an attitude was astute in that it lent the London League's sometimes rickety cultural projects a certain emotional resilience.

The Irishman was also distinctive in that it recounted the history of Irish London itself through its regular 'Pioneers' feature, which profiled the lives of activists who had first initiated revival activities in the city such as Fahy and Thomas Flannery.[67] These small but resonant acts of remembrance owed much to O'Hegarty's historicizing instincts – his Fenian-inspired belief that it is only as part of a tradition that individual acts gain significance – and it was through this initiative that Irish London began to know itself. More contentiously, the paper was willing to act as a forum for the discussion of the political disagreements and tensions that lay at the heart of the League's self-image as the manifestation of a national ideal. For instance, at the Branch's annual meeting in July 1911, a motion proposed by Pádraic Ó Conaire, the Irish language author and teacher, and Eoghan O'Sullivan questioned the London branch's long-established custom of sending London-Irish children to rural Ireland during the summer, and suggested that such interaction might have a harmful effect on the linguistic habits of the native Irish speakers living there. Alongside this they argued that the overall benefits of educating London-born Irish children in the language

---

[65] *The Irishman* (January 1911), 8 and *The Irishman* (February 1911), 7, 11.

[66] *The Irishman* (March 1913), 7.

[67] *The Irishman* (September 1911), 4.

were marginal and proposed instead that the League 'had better concentrate its spare energies on adult arrivals from Ireland'.[68] The motion was defeated and yet the fact that it had been tabled at all indicated that many continued to regard Irish nationality as a strictly circumscribed entity. Indeed the implications of the motion were such that had it been passed it would have effectively ended most of the League's work in the city. Perhaps for this reason, *The Irishman* responded passionately:

> The suggestion that London-born children of Irish parents necessarily cannot be Irish is simply beneath argument. When not used thoughtlessly it is based upon an utterly superficial notion of what constitutes race and individuality.
>
> Another notion, that the half-dozen or dozen children we send annually to an Irish-speaking district may do harm by speaking some English, is really laughter-moving. We find it quite impossible to take it seriously. Really some of our young friends are very harsh on those who live in Irish-speaking districts. They seem to assume that those Gaels have neither sanity nor sense of humour.
>
> The innocent and artless Irish speaker spoiled and corrupted by a few children from London! He hears English abounding from pulpit, press, and bench, and there is little woe or protest. But let a few London children – on the quest for more Irish mind you – go within measurable distance of his hearth and – ! Oh, the humour and the irony of it!

Other correspondents responded with a similar fury. 'Eilis ni F' declared that 'adult members of the League feel and resent the spirit of contempt underlying [O'Sullivan's] words' and continued:

> Does he know almost from babyhood we are proud of the land which should be ours? The sneers in school life, directly they know you were Irish, starts that fighting spirit, that makes us firm in our resolve to fight through life for our land, and only make us London-Irish prouder of being Irish. Ireland is to us, when children, a place of all that is noble and good, an ideal land, an ideal which when grown up is, alas, very often shaken. It is not by any heroic deed of their own, that our critical friends are born and bred in their own land, neither is it our fault we are London-born.[69]

The anger of this response, a reaction to the childhood 'sneers' of the English and their constant anti-Irish prejudice, was a crucial element of London life for the Irish at this time and yet it is rarely encountered in such overt terms in the League's various publications. This is partly due, no doubt, to the organization's policy of emphasizing the positive aspects of identity formation through its cultural activities, but, despite this, the rawness of the grievance was never far from the emotional surface. Indeed as O'Sullivan's and Ó Conaire's motion would have effectively trapped the London-born

---

[68] *The Irishman* (August 1911), 7.
[69] Ibid., 8.

Irish in a cultural ghetto, caught between the disdainful attitudes of both the English and the Ireland-born Irish, the intensity of the reaction was understandable.

Arguments about the possible dangers of assimilation were frequent and inevitably incendiary given that within Irish-London society any accusation of 'shoneenism' was regarded as a particularly vicious insult. In 1906 an anonymous writer to *Inis Fáil*, signing themselves 'CARRIGAFOYLE', condemned members of the Islington League for helping to facilitate, on the same night and in the same building as a League language class, 'a shoneen dance, to which they invited all their shoneen English friends, offering a very attractive shoneen programme'.[70] 'The English came and the shoneens came, and they fondled each other to their heart's content', the correspondent added. Given the seriousness of this allegation, rebuttal by the Islington Committee members was swift. 'The dance referred to was simply an entertainment organized by the Eden Grove Catholic Church and therefore the adjective "Shoneen" was inapplicable' wrote 'L. Dill Smyth' in response. 'And while holding no brief for the English people we must in common fairness concede them the right to organise English dances if they wish,' they continued.[71] While CARRIGAFOYLE's original letter had condemned a 'cowed down spirit of West Britonism and its secret effects', its pointed reference to 'fondling' suggests that their primary anxiety was less about damage to Irish language educational provision in N1 and more about the possibility of miscegenation. More generally, the League, like other Irish-Ireland cultural organizations in the city, tightly policed possible expressions of sexual desire, and occasions where the sexes might mingle were strictly regulated. This is not to say that such opportunities did not exist; ceilidhs organized by Irish organizations or the Catholic Church provided opportunities for fraternization, while the League's mixed language classes and occasional day trips offered other possibilities. In a slightly more surreptitious manner, there were mixed gatherings in private residences, such as the regular parties of younger Irish people organized by the Collins siblings at their flat in Shepherd's Bush. Even in these meetings, however, there could be no hint of impropriety and any trace of scandal had to be avoided.

In 1913 the Gaelic League relocated its headquarters from 'the seclusion of that old dingy building away at the back of Fleet Street' to new premises on Lamb's Conduit Street in Holborn, a move that 'has brought us into touch with the world again'.[72] Yet this sense of renewal was misleading. By this point the *Irishman* was making heavy losses and O'Brien tabled a motion at the League's annual meeting in June to shut it down. Ó Conaire spoke (in Irish) against the motion, praising the paper's value as propaganda, while O'Hegarty, Collins and de Blacam also opposed.[73] The motion was defeated but when O'Hegarty announced his return to Ireland two months later ('It is likely that I shall be gone before many members have even heard that I am going,' he declared dramatically), it was clear that the paper could not continue without his energy and O'Brien's wish was fulfilled.[74] 'We have not, and have not had for some

[70] 'STRONG LETTER TO THE EDITOR', *Inis Fáil* (February 1906), 8.
[71] 'Replies to "CARRIGAFOYLE"', *Inis Fáil* (March 1906), 6.
[72] *The Irishman* (January 1913), 3.
[73] *The Irishman* (July 1913), 5.
[74] Ibid.

time, sufficient workers with enthusiasm and initiative to keep this or any of our other activities going with success', he complained.[75] O'Brien's overall strategy at this point was to refocus the League's activities more determinedly on its core activity of language teaching, and his desire to close the *Irishman* indicated the extent to which he was uneasy with the organization's growing preoccupation with wider political and cultural activities. This had some support from the membership. The internal politics of the League was such that there was always extreme sensitivity about any suggestion that its key activity was being diluted. However, the loss of *The Irishman* deprived Irish London of its most vibrant voice and it was one that was never adequately replaced.

As the vibrancy of *The Irishman*'s coverage indicates, the Gaelic League was able to adapt to changing political contexts but, alongside this flexibility, it always maintained its emphasis on placing Gaelicization at the heart of the project of national liberation. However, the profiles of other Irish cultural organizations in London were less clearly defined and as a result they risked becoming marginalized by rapidly changing circumstances. For instance, although the ILS continued to run a full programme of events, including lectures, trips to Ireland, tea dances and 'Original Nights', many of the newer generation of Irish activists regarded its work as, at best, eccentric and, at worst, elitist and politically compromised. Such criticism was not without substance. As Mo Moulton has observed, ILS formal dinners had become of sufficient social standing to be reported in *The Times*, and in general the Society was at ease with itself as a 'happy family' located at the interface between Ireland and Britain.[76] For many this situation was far from satisfactory. 'Why is it that the lectures of the Irish Literary Society so often leave behind them a peculiar sense of respectability, rarely obtained at other Irish gatherings?', asked *Inis Fáil* mischievously in 1906.[77] The answer was clearly so obvious that it seemingly required no answer. The League would intensify its criticism in the following years, condemning an ILS lecture by Conal Holmes O'Connell O'Riordan in 1913 as a 'denial of the value of Gaelic as a living language', and suggesting that overall the organization 'has ceased to be very Irish at all nor literary for that matter'.[78] To some extent this attitude was part of a more widespread mistrust of 'old' revival organizations on the basis that such bodies, in Foster's words, 'repudiated simplistic nationalist rhetoric', but in the often intense atmosphere of Irish London specifically there was also the perception that the ILS had reneged on whatever small obligation it had once felt to the diaspora's cultural needs.[79] This does not mean that the ILS was entirely abandoned by Irish London's more radical figures; O'Hegarty, Lynd and Collins, for instance, were either members (and in O'Hegarty's case, a deeply committed member) or attended its lectures, while the fact that the ILS placed advertisements in *The Irishman* (possibly as a way of helping the newspaper's financial difficulties) indicates a certain goodwill. But, despite this, by 1913 it was clear that the two organizations represented quite different

---

[75] Ibid., 3.
[76] Mo Moulton, *Ireland and the Irish in Interwar England* (Cambridge: Cambridge University Press, 2014), 228.
[77] 'Hanover Cult in Hanover Square', *Inis Fáil* (February 1906), 6.
[78] *The Irishman* (January 1913), 7 and *The Irishman* (June 1913), 5.
[79] Foster, *Vivid Faces*, 24.

visions of what Ireland might be and as the decade progressed it would be increasingly difficult for individuals to maintain an allegiance to both. This was not the only tension to emerge among the city's various Irish organizations and it is significant that when a new Irish club in the city was proposed in 1911 (the 'Union of the Four Provinces of Ireland Association') one of its functions was to 'dissipate any suspicions or jealousies which may exist between some of them'.[80] The Union had some success in this and its headquarters played host to what would be the most important collaboration of Irish organizations in London in this period when the 'United Irish Societies Association' was formed to raise money for the victims of the Dublin Lockout in the autumn of 1913. This was a Gaelic League initiative chaired by O'Brien, and, as Pádraig Yeates records, it brought together representatives from 'the Ancient Order of Hibernians, the GAA, the Gaelic League, the Irish Association, the United Irish League, the Irish Literary Society, the Irish Athletic Club, the London Irish Football Club, the Irish League for Women's Suffrage, and the United Irishwomen'.[81] Its success was such that it continued to operate through the revolutionary years and provided funds for the families of those nationalists killed or imprisoned during the Easter Rising.

Alongside the ILS, another centre for what might be considered the older school of literary revivalism was Yeats's residence at 18 Woburn Buildings (see Figure 9), which he maintained as his London base and a 'Celtic stronghold' from 1896 to 1919, a period when he was extraordinarily peripatetic.[82] An atmospheric building with what John Masefield described as 'a kind of blackguard beauty', the Woburn Buildings were, as Foster notes, 'symbolically, across the road from Euston Station, where the Irish Mail departed every evening and arrived very morning'.[83] This had a practical purpose in that it was conveniently located in order to meet those newly arrived from Ireland and glean what news they brought with them, but it also indicated something of Yeats's ambivalent relationship to London and what David Pierce has identified as his 'ability to drift in and out of things'.[84] Regarded by the other residents as 'the toff what lives in the Buildings', the cheap if shabby apartment enabled Yeats to maintain a permanent base in London, and to do so strictly according to his own eccentric values. Although lacking electricity and with only the most rudimentary plumbing, the arrangement suited him well (as well as its proximity to Euston it was also a short walk for the British Museum's Reading Room) and he would gradually expand his living space into the floors above and below as his circumstances allowed.[85] He initiated a long-running salon on Monday evenings, which entertained figures as diverse as his old Rhymers' Club colleagues Ernest Rhys and Arthur Symons, J. M. Synge, Standish O'Grady,

[80] *The Irishman* (March 1911), 4.

[81] Pádraig Yeates, *Lockout: Dublin 1913* (Dublin: Gill and Macmillan, 2000), 319.

[82] Douglas Goulding, *South Lodge: Reminiscences of Violet Hunt, Ford Madox Ford and The English Review Circle* (London: Constable, 1943), 48.

[83] John Masefield, 'My First Meeting with Yeats', in *W. B. Yeats: Interviews and Recollections*, Vol. 1, ed. E. H. Mikhail (London: Macmillan, 1977), 47. Foster, 'Marginal Men and Micks on the Make', 296. The meeting between Yeats and Masefield took place on 5 November 1900.

[84] David Pierce, *Yeats's Worlds: Ireland, England and the Poetic Imagination* (New Haven: Yale University Press, 1995), 108.

[85] Masefield, 'My First Meeting with Yeats', 47.

Augusta Gregory, the illustrator and occultist Pamela Colman Smith, Rabindranath Tagore, and, perhaps most significantly, a domineering Ezra Pound. Beginning as a fairly conventional literary circle appealing to, what Masefield termed, 'the last of the Pre-Raphaelite followers', it would soon be reshaped according to Yeats's restless interest in poetry and performance becoming a forum where experimental methods of literary reading – most notably through the medium of chant – could be explored.[86] As the artist William Rothenstein recalled: 'when Yeats came down, candle in hand, to guide one up the long flight of stairs to his rooms, one never knew what company one would find there. There were ladies who sat on the floor and chanted stories, or crooned poems to the accompaniment of a one-stringed instrument'.[87] Indeed, such was Yeats's interest in this subject that he delivered a lecture with Florence Farr titled 'Chanting' to the ILS in May 1903. The apartment would also host evenings dedicated to Yeats's fascination with occult rituals although these were not universally popular; according to his wife George, Yeats 'lost many of the habitués of his Woburn Buildings Mondays because he insisted on talking about occult experiments – none of which went much further than the ones before'.[88] Partly because of this activity Yeats was regarded as something of a curiosity by many of the younger generation of Irish revivalists in London. In Terence Brown's words, he was 'an exotic figure in the English capital's literary and social scene', and, indeed, much of what happened inside the esoterically decorated walls of his home might now be regarded as faintly ludicrous.[89] That said, it would be a mistake to let these moments obscure the overall cultural importance of the Monday meetings and the manner in which they enabled the worlds of Irish cultural politics, the European literary avant-garde, and occultism to meet (and occasionally collide).

Despite the fact that Yeats maintained his rooms at the Woburn Buildings for what was (by his standards) an extraordinarily lengthy period, his attachment to London was always conditional and after a period of city life he would typically relocate elsewhere – often to Gregory's Coole Park in Galway – and declare himself heartily tired of its crowds, noise and gossip. He would, however, always return. In this regard his ambivalence about the city was similar to Roger Casement's, another startlingly single-minded and charismatic Protestant nationalist, albeit one with a quite different set of political priorities. For Casement the city provided an opportunity to build networks within Irish nationalism through his close friendships with figures such as Lynd, while also serving as a vast resource of sexual pleasure. He would initiate the latter through impromptu sexual encounters at busy railway stations such as Victoria and Euston, and the crowded exhibition halls of Earl's Court and White City.[90] As this

---

[86] John Masefield, *So Long to Learn: Chapters of an Autobiography* (London: William Heinemann, 1952), 143.

[87] Ronald Schuchard, 'The Countess Cathleen and the Revival of the Bardic Arts', *South Carolina Review*, 32:1 (1999), 24–37, 32.

[88] Ann Saddlemyer, *Becoming George: The Life of Mrs W. B. Yeats* (Oxford: Oxford University Press, 2004), 108.

[89] Terence Brown, *The Life of W. B. Yeats* (Oxford: Blackwell, 1999), 110.

[90] Jeffrey Dudgeon, *Roger Casement: The Black Diaries with a Study of His Background, Sexuality, and Irish Political Life* (Belfast: Belfast Press, 2016), 297.

Figure 9 William Butler Yeats in his study in Woburn Buildings (*The Tatler*, 29 June 1904).

indicates, although by this stage of his life he was intensely Anglophobic in his politics, Casement made London his own; in the words of his biographer Jeffrey Dudgeon, his trips to the city were typified by a 'relentless wandering' and certainly no other figure in this book traversed London so extensively or recorded their excursions in such detail.[91] Most strikingly, his private cash ledger and diary of 1911 describes a period of his life in which he combined burgeoning political activism with a considerable appetite for cruising in a remarkably intense manner. In just January and February of that year it details assignations with, among others, an 'Ahmed Khaled', two rent boys called Ernest and Fred, a young Italian, a Welsh Grenadier, a 'Harrow Jew', a Japanese sailor, and an unnamed Scotsman, at locations as diverse as New Oxford Street, Farringdon Road, Tottenham Court Road corner, Clerkenwell Road, an unnamed Turkish baths, the public toilets at Piccadilly Circus, the West Indies Docks in the East End, St James Park, Hyde Park Corner, Clarence Gate in Marylebone, Victoria Station, Sloane Square and Putney Bridge. Key to this activity was the anonymity the city afforded him. At a time when he was increasingly well known – he was knighted in July 1911 for his work in exposing human rights abuse in the Putamayo district of the Amazon Basin and was a significant figure in Irish Ireland circles – Casement could effectively disappear into London and live a quite unrecognizable life. Such episodes were usually time-limited; like Yeats, after a while he would pronounce that he was 'very tired of London' and leave, but (also like Yeats) he would inevitably return for further experiences.[92] Given this habit, it was, perhaps, morbidly appropriate that the final days of his life would also take the form of a London odyssey. Following his arrest at Banna Strand in Kerry in April 1916 having been put ashore from a German U-Boat, an ill and despairing Casement was taken to the city. He was held in Brixton Prison and then the Tower of London, charged with treason at Bow Street Magistrates Court, and had his appeal heard at the Royal Courts of Justice in July. Finally, with all further options exhausted, he was hanged at Pentonville in Islington on 3 August 1916. One hour before his execution a crowd gathered on Caledonian Road outside the Prison. It consisted mostly of women, children and munitions workers from the locality. When the prison's minute bell struck indicating that the execution had taken place some in the crowd 'fell to their knees and with bowed heads remained a few minutes silently praying for the repose of the dead'.[93] Others, however, raised a celebratory cheer – a moment that inspired the indefatigable Irish poet, dramatist and propagandist Alice Milligan, who had remained in what she called 'gay, blood-guilty London' after Casement's trial, to compose one of her most powerful poems:

> How from England's beauty
> Can I my heart withhold?
> *By thinking of her crowds that cheered*
> *When a death bell tolled.*[94]

---

[91] Ibid., 281.
[92] Ibid., 230.
[93] 'Casement's Fate', *Irish News* (4 August 1916), 3.
[94] Alice Milligan, 'In the Wirral' (1917, ms17630, Joseph McGarrity Papers 1789–1971, National Library of Ireland).

As Milligan's frozen moment of appalled recollection illustrates, the series of events that culminated in the Rising of 1916 crashed over Irish London in waves, transforming many individual lives in ways that could scarcely have been anticipated. And yet even in 1912 there were ominous signs of what lay ahead; in September an anti-Home Rule meeting in Bermondsey was disrupted by what Belfast's *Northern Whig* described as a 'band of Irish and Radical roughs' who caused an 'almost incessant uproar'.[95] The *Whig's* perspective on this event was hardly impartial, but, even allowing for this, it is clear that the atmosphere across the city was increasingly incendiary. Indeed, the establishment of the Irish Volunteers in November 1913 in response to the formation of the Ulster Volunteers in the previous year was simply one in a series of increasingly portentous anticipations of violence. Dedicated to preventing Home Rule by military means, the (overwhelmingly Protestant) Ulster Volunteers were a well-funded paramilitary force, armed with German weaponry smuggled into Ulster through gun-running operations. It was able to draw on substantial military experience from sympathetic ex-Army officers in its leadership. Unionism was also mobilizing in London. In July 1914 the anti-Home Rule leader Sir Edward Carson addressed a gathering of around ten thousand people at the London County Athletic Ground in Herne Hill. In an overtly paramilitary atmosphere he was escorted by a bodyguard drawn from the 'Walworth section of the British League for the Defence of Ulster and the Union', and delivered a fiery address in which he pledged 'to go any length and to make any sacrifice' in defence of the Union.[96] It was, as the *Drogheda Independent* declared, 'a Twelfth of July speech from beginning to end'.[97]

When compared to the Ulster Volunteers, the Irish Volunteers had significantly fewer assets other than sheer weight of numbers. Committed to protecting the Home Rule cause and encompassing (frequently uncomfortably) a wide variety of nationalist opinion from ardent Home Rulers, who envisaged a devolved Ireland as part of the British Empire, to members of Sinn Féin and the Gaelic League, the organization lacked resources and military experience. It was also deeply infiltrated from its inception by IRB operatives at both national and local levels. The formation of the Volunteers in London was inspired by what local recruit William Daly termed 'a slashing speech' by the West Clare MP Colonel Arthur Lynch in Lambeth, and was given further urgency by nationalist outrage at the Curragh Mutiny in March 1914, when British Officers effectively refused to obey Government orders to prepare for possible military action against the Ulster Volunteers.[98] The inaugural meeting – consisting of just thirty men – took place that month at Highgate. The first members were mostly from the North London GAA, but as the movement gathered momentum it gained recruits from all the major Irish organizations across the city, including the United Irish League of Great Britain and the Ancient Order of Hibernians, which let the Volunteers use its headquarters in West London for meetings. Drill sessions with wooden rifles took place at Highgate Woods, the German Gymnasium by St Pancras

[95] *The Northern Whig* (20 September 1912), 7.
[96] *Sheffield Daily Telegraph* (6 July 1914), 9.
[97] *The Drogheda Independent* (11 July 1914), 5.
[98] William D. Daly, BMH Witness Statement: 291 (17 December 1949).

Station and, as the organization grew, at St George's Hall in south London and the GAA grounds at Lea Bridge to the east. They possessed very little worthwhile equipment, although, according to North London Volunteer Joe Good, 'even as far back as 1913, small amounts of arms were being smuggled into Ireland; some of these were taken from Woolwich Arsenal. They comprised only revolvers and revolver ammunition'.[99] Woolwich Arsenal was a significant employer of Irish people so the fact that its security proved to be occasionally porous is unsurprising. There were other opportunities too; for instance Liam de Róiste, the Cork Sinn Féin activist, was able to purchase a new Mauser rifle in a London gunsmith's shop and smuggle it back to Ireland with no serious difficulty while attending a summer lecture course at the London School of Economics in 1914.[100] However, given the rapidly escalating militarization of Irish society these individual initiatives were far less than what was required.

In June 1914, the organization's national newspaper, *The Irish Volunteer*, reported that the fledgling London branch had accepted an offer of assistance from the London-based Irish Piper's Club, which included the use of its band during manoeuvres.[101] This arrangement had been facilitated by Collins (using his old Post Office connections) with the hope that sympathetic ex-Army drill instructors would provide military training for what was essentially an inexperienced group of civilians. As Louis Noble, the first drill instructor and piper, recalls:

> In March, 1914 Michael Collins and Maurice Sheahan came to me at the Pipers Club and asked me to take charge of the drilling and instruction of the First Company of the Irish Volunteers then being formed at the German Gymnasium, St. Pancras Road, London, NW. They knew I held a proficiency Certificate for Drill and Musketry from the English Volunteers. I had in my Company men who were to make history in Ireland, I can remember a number of them: Michael Collins, Maurice Sheahan, Sean Hurley, Sean and E. [Ernie] Nunan, Dan Sheehan, M. [Michael] Cremins, J. [Joseph] O'Brien, Francis Fitzgerald, Con Crowley, Padraig O'Conaire, Joe and Matt Furlong; there were seventy-seven names on my roll. After the split in volunteers I carried out training at Highgate Woods and Hammersmith.[102]

As this account suggests, Collins and Maurice Sheahan (a London-based Gaelic League activist and hurler who would die a year later from pneumonia contracted while training Volunteers in the Wicklow Mountains) were at the heart of the London organization from the beginning. Indeed, such was Collins's self confidence that, according to Good, he behaved as if he was 'meant to be in command'.[103] Alongside

---

[99] Good, BMH Statement: 388.
[100] Liam de Róiste, BMH Witness Statement: 1698 (27 November 1957).
[101] *The Irish Volunteer*, 1:20 (20 June 1914), 12.
[102] James Langton, 'The Volunteers Irish Citizen Army IRA Cumann Na mBan Photo File Part 3', Available online: https://irishvolunteers.org/the-volunteers-irish-citizen-army-ira-cumman-na-mban-photo-file-part-3/ (accessed 5 November 2019).
[103] Good, BMH Statement: 388.

drill practice and military manoeuvres, the Volunteers organized educational and social events such as céilís and concerts. These raised funds which were used, in part, to purchase weaponry. As noted earlier in the chapter, Cumann na mBan was centrally involved in this aspect of Volunteer activity, and would develop a semi-autonomous existence, working alongside the Volunteers as paramilitaries (at least initially), fund-raisers, medical practitioners and (ultimately) intelligence gatherers.

Although the bulk of the Volunteers were recruited from Irish-London's clerical lower-middle class, the organization gained some unlikely allies from other sectors of London-Irish society. For instance, perhaps the landmark event in the history of the Volunteers – the gunrunning of 1,500 Mauser rifles at Howth harbour in Ireland on 26 July 1914 – had its origin in a lunch hosted by the historian Alice Stopford Green at her exclusive London residence on Grosvenor Road in April of that year. Described fawningly by O'Hegarty as 'a natural aristocrat, but an aristocrat of the intellect and not of any ignoble or materialistic concept', Stopford Green was a key figure in liberal and elite Irish London and a mobilizer whose weekly salons provided an opportunity for Irish nationalists to meet with British liberals and anti-imperialists on relatively neutral terms.[104] As a result of the lunch, at which were present senior figures in the Volunteer movement including Eoin McNeill (a co-founder of the Gaelic League and Professor of early Irish history), Casement and Darrell Figgis (a bookseller, literary critic, and novelist from Dublin), she agreed to loan most of the money required for the armaments and to act as treasurer for the venture. The IRB later repaid the sum to her. The weapons were purchased from an arms dealer in Hamburg in May and were transported back to Ireland in two yachts: the *Asgard*, which belonged to Erskine Childers and his wife Molly, and Conor O Brien's vessel, the *Kelpie*. The *Asgard* landed at Howth Head and the weapons were swiftly removed and concealed by local Volunteers. When an attempt by troops of the King's Own Scottish Borderers to prevent the smuggling resulted in the deaths of four civilians in what became known as the Bachelor's Walk massacre it only further emphasized the fact that the British military was scarcely a neutral observer of the unfolding crisis. Much of the significance of the Howth gunrunning was symbolic rather than practical – the smuggling was on a much smaller scale than that undertaken by the Ulster Volunteers previously and the weapons themselves were antiquated – although the arms would still play an important role in the Easter Rising two years later. Alongside this, the involvement of Stopford Green, as well as other London Irish liberals such as the Childers, indicates the degree to which elite Irish London was prepared to engage and support a violent and militarized vision of Irish politics in a manner which would have been unthinkable only a few years earlier. Certainly the extent of the radicalization that took place was profound. Stopford Green, for instance, began her adult life with little interest in Irish politics, then became a Home Ruler of varying degrees of commitment, until finding herself so immersed in militant Irish nationalism that she was happy to let IRA leaders use her Dublin home to plan strategy during the war of independence.[105] Erskine Childers' hectic journey from a House of Commons junior committee clerk with unionist beliefs

---

[104] O'Hegarty, BMH Statement: 839.
[105] Angus Mitchell, 'The Stopfords of Blackwater House: Alice Stopford Green's Family Circle', *Riocht na Midhe*, xxx (2019), 176–212, 206.

in 1895 to a committed revolutionary executed by pro-Treaty forces during the civil war for possession of a weapon in 1922 was more remarkable still. But beyond these specific details, the trajectory of their political development indicates something of the manner in which London-Irish experience more generally was transformed during this period as the Home Rule crisis and the events that it set in train polarized political life.

Galvanized by the success of the Howth adventure and the anger provoked by the Bachelor's Walk massacre, enthusiasm for the Volunteers increased and there was soon something close to 5,000 members in London alone. However, the situation would be changed profoundly by Britain's declaration of war with Germany on 4 August 1914. John Redmond, the leader of the IPP, committed the Volunteers to supporting the British and Allied war effort in September 1914 and in London, as elsewhere, the resultant split in the organization revealed a stark schism in the broad range of nationalist opinion. While the large majority of Volunteers supported Redmond's policy and reconstituted as the 'National Volunteers', a small but radical minority separated, kept the name Irish Volunteers, and immediately attempted to seize the organization's weaponry and resources. According to Maguire, Collins was a crucial figure in negotiating the split in the London Volunteers, swiftly commandeering what few weapons and funds existed for the more militant (if comparatively much smaller) faction.[106] A similar operation was attempted in south London; as Daly recalled, 'we had a small, but determined band of Irish-Irelanders [...] who, when the split took place, immediately grabbed control of Hall, money, equipment and anything of value in regard of our progress'.[107] This decisiveness was impressive, but there was no disguising the fact that as a result of the split the Irish Volunteers in London were reduced to a tiny company consisting of about sixty committed members. Naturally this included all the IRB operatives who had infiltrated the movement in its previous incarnation. For this reason the new body was much more unified in its political purpose, functioning as 'the military wing of the counter-culture', as Peter Hart describes it.[108]

Despite the drastically reduced numbers, the Irish Volunteers continued their operations in London, concentrating their resources south of the river and making St George's Hall their headquarters. These activities included parading through the suburbs of south London with a pipe band and, according to Daly, 'all the evolutions of military drilling including bayonet attacks and counter attacks'.[109] With the benefit of post-Rising hindsight, this conspicuous visibility is perhaps the most peculiar aspect of the London Volunteers' activity. Considering that the organization was essentially a hostile foreign army parading through the streets of the British capital, it is remarkable that they did not attract more scrutiny from the security services and were left unmolested by a general population fed on a constant diet of jingoistic propaganda. Rather than a manifestation of typical London incuriosity, this was more likely due to a mistaken understanding of the Volunteers' purpose; as Daly suggests, 'the Londoners looked upon us as a body of men who would soon be fighting for

---

[106] Dolan and Murphy, *Michael Collins: The Man and the Revolution*, 43.
[107] Daly, BMH Statement: 291.
[108] Hart, *Mick: The Real Michael Collins*, 67.
[109] Daly, BMH Statement: 291.

England (little did they know)'.[110] Either way the very fact that the Volunteers survived in such an atmosphere was, in itself, a considerable achievement. As *The Irish Volunteer* reported in October 1915 following a visit to London by the Volunteers' director of organization, Patrick Pearse, 'the difficulties of Irish Volunteering in London under war conditions may be imagined, but this hardy group is able to keep up training in all the essentials'.[111] But despite these encouraging noises, the organization struggled to maintain its membership. This was, in part, because of the fear of conscription but also because Volunteers frequently had to remove themselves to Ireland if they came under police suspicion. Under wartime conditions such movement was increasingly difficult. As London IRB member and Volunteer Richard Connolly recalled, 'it was very difficult for anyone in England to get across at the time. The conscription affair was on and permits were now being issued […] no one could come from England without going through Scotland Yard'.[112] The fact that London Cumann na mBan developed particular expertise in facilitating these covert relocations was a great asset. The introduction of conscription in January 1916 in Britain (though not Ireland) forced the hand of the remaining Volunteers. Following a hurried meeting in St George's Hall, thirty-two of them (including some Cumann na mBan members) left London amidst constant rumours that some kind of major military operation was being planned in Dublin. Collins and his closest confidants were in this group. For many, particularly those Volunteers born in London, this was the biggest adventure of their life. Daly, especially, could scarcely have anticipated the experience that lay ahead. Born in Dockhead, 'a rough and ready quarter of London', and 'never out of London (except on a holiday) in my life', he knew 'nothing of Ireland except in a hazy kind of way'. His BMH Witness Statement captures something of the apprehension, excitement and fear of the journey:

> I met Dave Begley and Jimmy Riley at Euston Station at 8 p.m. on 10th Jan. and we travelled to North Wall via Holyhead. I had my rifles with me, one taken asunder and packed in a large portmanteau, the other hanging under my long overcoat and I had to stand the whole distance from London to Dublin. My companions had saloon tickets and got to bed on board, while I stayed on deck through that stormy night, stretching myself occasionally on a big box against the deck rails. The train and boat was packed with soldiers coming to Ireland and I felt that everyone knew I was skipping the country. I managed to get safe and sound to L.&N.W.R. Station, North Wall, without arousing suspicion. I had feelings of fear while walking along the North Wall to O'Connell Bridge as there appeared to me to be a very big policeman every 20 yds along that route and I had never seen such big men in uniform before; with the possible exception of the City of London Police, the D.M.P. [Dublin Metropolitan Police] were a body of [the] biggest men I had seen.[113]

[110] Ibid.
[111] 'Notes from Headquarters', *The Irish Volunteer*, 2:45 (16 October 1915), 5.
[112] Richard Connolly, BMH Witness Statement: 523 (5 June 1951).
[113] Daly, BMH Statement: 291.

Along with other Volunteers from Britain, the London members billeted in a derelict mill on Joseph Plunkett's Kimmage estate south of Dublin where they drilled and made ammunition in preparation for the coming insurrection. During the Rising itself they became known as the 'Kimmage Garrison' and, despite the initial mistrust they occasionally encountered from their Irish-born fellow Volunteers, were in the vanguard of the fighting around the GPO and Sackville Street. Indeed, as the Belfast IRB operative Séumas Robinson recalled, the Kimmage Garrison functioned as 'the Standing Army or "Shock Troops" of GHQ, before and during Easter Week'.[114] It is unsurprising, then, that for Daly the experience was 'the turning point in my life'. Certainly participation in the Rising gave British-born Volunteers unimpeachable Irish nationalist credentials and thus laid to rest any lingering doubts about their national identity – doubts that had been raised in the past by individuals such as Ó Conaire. As Daly put it with touching simplicity, 'I adopted Ireland as my own country until it adopted me at Easter 1916'.[115]

Other London Irish Volunteers that fought in the Rising and survived included Sean Nunan and his seventeen-year-old brother Ernie from Brixton, Joe Good, the civil servant Con Collins and John 'Blimey' O'Connor, a colourful figure from Islington who gained his nickname at Kimmage because of his broad cockney accent. O'Connor had the scarcely believable task of climbing up a pole to fix an aerial while under sniper fire in order that the proclamation of the Republic might be broadcast. As fellow Volunteer Liam Tannam recalled, 'how he had the pluck to carry on and how he was not riddled beats me'.[116] A number of other London-Irish combatants were less fortunate. According to Arthur O'Brien, President of the London Gaelic League at the time, London League members Patrick Shortis, Seán Hurley, Michael Mulvihill, Patrick O'Connor, Donal Sheehan and Con Keating were killed.[117] Keating and Sheehan drowned alongside another volunteer, Charlie Monahan, on Good Friday when their car plunged off Ballykissane pier in Kerry. They had been driving to Cahersiveen in order to seize the wireless station at Valentia Island with the aim of setting up radio communications with Casement and the German arms ship the *Aud* and (as a diversionary tactic) of sending signals to the Royal Navy about a hoax imminent German attack on Scottish naval bases. They are usually regarded as the Rising's first casualties. Hurley was shot dead fighting with the Four Courts garrison, while Mulvihill, Shortis and O'Connor died in what became known as the 'O'Rahilly Charge', an attempt to break the British barricade of the GPO at the Moore Street junction with Parnell Street after four days of exhausting resistance. Of this moment Limerick Volunteer Éamonn Dore recalled that 'my nearest comrade, Pat O'Connor, was killed in front of me and, falling on me, pinned me under him'.[118] O'Connor had worked for the Post Office in London from 1900 to 1912 and later transferred to the

---

[114] Séumas Robinson, BMH Witness Statement: 1721 (16 April 1957).
[115] Daly, BMH Statement: 291.
[116] Liam Tannam, BMH Witness Statement: 242 (30 April 1949).
[117] Art Ó Bríain, 'Gaedhil thar sáile: Some Notes on the History of the Gaelic League of London', *The Capuchin Annual* (1944), 116–26, 126.
[118] Eamon T. Dore, BMH Witness Statement: 153 (19 September 1948).

GPO in Dublin where he worked as a sorter. That his sometime mundane place of work had been transformed into the epicentre of revolutionary violence must have provoked one of the Rising's more peculiar moments of cognitive dissonance.[119] The Nunan brothers and Denis Daly, another volunteer who had served in the London civil service, survived the assault. Altogether, such was the number of London-Irish Volunteers who took part in this particularly terrifying episode in the insurrection that it can be understood as the landmark moment in their story.

Back in London, the events of Easter 1916 also proved to be traumatic. Although some activists may have had an approximate sense of what was being planned as a result of communications from the Kimmage Garrison – Cis Sheehan's recollection that 'we in London did not know the Rising was coming off, but we were not surprised when it did' was typical – the scale of the operation and the devastation it caused was of a different order.[120] For this reason in the immediate aftermath of the Rising, the dominant emotions were of shock and confusion. With communications from Dublin sporadic and wartime reporting restrictions in place, London newspapers' coverage was haphazard and misleading, initially underplaying the scale of the event before suddenly declaring that it was, in fact, part of an international conspiracy masterminded by Casement and his German allies. In this manner the *Globe* was content to declare the matter closed after the first day of fighting, reporting that 'a mob seized the post office; troops were brought down from the Curragh and the situation is now well in hand'.[121] On the next day, 'Sinn Feiners' were (also erroneously) identified as responsible, but the event continued to be reported as a minor disturbance, a 'riot rather than a rising' as the *Guardian* pronounced it.[122] On 30 April, six days after it had begun, the *People* described the Rising as part of a coordinated operation which included Zeppelin raids into Norfolk and Suffolk and the bombardment of Lowestoft and Yarmouth by a German battle cruiser squadron. Despite this, it still stressed the limited nature of the operation. 'The great scheme has failed lamentably. The Dublin insurrection, organized by traitors, has been nipped in the bud, and it obviously never had the slightest chance of successes,' it crowed, slightly desperately.[123] It was not until a little time had passed that a dim awareness of the significance of the Rising began to emerge and, with this, some recognition that English ignorance of Irish opinion was partly a cause. As the exotically named Major Charles de Brézé Darnley-Stuart-Stephen reflected:

> Unfortunately many Englishmen and North Britons take little or no notice of affairs in the Sister Isle, believing them to be matters of merely local interest. Then comes a morning when the self-superior cockney reads of an outbreak of

---

[119] The occupations of the other London Irish dead were as quotidian as O'Connor's: Sheehan was a bookkeeper at the shipping company J&C Harrisons, Mulvihill was a post-office clerk (and friend of Collins), Keating was a wireless operator, while both Hurley and Shortis worked in Harrods department store.

[120] Cremin, BMH Statement: 924.

[121] *The Globe* (25 April 1916), 1.

[122] *The Guardian* (27 April 1916), 4.

[123] *The People* (30 April 1916), 9.

Milesian aborigines who are distinguished by a tribal name unpronounceable by the Sassenach, and he mutters while surveying the news-paper scare-heads, 'Who would have thought it?'[124]

The point was well made. If nothing else, one result of the Rising was to focus London's political class on the matter of Ireland to a remarkable degree; the fleeting attention of 'self-superior cockneys' was no longer adequate to a political situation that was about to conflagrate in the most spectacular manner. It was not as if there had been no clues as to what was about to unfold; it was only in the wake of the event that *The Globe* drew attention to the fact that what it called 'treasonable literature' had been circulating across London for months.[125]

Given media coverage of the Rising, it is unsurprising that the great majority of the London Irish followed British public reaction in expressing shock and disgust at what had taken place. Seen as a distraction from the major theatres of war in Europe, it also exacerbated a deep suspicion among the British public about the extent of Irish commitment to the war effort. In this context the reassurances of the *Illustrated London News*, which argued that 'the few misguided fanatics who engineered the Sinn Fein rebellion are in no sense representative of Irish feeling [...] the real Ireland is rather to be found among the gallant Irish troops at the front', were not entirely persuasive.[126] For this reason, denunciations of the event by London Irish groups were, if anything, over-effusive. A meeting of the UIL in Caxton Hall in Westminster on 3 May passed a motion 'that this meeting of London Irish Nationalists expresses its strongest condemnation of the wickedness and insanity of the recent rising of Sinn Feiners in Ireland, and heartily approves of the attitude of Mr John Redmond and the Irish party, and reiterates its complete confidence in them'.[127] With thousands of British UIL members on military service via the National Volunteers there was no other response possible, although it would do nothing to halt the steady decline of an organization already suffering from greatly reduced membership levels. Like the UIL, the *Catholic Herald* group of newspapers – another traditional voice of the Irish in Britain – came out strongly against the Rising, maintaining its enthusiastic Redmondite position and the support for the war effort that this demanded. Deeming it nothing more than a 'Pocket Edition of a Revolution' intended 'to hand Ireland over to Germany for that country to impose its beneficent will upon the people', its London edition reserved particular disdain for James Connolly (because of his 'Socialistic, Anti-Clerical and Anarchical' tendencies) and for Casement (whom it accused of 'being in the pay of the German government').[128] 'It has been necessary on many occasions to point out that the renegade had never been known inside the Irish Nationalist movement. He is

---

[124] Charles de Brézé Darnley-Stuart-Stephen, 'The Sinn Feiners' Plan of Campaign', *The Review of Reviews*, 53:317 (May 1916), 424.
[125] 'Real Responsibility', *The Globe* (28 April 1916), 2.
[126] *Illustrated London News* (6 May 1916), 1.
[127] *Freeman's Journal* (6 May 1916), 3.
[128] *Catholic Herald* (London edition) (6 May 1916), 4. 'Sinn Féin and Its adherents', *Catholic Herald* (London edition) (29 April 1916), 4.

a native of Co. Antrim, a Protestant, and up to a few years ago he was in the pay and service of the British Government as a consular agent', it thundered.[129] Such casual sectarianism aside, overall the *Catholic Herald*'s assumptions about the Rising and its likely impact were almost comically ill-judged but it did, at least, call for mercy for those 'to whom drilling and arming appealed as romantic achievements' and, as such, recognized the grave error of undertaking what would soon appear to be vengeful executions.[130]

For those who were more sympathetic to the cause of radical Ireland, the insurrection was yet more distressing. Too remote from its epicentre to be able to feel the exhilaration of the event but too closely connected to many of the combatants to be immune to the pain it caused, it left a number of Irish political activists in London entirely bereft. Indeed, as this book's epilogue will discuss, there were some, such as Dora Sigerson, who literally never recovered from the shock. There were also reprisals to contend with. The London Gaelic League's new headquarters in Fulwood House in Holborn were searched and ransacked by the Flying Squad (led by the Cahersiveen-born detective Jeremiah Lynch) in what O'Brien described as an 'act of intimidation'.[131] Certainly the raid was large and threatening, consisting of 'a military staff officer, a junior officer, a quartermaster-sergeant, two sergeants and some privates, two detective inspectors, and four or five subordinate detectives. The military officers were armed with revolvers which they kept very much in evidence throughout the proceedings'.[132] Items removed for further examination included a register of members, minute books, letters, pamphlets and magazines. According to Larry Ginnell, the independent nationalist MP for Westmeath North, the raid on 'a literary and non-political society appealing to all Irish people without distinction', as he described it, was part of a 'policy of exasperating the Irish in this country' which would likely extend 'to all Irish societies and Irish residents in Great Britain'.[133] The homes of prominent London Irish nationalists were also searched. Diarmuid O'Leary, who was taking part in the Rising in Dublin, recounts that as word of the raids spread all potentially incriminating correspondence at his London home was hastily destroyed, save for two letters from Roger Casement, which 'Dick Connolly's sisters insisted should be kept' and so were concealed 'inside the leg joint of a kitchen table'.[134] London's wider Irish community would also suffer repercussions. In the months that followed there were instances of police harassment of GAA and Gaelic League gatherings, including an incident at an Irish dance in Hackney where eight men were arrested and detained for not having their registration forms with them.[135] Many music halls, theatres and restaurants suspended the performance of Irish songs in the Rising's immediate aftermath, with the hugely

---

[129] 'Sinn Féin and Its adherents', *Catholic Herald* (London edition) (29 April 1916), 4.

[130] *Catholic Herald* (London edition) (6 May 1916), 4.

[131] 'London Gaels Annual Meeting', *An Claidheamh* Soluis (24 June 1916), 8.

[132] Art O'Brien, 'Raid on the Gaelic League of London', *Daily Herald* (20 May 1916), 10.

[133] 'Gaelic League, London (raid by military authorities)', HC Debate (15 May 1916), *Hansard*: Vol. 82 c.1127.

[134] O'Leary, BMH Statement: 1108.

[135] 'Petrol Supply', HC Debate (1 August 1916), *Hansard*: Vol. 85 c.191.

popular Irish song of the time 'A Little Bit of Heaven' (from the 1914 Broadway musical *The Heart of Paddy Whack*) regarded with particular suspicion. Indeed, such was the scale of this boycott that it led to a question in the House of Commons from IPP MP Alfie Burn, who wondered whether it was official Government policy.[136]

In London, as elsewhere, the execution of sixteen of the Rising's leaders would decisively shift Irish opinion towards a greater sympathy for their bravery. In turn this provoked impatience with the constitutionalism of the IPP and what was seen as its lack of regard for the dead, an insensitivity which would ultimately prove terminal for the party's fortunes. Cumann na mBan activist Nic Diarmada was at the Gaelic League's headquarters when the news of the executions of the Rising leaders was delivered:

> Desmond Ryan's father, W. P. Ryan, was literary editor of the *Daily Herald* and he was there on that occasion and he cried. Larry Ginnell who was also present cried. It was he brought us the news and also told us that the Irish Members of Parliament cheered when they heard the news. Pearse, MacDonagh and Clarke were executed on the 3rd May. I said; 'They are in Heaven'. But Ryan said, 'It is the quality of the men who are shot I am crying for'.

For Ryan – a veteran activist and journalist in Irish-London cultural circles since the 1890s and a figure with much experience in negotiating its various political factions – the shock must have been intense. At the annual meeting of the London Gaelic League in June, O'Brien, as its President, provided the organization's formal response and spoke movingly of the Rising and its victims:

> Once again Ireland lies silent and bleeding – more silent, and bleeding more profusely, than, perhaps, ever before in her long, chequered but unconquerable history.
>
> It is outside the province of the Gaelic League as an organisation to discuss or criticise the action of the Leaders in the recent Rising; but would it be possible or right, or proper for any gathering of Irish people to come together at the present moment without reference being made to events which have drawn from us tears of blood, and which sicken our hearts with anxiety for the future?
>
> Some of these victims .... were very near and dear to us, and whether we agree or disagree with their late action, our respect and love for them, will survive in our memories to the end of our days, and in the memory of Ireland for ever.[137]

O'Brien's vivid sense that in the immediate aftermath of the Rising Ireland lay 'silent and bleeding' is arresting, not least because it contradicts an easy assumption that the onset of a revolutionary period must somehow appear both energizing and vital. Of course, at this point neither O'Brien, nor any of his colleagues, could have known that the Rising would function in this way, although political visionaries like O'Hegarty,

---

[136] 'Places of Amusement (Irish Airs)', HC Debate (22 May 1916), *Hansard*: vol 82 c1808–9.
[137] 'London Gaels Annual Meeting', *An Claidheamh Soluis* (24 June 1916), 8.

Collins and Nic Diarmada may have been able to hazard an astute guess as to how things would transpire. But nevertheless, O'Brien's sense of Ireland – and Irish London more particularly – pausing in order to contemplate the immediate consequences of the violence, as well as his sense of heart-sickening anxiety for the future, indicates something of the degree to which previous political certainties could no longer be relied upon. It was clear that the old alliances and compromises which had held together the broad spectrum of nationalist opinion would not survive this new reality. More specifically, the Rising made a distinctive sort of Anglo-Irish liberalism quite impossible and, with this, finally extinguished the dying embers of a mode of cultural revivalism that had allied itself to the possibility of Home Rule. Katharine Tynan, a friend of Oscar Wilde in a previous age and a confidant of Yeats, was a revivalist of precisely this sort. Tynan had two sons fighting for the British in the war effort, had spoken at an army recruitment meeting in Ireland and was, in all ways, 'enthusiastically pro-Ally'.[138] For these reasons the Rising came as a profound shock: 'The shootings, the deportations, the peculiar trouble as it affected me personally, were with me all day, going on at the back of my mind as I wrote, lying down with me, haunting my dreams, rising up with me, treading the daily round with me: I was Rebellion-ridden'.[139] As this indicates, for Tynan the Rising was simultaneously a monstrous eruption of something wholly unexpected and a return of old and familiar passions she had previously considered long extinct:

> To me any bloodiness between England and Ireland was unthinkable. All that belonged to the bad old days. And here was '98 come again, and the people who were my own people were being shot and deported by the people with whom we had lived in amity and affection for eighteen long years. I had always been on the side of my own people. [...] We had grown up to the love of Ireland; and now came this sharp, bitter cleavage, in which, with incredible rapidity, the great body of the Irish were massing themselves in a hostility against England – and England, a great part of her, against Ireland.
>
> It was a tragedy many shared with us.[140]

Tynan's tone is bewildered and hurt, but it also contains an element of self-pity. It was, after all, only her family's material privilege that enabled her to 'believe that affection for England and love of Ireland could quite well go hand in hand' and one pointed outcome of the Rising was that, in the realm of politics at least, such equivocation was now impossible.[141] Perhaps as a result, the insurrection greatly reduced the fashion for Irishness among what she termed 'literary and Bohemian circles', and meant that no longer would 'those who were interested in the Arts [make] much of us because we were Irish'.[142] Perhaps it was time for such affectation, which in various forms had

---

[138] Katharine Tynan, *The Years of the Shadow* (London: Constable and Co., 1919), 204.
[139] Ibid.
[140] Ibid., 205.
[141] Ibid., 204.
[142] Ibid., 205.

been present in London since at least the Irish exhibition at Olympia in 1888, to be put out of its misery. London's thirty-year flirtation with a particularly sentimental vision of Ireland – a vision that emerged out of the shadow of the Famine – was over and it would not return for many years. A colder atmosphere typified by suspicion and disdain would take its place. Indeed, among the many other things that it ended, Easter 1916 acts as a watershed moment for the London Irish; it was the point when for many the possibility of a return to Ireland – a homeland that at times had appeared impossibly remote – would cease to be an aspiration and instead become a necessity.

Epilogue: The slow martyrdom of Dora Sigerson

HARK! in the still night. Who goes there?
  'Fifteen dead men.' Why do they wait?
'Hasten, comrade, death is so fair'
  Now comes their Captain through the dim gate.

Sixteen dead men! What on their sword?
  'A nation's honour proud do they bear.'
What on their bent heads? *'God's holy word;*
  All of their nation's heart blended in prayer.'

Sixteen dead men! What makes their shroud?
  'All of their nation's love wraps them around.'
Where do their bodies lie, brave and so proud?
  'Under the gallows-tree in prison-ground.'

Dora Sigerson, from 'Sixteen Dead Men'[1]

As the previous chapter described, the events of Easter 1916 fractured many old certainties and initiated an intense period of change that for many was experienced as a deeply personal crisis. As part of this process new political agents emerged, figures whose revolutionary instincts were strikingly different to that which had gone before and whose priorities would have been unrecognizable in the pre-1916 period. Although the epicentre of this sometimes feverish activity was, of course, Ireland (which now demanded the attention of the London Irish to an overwhelming degree) London too was caught in the whirl of revolutionary politics. As the London Cumann na mBan member Sorcha Nic Diarmada recalled, 'money was rolling in at that time. You could get money for anything. People had not yet got over the feelings inspired by the Rising. We used to collect 3d. a week from everybody. This was for the prisoners' dependants'.[2] But while Nic Diarmada and others like her were galvanized by this changed reality, many individuals and organizations were effectively traumatized by

---

[1] Dora Sigerson Shorter, *Sixteen Dead Men, and Other Poems of Easter Week* (New York: Mitchell Kennerley, 1919), 15.
[2] Sorcha Nic Diarmada, BMH Witness Statement: 945 (13 May 1954).

what had occurred in Dublin's General Post Office, while others appeared to be in a form of deep denial. The (now almost entirely genteel) Irish Literary Society (ILS) maintained its annual series of lectures and recitals but these were usually politically quiescent; a 'show of water-colours of Irish bog and mountain scenery' by Percy French at its headquarters in Hanover Square in Mayfair being a typical reflection of its interests.[3] Alongside this it reaffirmed its support for the British war effort and for those injured at the Front; an ILS-sponsored afternoon tea for wounded Irish soldiers held only one month after the Rising had occurred constituting a particularly vivid indication of where its sympathies lay.[4] The London Gaelic League also pronounced business as usual. Despite the profound shock the Rising caused its President Arthur O'Brien, the significant number of its members who had taken part in the fighting, and the Police raids the organization endured as a consequence, it continued its normal activities of classes, lectures and concerts, with speakers that included Alice Stopford Green ('The Spanish Armada and Ireland'), Francis Joseph Bigger, the antiquarian and solicitor over from Belfast for one of his sporadic visits ('Irish Art and Architecture') and the British Museum's manuscript expert, Robin Flower ('Irish Poetry in Ulster in the Seventeenth Century').[5]

Dora Sigerson's poem 'Sixteen Dead Men', which emerged from the unlikely location of affluent St John's Wood where she lived with her husband Clement K. Shorter, the English historian and editor of the *Illustrated London News* and *Sketch*, was a more explicit reaction to dramatically changed times. One of the earliest literary commemorations of the Rising's dead leaders, and part of a series of poems she wrote about 1916 and its aftermath, it is sharp-cornered in its certainty about the moral justification for the event and absolute in its depiction of the dead as guardians of the nation's conscience. As such, and following Patrick Pearse's lead, it celebrates the Rising as nothing less than a historical death cult: 'a regiment, where Sarsfield leads; Wolfe Tone and Emmet, too'. Given the instabilities of the time such material was potentially dangerous; even Sigerson's old friend W. B. Yeats, writing to her husband in 1918, considered her 1916 poems too politically inflammatory to be widely circulated in an Ireland facing the possibility of imminent conscription.[6] Yeats's fear was that her poems would 'encourage men to risks I am not prepared to share or approve', and indeed, in its absolute rejection of what he would call in one of his own commemorations of the Rising the 'breath of politic words' and its desire for further sacrifice 'Sixteen Dead Men' lodges itself at the extremity of Irish – and indeed London-Irish – cultural politics.[7]

Sigerson was an important if enigmatic figure in the world of Irish London at this time (see Figure 10). A writer and sculptor who was energetic in her coterie-building activities on behalf of Irish Ireland, she was from one of the elite families of the literary revival in Dublin. Her father, George Sigerson, was a noted Gaelicist and her mother

3   *Westminster Gazette* (30 November 1918), 11.
4   *The People* (21 May 1916), 5.
5   *Daily Herald* (27 October 1917), 14.
6   Matthew Campbell, '"A Bit of Shrapnel": The Sigerson Shorters, the Hardys, Yeats and the Easter Rising', in *Sacrifice and Modern War Literature: the Battle of Waterloo to the War on Terror*, ed. Alex Houen and Jan-Melissa Schramm (Oxford: Oxford University Press, 2018), 124–44, 135.
7   W. B. Yeats, 'The Rose Tree', in *The Collected Poems of W. B. Yeats* (London: Macmillan, 1989), 183.

Hester (née Varian), a novelist and painter. Dora, the third of their four children, was born in 1866. A striking and charismatic figure, according to her close friend the poet and memoirist Katharine Tynan, in her youth 'she was wild and gay, with a deep Irish streak of melancholy'.[8] The family's house on Clare Street was for an intense period the epicentre of revival activity in Ireland, with frequent visits from figures such as the Roger Casement, Pearse and Yeats, who performed psychic experiments at their home in August 1891.[9] Dora, her sister Hester, and Tynan lived the ideals of Irish Ireland deeply and, as passionate Parnellites, were familiar figures in the politics and culture of nationalist Dublin. As Tynan recalled, 'together we exulted; together we mourned; together we followed our chief to the grave'.[10] Tynan's memoirs of this period describe it as an idyllic time as the circumstances of their youth, the new freedoms gradually becoming available to middle-class urban women in Ireland during the 1880s, the Sigerson family's relative wealth, and the vibrancy of the Irish national movement combined to create a moment of unusual individual possibility.[11]

Possessing what one early critic described as an 'ardent and multi-faceted mentality', Sigerson displayed considerable artistic talent and for a period attended Dublin's Metropolitan School of Art alongside Yeats.[12] Her family connections were an advantage in promoting her work and she was soon publishing her poetry in significant journals such as *The Irish Monthly, The Nation, The United Ireland* and, later, *Samhain*. In striking contrast to what Tynan describes as her *'joie de vivre'*, this early poetry was remarkably dark, exhibiting a gothic bleakness in which, as Lucy Collins observes, 'death by drowning is a recurrent trope'.[13] Sigerson also had a particular talent for the ballad form; Douglas Hyde, in a widely quoted posthumous appraisal of her career from 1918, declared her 'the greatest mistress of the ballad, and the greatest story-teller in verse that Ireland has produced'.[14] Given her recent death and Hyde's close association with her father, there may be an element of hyperbole about this assessment, though his recognition that 'in verse she was a facile and a fluent story-teller, with a marvellous invention in the matter of plots' is accurate.[15] Virginia Woolf, who was better positioned to provide a more nuanced perspective on Sigerson's work, saw the scale of her achievement more clearly, observing that 'the ideas behind several of her poems are subtle and difficult, and have evidently broken through her powers of expression so that they remain sketches rather than completed poems'.[16] For Woolf this

8   Katharine Tynan, *Memories* (London: Eveleigh Nash and Grayson, 1924), 255.
9   John Kelly, *A W. B. Yeats Chronology* (Basingstoke: Palgrave, 2003), 22.
10 Tynan, 'A Tribute and Some Memories', from Dora Sigerson Shorter, *The Sad Years* (London: Constable and Company, 1918), x.
11 Tynan, *Memories*, 259.
12 Evelyn A. Hanley, 'Dora Sigerson Shorter: Late Victorian Romantic', *Victorian Poetry*, 3:4 (Autumn 1965), 223–34, 223.
13 Tynan, 'A Tribute and Some Memories', x and Lucy Collins, ed., *Poetry by Women in Ireland: A Critical Anthology 1870–1970* (Liverpool: Liverpool University Press, 2012), 102, 109.
14 Douglas Hyde, 'Dora Sigerson Shorter', *Studies: An Irish Quarterly Review*, 7:25 (March 1918), 139–44, 144.
15 Hyde, 'Dora Sigerson Shorter', 140.
16 Virginia Woolf, Review of *The Sad Years* by Dora Sigerson Shorter, *Times Literary Supplement* (29 August 1918), 403.

Figure 10 Dora Sigerson Shorter (1866–1918) (litho).

indicated a 'faultiness of technique' which left the poetry appearing 'unduly personal'. 'She cannot give her melancholy or her indignation the impersonal stamp which perfect expression bestows, so that we forget the particular grief and the particular writer,' she concluded in a withering *coup de grâce*.

Sigerson married Shorter in Hampstead in 1896, a union facilitated, unwittingly or not, by Tynan who had described her as a 'lovely creature' in a letter to Shorter in September 1893, subsequently sending him her picture.[17] She moved to London,

[17] Letter to Clement King Shorter (6 September 1893). *The Selected Letters of Katharine Tynan: Poet and Novelist*, ed. Damian Atkinson (Newcastle: Cambridge Scholars Press, 2016), 173.

reuniting with Tynan who by this stage was married and living in Ealing, and would spend the rest of her life in the city weaving networks of political and cultural influence from the marital home at 16 Marlborough Place. This was enabled, at least in part, by the fact that Shorter was wealthy, extremely well-connected and generally sympathetic to his wife's political opinions. He became, in George Bernard Shaw's phrase, an 'Irish patriot by sexual selection', and even after her death he continued to fly the Irish flag above Knockmoroon, a cottage in Great Missenden in Buckinghamshire that the couple had built together in 1904.[18] Indeed Shorter records in his autobiography that he wished to be buried alongside Sigerson in Glasnevin Cemetery in Dublin but that this 'was found impossible'.[19] However, despite this solicitousness and the couple's material comfort, it is clear that Sigerson's life in London was frequently anguished. As Tynan put it in a posthumous memoir, 'her heart was always slipping away like a grey bird to Ireland', while Bridget Lawlor, another friend, was more direct again, asserting that 'her life in England was in a way a slow martyrdom, though it was only during the last few years before her death, the Sad Years, as she called them, that it became quite unendurable for her. Always this hunger for home was in her heart'.[20] Only Shorter's own memoir of his wife's life and death would challenge this narrative, and even then his corrective was slightly half-hearted.[21]

Possibly as a result of her homesickness, Sigerson's commitment to the cause of Irish nationalism – and Pearse-inspired radical separatism more specifically – increased in the years leading up to 1916. Indeed, so consuming did this become that the Easter Rising and the subsequent executions of its leaders left her ideologically and emotionally traumatized. She would never recover; as Tynan noted, 'never for one moment did she go back to play and laughter as so many of us are able to do so that we may live, and she died of this constant prepossession and fierce pity'.[22] While Sigerson was not alone in reacting to the Rising in this way, her trauma was extreme and had specific features; an obituary in the *Dominion* asserted that 'she made all the sorrows of men and women of Ireland intimately and poignantly her own', while Lawlor recalls that 'she suffered personally for everyone who went through the fire of Easter week'.[23] Alternatively, her grief was described by Deirdre O'Brien as 'the wild sorrow of a child for an idolised mother'. 'She never seemed to rally from the shock of being absent at a time when, it seemed to her, Ireland needed every friend,' she continued.[24] This is not to suggest that Sigerson was inactive in this period or negligent in her political concern – she

---

[18] Jeffrey Dudgeon, *Roger Casement: The Black Diaries with a Study of His Background, Sexuality, and Irish Political Life* (Belfast: Belfast Press, 2016), 593.

[19] Clement Shorter, *CKS: An Autobiography. A Fragment by Himself*, ed. J. M. Bulloch (London: privately published, 1927), xxi. In fact the urn containing his ashes was buried in Sigerson's grave in 1926.

[20] Tynan, 'A Tribute and Some Memories', xii. Bridget F. Lawlor, 'Dora Sigerson Shorter. An Appreciation', *The Irish Monthly*, 48:560 (February 1920), 100–6, 102.

[21] Shorter, *CKS*, 139.

[22] Katharine Tynan, 'Dora Sigerson's Last Poems', *The Observer* (1 September 1918), 4.

[23] 'The Late Dora Sigerson Shorter', *Dominion*, 11:155 (20 March 1918), 2. Lawlor, 'Dora Sigerson Shorter. An Appreciation', 106.

[24] Deirdre O'Brien, 'Dora Sigerson Shorter', *The Irish Monthly*, 56:662 (August 1928), 403–8, 407.

was, for instance, one of the founders of the London-based Irish National Relief Fund intended to help the victims of the violence and she contributed a scathingly ironic piece about the British military response to the Rising to the *Daily Herald* titled 'How to Settle the Irish Question' – but clearly she considered this to be peripheral activity given the momentous events taking place elsewhere.[25] As a result, guilt mingled with a feeling of abandonment and she was left, in Tyson's phrase, 'bitterly isolated'.[26] These external impressions of her suffering tally with Sigerson's own interpretation of events. Following a visit to Kilmainham Gaol, the site of the executions of a number of the Rising's leaders, Sigerson wrote to the prominent Dublin republican Lily O'Brennan of her sense that 'every bullet went through my own heart'.[27] 'But it was good to live through such a time – and good to die,' she continued, again echoing Pearse's mantra of blood sacrifice. Her poem of this period 'Sick I Am and Sorrowful' expresses a similarly dark sentiment.[28] Scarred not just by the violence of the Rising but also the endless slaughter of the First World War, it is a poem of despair that poses a series of increasingly distraught questions:

> Sick I am and sorrowful, how can I be well again
> Here, where fog and darkness is, and big guns boom all day,
> Practising for evil sport? If you speak humanity,
> Hatred comes into each face, and so you cease to pray.
> How I dread the sound of guns, hate the bark of musketry,
> Since the friends I loved are dead, all stricken by the sword.
> Full of anger is my heart, full of rage and misery;
> How can I grow well again, or be my peace restored?

The remedy that the poem proposes – predictably given Sigerson's state of mind at this time – is to seek a return home, and so it takes flight on a series of ecstatic reveries revisiting the Ireland that Sigerson lost when she moved to London. Before 1916 the power of this incantation might have been sufficient to enable some comfort to be found, but now no transcendence is achieved and the poem returns to London with a thud, lamenting: 'but 'tis sick I am and grieving, how can I be well again/Here, where fear and sorrow are my heart so far away?' This desolate sentiment was reflected in the circumstances of the poem's production. As Shorter notes in his editor's introduction, the publication of *Sixteen Dead Men and Other Poems of Easter Week* represented 'a sacred obligation to one who broke her heart over Ireland. Dora Sigerson in her last few weeks of life, knowing full well that she was dying, designed every detail of this little volume'.[29] As a result, the collection became a reflection on mortality and, ultimately, a comfortless final testament for those she left behind.

---

[25] *Daily Herald* (15 July 1916), 4.

[26] Tynan, 'A Tribute and Some Memories', xii.

[27] Undated letter from Dora Shorter to Lily O'Brennnan concerning poetry and memories of the Easter Rising (1916–1918?) (MS 41,491/5/9, Ceannt and O'Brennan Papers, 1851–1953, National Library of Ireland).

[28] Sigerson Shorter, *Sixteen Dead Men*, 19–21.

[29] Ibid., 5.

As Shorter's note indicates, Sigerson knew that she was going to die, but, at another level, it also appears that she made a conscious decision *to* die, a decision she shared with her husband and friends. The process was protracted – newspaper reports in June 1917 stated that she 'was lying so seriously ill that she is only permitted to see her most intimate friends' – but death came, finally, on 6 January 1918.[30] Tynan noted bluntly, 'She broke her heart over it all; and so she died, as she would have chosen to die, for love of the Dark Rosaleen.'[31] Given the relentless mythologizing of her protracted illness during her final years it is perhaps unsurprising that the physical cause of her death remains uncertain. Wayne K. Chapman asserts that it was cancer, Matthew Campbell, citing the death certificate, proposes that she suffered a stroke (although he also refers to it as a 'mystery illness'), while Jeffrey Dudgeon believes it to have been suicide 'due to a psychosis brought on by Casement's execution and the Easter Rising deaths'.[32] Either way, it is significant that her contemporaries preferred the more aestheticized version of her death as summarized by O'Brien's belief that 'she died because she could not bear to live.'[33] Sigerson's remains arrived in Dublin on 8 January and were transferred to St Andrew's Church on Westland Row. The funeral was held in private but was attended by the elite of revolutionary Ireland, including Éamon de Valera, Count George Noble Plunkett, Maud Gonne (who had travelled from London in disguise to escape the attentions of Scotland Yard detectives), W. T. Cosgrave, Nancy O'Rahilly (the O'Rahilly's widow) and Margaret Pearse (Patrick Pearse's mother).[34] In line with her wishes she was buried at Glasnevin cemetery. As part of her own monument Sigerson designed a memorial to the martyrs of 1916 and Shorter ensured there were funds for its erection from the sales of *Sixteen Dead Men*. Typical of its time, this depicts a 1916 rebel – most obviously Pearse – lying in the lap of Cathleen ni Houlihan in the manner of a pietà. Its symbolism is conventional, although it remains a powerful piece of work and was central to the centenary commemorations of the Rising in 2016. Ironically given the guilt she felt at her lack of involvement, one powerful effect of the monument's design and positioning is the manner in which it weaves Sigerson herself into the overall 1916 narrative. In short, she achieved in death what she could not achieve in life.

Contemporary accounts of Sigerson's despair-laden decline tend to be recounted with a surprising lack of critical reflection. As a result she became an embodiment of the unrequited grief many felt for the dead of 1916, a sentiment that was not uncommon among the radical edges of Irish London specifically; the place where many of the combatants had gained their political education. In this the suffering of Sigerson symbolized a larger apprehension of loss – the exile's loss of homeland – and an uneasy (if rarely articulated) guilt at being absent from Ireland at such a momentous time. Key

---

[30] *Belfast Telegraph* (29 June 1917), 7.

[31] Tynan, 'A Tribute and Some Memories', xii.

[32] Wayne K. Chapman, 'Joyce and Yeats: Easter 1916 and the Great War', *New Hibernia Review/Iris Éireannach Nua*, 10:4 (Winter 2006), 137–51, 143. Campbell, 'A Bit of Shrapnel', 124 and Dudgeon, *Roger Casement*, 593.

[33] O'Brien, 'Dora Sigerson Shorter', 406.

[34] *Freeman's Journal* (10 January 1918), 4. Caoimhe Nic Dháibhéid, *Seán MacBride: A Republican Life, 1904–1946* (Liverpool: Liverpool University Press, 2011), 21.

to this mythologization was a pamphlet of poems Sigerson's husband collected and published privately after her death. *In Memoriam Dora Sigerson 1918–23* had a tiny print run of just twenty-five copies and its circulation 'among **her** friends', as the title page put it (conspicuously underlining and placing in boldface that '**her**'), indicated something of the pamphlet's purpose as well as lending the project an air of slight paranoia.[35] The contributors to the collection were united in their mourning and also in their belief that political events in Ireland had broken Sigerson's heart and eventually killed her. In this manner the first poem in the collection, Eva Gore-Booth's 'To Dora Sigerson Shorter', expresses common cause with Sigerson – despite the fact that the two poets did not know each other personally – in that she 'died of the grief that tore my heart'. Alice Furlong's eulogy, 'Ours', returns to the perception propagated by Tynan and others that Sigerson was essentially out of place in London and concludes that, as a result, holding her there was little more than an act of cruelty.[36] In that spirit the poem summons the 'dead woman' back 'over the perilous midnight sea', culminating with considerable bitterness: 'No alien earth shall have or hold/Dust that was once your heart of gold!' Certainly Furlong was well-placed to recognize something of Sigerson's misery: she had also suffered a breakdown induced by the executions of 1916 and subsequently withdrew into a long period of seclusion in Tallaght until her death in 1946. Other contributors to the collection included William Norman (W. N.) Ewer, a journalist and Fabian socialist (and soon to be Soviet spy), William Kean Seymour, a minor poet and bank manager, and Tynan. For Ewer, Sigerson was 'the poet and the rebel' with 'the burning heart/that broke for Ireland', while Seymour's 'In Memoriam: Dora Sigerson' again returned to the 'desolate days' and the 'bitterness and wrong' she endured at the end of her life. In these accounts no alternative perspective on Sigerson's life can be glimpsed. The effect of this unanimity was to ensure that in the years following her death it became commonplace for critics to refer to her work only in the context of her grief-laden final days, as Stuart Petre Brodie (S. P. B.) Mais would attempt in especially overheated fashion in 1920:

> A lonely, tragic figure, unable to find consolation even among those who loved her most dearly, she was broken in pieces by the savagery of war and the wreck of her ambitions for her own country. Naturally fragile, she could not withstand the avalanche of blood; she had not the capacity of becoming more and more hardened by the holocaust.[37]

A romanticized, posthumous, portrait of Sigerson by Sir John Lavery, commissioned by Shorter and presented to the National Gallery of Ireland in February 1921, would further reinforce this message, although by this point it was scarcely required.

Although Shorter facilitated the publication of *In Memoriam Dora Sigerson*, he disliked the belief persistently expressed by Tynan and others that Sigerson had

---

[35] Clement Shorter, ed., *In Memoriam Dora Sigerson 1918–23* (London: privately published, 1923).

[36] Also reprinted in *The Irish Monthly*, 46:536 (February 1918), 123.

[37] S. P. B. Mais, Review of *A Dull Day in London* by Dora Sigerson Shorter, *Aberdeen Press and Journal* (5 July 1920), 2.

been happier in Ireland than with him in London and made a point of noting in his autobiography that 'she loved London in a way, as readers of her essay, "A Dull Day in London", will know' as a mild rebuttal.[38] As might be guessed, that 'in a way' has to work especially hard to justify Shorter's assertion, and indeed 'A Dull Day in London', which was published posthumously in 1920, scarcely corroborates his claim. In fact, its vision of the city is extraordinarily bleak, depicting London as a locus of emotional desolation and a place where only the company of anthropomorphized animals provides the protagonist with any relief.[39] The other pieces in the collection, also called A Dull Day in London, are best described as prose fragments as few of them have a substantial unfolding narrative, and they develop the tone of psychological enervation established by the opening essay, exploring the extremities of mental distress from different perspectives. 'The Eyes', for example, describes life as a process of constant and debilitating surveillance: 'From the hour we are born until the day we die they are upon us, watching us always. The eyes. Loving, kindly, pitying, agonised eyes. Cold, jealous, scornful, evil eyes. Watching us always.' [...] 'they devour us with their eagerness.'[40] At times, as in the final fragment 'Sunshine in Rain', a half-hearted liberal humanism flickers into life – suggesting, for instance, that the positive act of one individual can mitigate, at least for a moment, some of the worst of this suffering – but these occasional moments of light are soon extinguished by the general enveloping misery of London's streets, where the certainty that 'I am cold. I am miserable. I hate every passer-by as I am sure he or she hates me' is the only proportionate response.[41]

Clearly it is dangerous to intuit too much about the depth of Sigerson's mental distress from such pieces and yet the relentlessness of the anguish they describe accords with what we know of the final years of her life as her friends and husband recorded them. Moreover, a comparison of A Dull Day in London with Sigerson's own account of her post-Rising torment (which Shorter included in his autobiography) provides an illuminating juxtaposition:

And the world came hard on me till the years brought knowledge – then I died, a child yet, but dead, stricken by infirmities. When my blood was hottest and my heart cried out in its anguish and its grief and my mind in its excitement, rising with the soul of my land, dying with the death of my countrymen and friends. Fifteen times was I shot thro' the heart, and once stood by the hangman's noose, but I rose in the glory of the dead, as I had risen before, from the murdered corpses that make the soul of my country. Why have you stricken me now, oh Lord, when the blood runs light in my pulses and even to me some little duty may have passed? Like a prisoner I peep from my window. And at night am I haunted by the reproachful dead. Like a dead drone do I lie on the hive of the bees. Like the

---

[38] Shorter, CKS: An Autobiography, 139.
[39] Dora Sigerson Shorter, A Dull Day in London and Other Sketches with an Introductory Note by Thomas Hardy (London: Eveleigh Nash, 1920), 11.
[40] Sigerson Shorter, A Dull Day in London, 57.
[41] Ibid., 121.

stricken hearts do I creep into a corner to die. Strike then, oh Lord, that all of me may cease! Or let me live now that the spring comes.[42]

Written in the winter before her death, this extraordinary testimony revisits and condenses many resentments and grievances. The nightmares of surveillance she describes in *A Dull Day in London* become the constant hauntings of 'the reproachful dead' of Easter 1916, those shot at Kilmainham and Roger Casement, who met the 'hangman's noose' at Pentonville on 3 August 1916. As such, the fate of these martyrs and their insistent demands for reparation from beyond the grave – the constant preoccupation of her final years – become a mode of gothic intervention. In Sigerson's imagination revolutionary Ireland buzzes like a hive while she, in a chilling phrase, is its useless 'dead drone'. Described as such her pain derives from the lack of political agency she experienced as a woman domiciled 'like a prisoner' in St John's Wood. Hyde was sensitive to this aspect of Sigerson's plight and in his 1918 review of her work noted the manner in which she especially resented 'the trivialities of the hour which made it impossible to live a wide and open life'. As he observed, 'the petty conventionalities that make up so large a part in the existence of the modern man, and still more of the modern woman, disgust her'.[43]

Interpreted in this way Sigerson's life reveals itself as a stark binary wherein the first act can be summarized as youthful, Irish, female and social, and the second as mature, London-based, married and lonely; 'a child yet, but dead, stricken by infirmities', as she describes her latter condition. Strikingly, it appears that something of this was anticipated at the time of Sigerson's departure from Ireland in 1896, as Tynan recalled:

> When she was about to leave Dublin her friends gathered at her father's house, and presented her with an antique Irish writing desk, in which their names were carefully secured in a secret drawer. And whether Mrs Shorter, from that day to this, had ever discovered that little bit of hidden parchment in the old escritoire, not one of those concerned in the compliment ever found out.[44]

In the context of Tynan's posthumous tribute, the leaving gift symbolized the importance of female collectivity, the centrality of that collectivity to the act of literary creation and an awareness that this would end with Sigerson's marriage and relocation to London. It is a poignant anecdote, but not one that entirely dispels the sense that ultimately Tynan's role in Sigerson's life was ambiguous. While, at one level, her self-described best friend (at least in her younger years), Tynan was also the figure keenest on defining a particular sense of who Sigerson was, and the most energetic promulgator of that definition in the years after her death. Alongside this, she appears to have been an energetic match maker for the Sigerson family, finding husbands for both Hester and Dora. As I have previously discussed, in Dora's case her role was particularly crucial in that she sent Shorter pictures of Sigerson and arranged their first introduction at

---

[42] Shorter, *CKS: An Autobiography*, 149–50.
[43] Hyde, 'Dora Sigerson Shorter', 141.
[44] 'Death of Dora Sigerson Shorter', *Freeman's Journal* (7 January 1918), 2.

her house in Ealing. The two friends must have diverged in their politics later in life as Tynan was active in encouraging the British war effort, spoke at an army recruitment meeting at Ballinasloe in Galway and was, in her own words, 'enthusiastically pro-Ally'.[45] However, if this was the case Tynan makes no record of it, and perhaps it is appropriate that in one of her last reflections on Sigerson's life she chooses to overlook the final years entirely, noting instead that 'she belonged to the golden days of my girlhood. There I prefer to leave her, in the country of both our loves'.[46]

Possibly the best poem about Sigerson's death, Thomas Hardy's 'How She Went to Ireland', stands in direct opposition to the kind of mythologizing Tynan's memoirs encouraged; indeed in its sardonic acknowledgement of the mysteries of personal motivation it can be read as a direct rebuke to the persistent romanticization of her final days that the Sigerson Shorter circle had engaged in through the publication of *In Memoriam Dora Sigerson*. Hardy knew Sigerson well through his long friendship with Shorter, although he frequently found her to be perplexing and was unsympathetic to her politics. Indeed Robert Gittings and Jo Manton go so far as to suggest that ultimately Hardy 'did not greatly care for' either Shorter or Sigerson, although such an assertion is challenged by the simple fact of the friendship's longevity.[47] According to Campbell, the poem was composed at Shorter's request, although its final form can hardly have been what he anticipated:

Dora's gone to Ireland
　　Through the sleet and snow;
Promptly she has gone there
　　In a ship, although
Why she's gone to Ireland
　　Dora does not know.

That was where, yea, Ireland,
　　Dora wished to be:
When she felt, in lone times,
　　Shoots of misery,
Often there, in Ireland,
　　Dora wished to be.

Hence she's gone to Ireland,
　　Since she meant to go,
Through the drift and darkness
　　Onward labouring, though
That she's gone to Ireland
　　Dora does not know.[48]

45 Tyson, *The Selected Letters of Katharine Tynan*, 204.
46 Katharine Tynan, *Memories* (London: Eveleigh Nash and Grayson, 1924), 271.
47 Robert Gittings and Jo Manton, *The Second Mrs Hardy* (London: Heinemann, 1979), 34.
48 Thomas Hardy, *Winter Words in Various Moods and Metres* (London: Macmillan and Co., 1928), 174.

Without some knowledge of the manner in which Sigerson's death had been romanticized by those close to her, Hardy's poem might seem mysterious in its occasional banality or even perhaps slightly callous in its presumption that all her mortal desires were suitable only for mockery. In context, however, it reads instead as a necessary corrective to those narratives of Sigerson's life that understood it only as a protracted form of futile political martyrdom. In opposition to this, the poem asserts what Margaret Mahar identifies as a 'negative meaning' or 'unreason', which 'lies in the blank space between desire and fulfilment'. Indeed, Mahar's summary of the poem's overall effectiveness is illuminating: 'What is significant is the degree of unreason which can be carried, so gracefully, within rhyme. The final "Dora does not know" echoes "Since she meant to go" and the echo seems nearly an answer to the poem's problem'.[49]

Hardy's emphasis in 'How She Went to Ireland' on the enigmatic nature of motivation and the limited extent to which one can fully comprehend the life decisions of another was a tactful gesture to a grieving widower but also highly astute. After all, the reasons why Sigerson felt anger at the bloodletting of 1916 are certainly explicable, but comprehending the *extremity* of these feelings – feelings of such strength that they literally killed her – is a more difficult task. As Campbell observes, she remains an enigma – a figure of 'extreme inwardness' who, despite her 'impeccable liberal and Labour English literary connections' and the fact that she was seemingly neither a member of Sinn Féin nor Cumann na mBan, demonstrated an Irish 'savage resentment' that the British were never able to fully comprehend.[50] In this way, the seeming extremities of Sigerson's political position were played out against a backdrop of English liberalism that was constitutionally incapable of understanding why British actions in Ireland were suddenly so detested. As such, the very idea of Sigerson's 'unknowability' takes its place as part of a wider critique of the dominant political order.

Even in the particularly intense atmosphere of Irish London in the years leading up to and immediately following the 1916 Rising Dora Sigerson stands out as a vivid presence. However, although her life was exceptional in the extremity of its suffering, it still had elements in common with more widely shared aspects of London-Irish experience. Most notably, although she was in many ways securely embedded in liberal English elite culture with personal wealth and politically sympathetic friends and social networks, she remained troubled by the persistent call of obligations – both practical and emotional – from Ireland. She encountered these obligations in the form of the 'reproachful dead', the restless souls of the 1916 martyrs whose nocturnal hauntings dominated her final days. Elsewhere in this book I have referred to such insistent demands as the 'matter of Ireland', and for many London Irish this matter could never be entirely relinquished, regardless of the length of time they lived in the city. Indeed, in a manner similar to revolutionary figures such as P. S. O'Hegarty, Robert Lynd and Michael Collins, Sigerson's commitment to Irish separatism actually increased during her time in London. Certainly there is evidence that the sometimes

---

49 Margaret Mahar, 'Hardy's Poetry of Renunciation', *ELH*, 45:2 (Summer 1978), 303–24, 306.
50 Campbell, 'A Bit of Shrapnel', 135, 140.

insular environment of Irish cultural nationalism in the city could act as a political hothouse. Indeed, while bodies such as the London Gaelic League sounded constant warnings about the danger of cultural assimilation into the host community – in other words, Anglicization – there were always powerful political countercurrents at work. These forces galvanized exiles who had experienced life in Ireland first hand, but they were just as effective in inspiring the second generation of London Irish, figures such as the GPO combatants John 'Blimey' O'Connor and William Daly, for whom Ireland itself was often a fantasy projection. The difficulties created by the lure of London's competing cultural and political realms should also be recognized. Sigerson, for instance, was pulled in two directions simultaneously: in one way towards middle-class liberal Englishness with its humanist tendencies and Home Rule sympathies, and in another towards the irreducible conviction that Irish life was distinct and should be separated – by force if necessary – from English influence. As the examples of Francis Fahy or Tynan demonstrated, during times of relative political quiescence it was possible for the London Irish to balance conflicting political instincts through either a constant process of dialectical adjustment (Fahy) or a strategic forgetting of underlying political realities (Tynan), but at moments of crisis these delicate arrangements were liable to collapse. The effect of this could be personally shattering. There was nothing unusual about Sigerson's distress at the fate of the 1916 leaders as the responses of other prominent London-Irish figures including William Patrick (W. P.) Ryan and Arthur O'Brien to the executions testify. During times of Irish political emergency it was common for the London Irish to feel too remote from the course of events to wield influence or demonstrate meaningful political agency, and yet they would invariably be buffeted by the shockwaves. Finally, and in a manner similar to other London Irish writers as otherwise different from Sigerson as Pádraic Ó Conaire, her writing illustrates how the idea of a received Irish culture was not an encumbrance to be discarded but instead served as a resource that would provide comfort at times of psychological and material duress. In this way it was not regarded as uselessly archaic or inimical to the sometimes harsh modernity of London life but rather functioned as an essential element in the constitution of a distinctive (if frequently bifurcated) shared identity.

Bibliography

Archives and Papers

Archive of the Irish in Britain, London Metropolitan University
Hansard Parliamentary Debates
National Library of Ireland, Manuscript Collections
Bureau of Military History, Irish Defence Forces Military Archives:
    Barry, Thomas. Witness statement: 1. 22 February 1947.
    Connolly, Richard. Witness statement: 523. 5 June 1951.
    Cremin, Michael (Mrs) ('Cis Sheehan'). Witness statement: 924. 25 February 1954.
    Cusack, Brian. Witness statement: 736. 9 October 1952.
    Daly, William D. Witness statement: 291. 17 December 1949.
    de Burca, F. Witness statement: 105. Undated.
    de Róiste, Liam. Witness statement: 1698. 27 November 1957.
    Dore, Eamon, T. Witness statement: 153. 19 September 1948.
    Good, Joseph. Witness statement: 388. 19 May 1950.
    McCullough, Denis. Witness statement: 915. 11 December 1953.
    Nic Diarmada, Sorcha. Witness statement: 945. 13 May 1954.
    O'Hegarty, P. S. Witness statement: 839. 17–31 December 1952.
    O'Leary, Jeremiah J (Diarmuid). Witness statement: 1108. 2 March 1955.
    Robinson, Séumas. Witness statement: 1721. 16 April 1957.
    Shouldice, John. Witness statement: 162. 16 November 1948.
    Tannam, Liam. Witness statement: 242. 30 April 1949.
Trinity College, Dublin, Archives

Newspapers and Periodicals

Aberdeen Press and Journal
An Claidheamh Soluis
Belfast News-Letter
Belfast Telegraph
Blackwood's Edinburgh Magazine
Capuchin Annual
Catholic Herald
Daily Herald
Daily Telegraph & Courier
Dial
Dominion
Drogheda Independent
Dublin Weekly Nation
Era
Flag of Ireland
Freeman's Journal and Daily Commercial Advertiser

Funny Folks
Globe
Graphic
Guardian
Guth na nGaedheal: Half-Yearly Magazine of the Gaelic League of London
Holborn Journal
Illustrated London News
Illustrated Police News
Inis Fáil: A Magazine for the Irish in London
Ipswich Journal
Irish Home Reading Magazine
Irish News and Belfast Morning News
Irish Volunteer
Irish World
Irishman
John Bull
Link
London Daily News
McClure's Magazine
Middlesex Chronicle
Moonshine
Morning Chronicle
Morning Post
Music Hall and Theatre Review
New Ireland Review
New York Times
North-Eastern Daily Gazette
Northern Whig
Observer
Pall Mall Gazette
Penny Satirist
People
Pick Me Up
Punch
Review of Reviews
Sheffield Daily Telegraph
South London Press
Standard
Sunday Independent
Tablet
Times
Times Literary Supplement
Ulster Guardian
United Ireland
United Irishman
Weekly Freeman's Journal
Westminster Gazette
Wexford People
York Herald

Books and Articles

Ackroyd, Peter. *London: The Biography*. London: Chatto and Windus, 2000.

Anderson, Robert. *Sidelights on the Home Rule Movement*. New York: Dutton and Company, 1906.

Anthony, Barry. *Chaplin's Music Hall: The Chaplins and their Circle in the Limelight*. London: Bloomsbury, 2012.

Anthony, Sian. *Medieval Settlement to 18th-/19th-century Rookery: Excavations at Central St Giles, London Borough of Camden, 2006–8*. London: Museum of London Archaeology, 2011.

Appleton, Robert. *After the Manner of Men: A Novel of To-Day*. Boston: Franklin Publishing Company, 1894.

Avrich, Paul. *The Haymarket Tragedy*. Princeton: Princeton University Press, 1984.

Baker, Richard Anthony. *British Music Hall: An Illustrated History*. Stroud: Sutton Publishing, 2005.

Banham, Martin, ed. *The Cambridge Guide to Theatre*. Cambridge: Cambridge University Press, 2000.

Barclay, Tom. *Memoirs and Medleys: The Autobiography of a Bottle Washer*. 1934. Leicester: Coalville Publishing, 1995.

Baron, Wendy, et al. *Walter Sickert: 'Drawing Is the Thing'*. Manchester: Whitworth Art Gallery, 2004.

Baron, Wendy, et al. *Sickert: Paintings and Drawings*. New Haven: Yale University Press, 2006.

Barthes, Roland. *The Eiffel Tower and other Mythologies*. Translated by Richard Howard. New York: Noonday Press, 1979.

Beames, Thomas. *The Rookeries of London*. 1852. London: Frank Cass, 1972.

Béaslaí, Piaras. *Michael Collins and the Making of a New Ireland*. Dublin: Talbot Press, 1922.

Beckson, Karl. 'The Legends of the Rhymers' Club: A Review Article'. *Victorian Poetry* 19, no. 4 (Winter 1981): 397–412.

Benjamin, Harrington W. *The London Irish: A Study in Political Activism, 1870–1910*. PhD thesis, Princeton University, 1976.

Biletz, Frank A. 'Women and Irish-Ireland: The Domestic Nationalism of Mary Butler'. *New Hibernia Review/Iris Éireannach Nua* 6, no. 1 (Spring 2002): 59–72.

Booth, Charles. *The Booth Police Notebooks* B346, 30–3. Available online: https://booth.lse.ac.uk/notebooks/b346 (accessed 22 June 2019).

Booth, John Bennion. *Pink Parade*. London: Thornton Butterworth, 1933.

Bourke, Angela. 'Legless in London: Pádraic Ó Conaire and Éamon A Búrc'. *Éire-Ireland* 38, no. 3/4 (Fall/Winter 2003): 54–67.

Bourke, Marcus. *John O'Leary: A Study in Irish Separatism*. Georgia: University of Georgia Press, 1968.

Boyd, Ernest. *Ireland's Literary Renaissance*. Dublin: Maunsel, 1916.

Bratton, J. S., ed. *Music Hall: Performance and Style*. Milton Keynes: Open University Press, 1986.

Bromberg, Ruth. *Walter Sickert: Prints, a Catalogue Raisonné*. New Haven: Yale University Press, 2000.

Brown, Terence. *The Life of W. B. Yeats*. Oxford: Blackwell, 1999.

Busteed, Mervyn. *The Irish in Manchester c.1750–1921: Resistance, Adaptation and Identity*. Manchester: Manchester University Press, 2015.

Campbell, Matthew. '"A bit of shrapnel": The Sigerson Shorters, the Hardys, Yeats and the Easter Rising'. In *Sacrifice and Modern War Literature: The Battle of Waterloo to the*

War on Terror, edited by Alex Houen and Jan-Melissa Schramm, 124–44. Oxford: Oxford University Press, 2018.

Cave, R. A. 'Staging the Irishman'. In *Acts of Supremacy: The British Empire and the Stage, 1790–1930*, edited by J. S. Bratton, et al., 62–144. Manchester: Manchester University Press, 1991.

Chance Newton, H. *Idols of the 'Halls' Being My Music Hall Memories*. London: Heath Cranton, 1928.

Chapman, Wayne K. and James Helyar. 'P. S. O'Hegarty and the Yeats Collection at the University of Kansas'. In *Yeats Annual No. 10*, 221–38. Basingstoke: Macmillan, 1993.

Chapman, Wayne K. 'Joyce and Yeats: Easter 1916 and the Great War'. *New Hibernia Review/Iris Éireannach Nua* 10, no. 4 (Winter 2006): 137–51.

Chesney, Kellow. *The Victorian Underworld*. London: Penguin, 1972.

Clarke, Thomas J. *Glimpses of an Irish Felon's Prison Life*. Dublin: Maunsel and Roberts, 1922.

Clutterbuck, Lindsay. 'The Progenitors of Terrorism: Russian Revolutionaries or Extreme Irish Republicans?'. *Terrorism and Political Violence* 16, no. 1 (2004): 154–81.

Clutterbuck, Lindsay. 'Countering Irish Republican Terrorism in Britain: Its Origin as a Police Function'. *Terrorism and Political Violence* 18, no. 1 (2006): 95–118.

Collins, Lucy, ed. *Poetry by Women in Ireland: A Critical Anthology 1870–1970*. Liverpool: Liverpool University Press, 2012.

Coogan, Tim Pat. *Michael Collins*. London: Arrow Books, 1990.

Corkery, Daniel. *Synge and Anglo-Irish Literature*. Cork: Cork University Press, 1931.

Curtis, Keiron. *P. S. O'Hegarty (1879–1955): Sinn Féin Fenian*. London: Anthem Press, 2010.

Daly, Nicholas. 'Britain'. In *The Fin-de-Siècle World*, edited by Michael Saler, 117–130. London: Routledge, 2014.

Davin, Anna. *Growing up Poor: Home, School and Street in London 1870–1914*. London: Rivers Oram Press, 1996.

Davis, Tracy C. *Actresses as Working Women: Their Social Identity in Victorian Culture*. London: Routledge, 1991.

de Brémont, Anna. *Oscar Wilde and His Mother: A Memoir*. London: Everett and Co., 1911.

Denford, Steven L. J. *Agar Town: The Life and Death of a Victorian 'Slum'*. London: Occasional Paper of the Camden History Society, 1995.

Denvir, John. *The Irish in Britain from the Earliest Times to the Fall and Death of Parnell*. London: Kegan Paul, 1892.

Denvir, John. *The Life Story of an Old Rebel*. Dublin: Sealy, Bryers and Walker, 1910.

Devoy, John. *Recollections of an Irish Rebel*. 1929. Shannon: Irish University Press, 1969.

Dickens, Charles. *Bleak House*. 1853. London: Bantam, 1983.

Dolan, Anne and William Murphy. *Michael Collins: The Man and the Revolution*. Cork: Collins Press, 2018.

Dungworth, David. *Wild Court Rookery, City of London Scientific Examination of Early 19th-century Crucibles*. London: English Heritage Technology Report, 2010.

Dudgeon, Jeffrey. *Roger Casement: The Black Diaries with a Study of His Background, Sexuality, and Irish Political Life*. Belfast: Belfast Press, 2016.

Ellmann, Richard. *Yeats: The Man and the Mask*. London: Faber, 1948.

Ellmann, Richard. *James Joyce*. Oxford: Oxford University Press, 1982.

Emmons, Robert. *The Life and Opinions of Walter Richard Sickert*. London: Faber, 1941.

Engels, Friedrich. *The Condition of the Working-Class in England in 1844*. 1887. London: Allen & Unwin, 1943.

Fahy F. A. and D. J. O'Donoghue. *Ireland in London*. Dublin: Evening Telegraph, 1889.

Faulk, Barry J. *Music Hall and Modernity: The Late Victorian Discovery of Popular Culture*. Athens: Ohio University Press, 2004.

Featherstone, Simon. 'Vestal Flirtations: Performances of the Feminine in the Late Nineteenth-Century British Music Hall'. *Nineteenth Century Studies* 19 (2005): 99–112.

Felstead, S. Theodore. *Stars Who Made the Halls: A Hundred Years of English Humour, Harmony and Hilarity*. London: T. Werner, 1946.

Fitz-Simon, Christopher. '*Buffoonery and Easy Sentiment*': Popular Irish Plays in the Decade Prior to the Opening of The Abbey Theatre*. Dublin: Carysfort Press, 2011.

Fitzpatrick, David. 'A Curious Middle Place: The Irish in Britain, 1871–1921'. In *The Irish in Britain 1815–1939*, edited by Roger Swift and Sheridan Gilley, 10–59. London: Pinter Publishers, 1989.

Flanagan, Frances. *Remembering the Revolution: Dissent, Culture, and Nationalism in the Irish Free State*. Oxford: Oxford University Press, 2015.

Foster, R. F. *Paddy and Mr Punch: Connections in Irish and English History*. London: Penguin, 1993.

Foster, R. F. *W. B. Yeats: A Life, Vol 1: The Apprentice Mage 1865–1914*. Oxford: Oxford University Press, 1997.

Foster, R. F. 'An Irish Power in London: Making it in the Victorian Metropolis'. In '*Conquering England*': Ireland in Victorian London*, edited by R. F. Foster and Fintan Cullen, 12–25. London: National Portrait Gallery, 2005.

Foster, R. F. *Vivid Faces: The Revolutionary Generation in Ireland, 1890–1923*. London: Allen Lane, 2014.

Frank, Michael C. 'Plots on London: Terrorism in Turn-of-the-Century British Fiction'. In *Literature and Terrorism: Comparative Perspectives*, edited by Michael C. Frank and Eva Grube, 41–65. Amsterdam: Rodopi, 2012.

Furlong, Alice. 'Ours'. *The Irish Monthly* 46, no. 536 (February 1918): 123.

Furlong, Sharon. '"Herstory" Recovered: Assessing the Contribution of Cumann na mBan 1914–1923'. *The Past: The Organ of the Uí Cinsealaigh Historical Society* 30 (2009–2010): 70–93.

Gardner, Joan. *Yeats and the Rhymers' Club: A Nineties Perspective*. New York: Lang, 1989.

Garratt, Evelyn R. *Life and Personal Recollections of Samuel Garratt*. London: James Nisbet and Co., 1908.

Garratt, Samuel. *The Irish in London. A Lecture. Delivered on Monday Dec. 6th, 1852, at the Music Hall Store Street by the Rev. Samuel Garratt, B.A. Minister of Trinity Church, Little Queen Street, Lincoln's-Inn-Fields*. London: Sampson Low and Son, 1853.

Gilbert, Pamela K. *Mapping the Victorian Social Body*. Albany: State University of New York, 2004.

Gillies, Midge. *Marie Lloyd: The One and Only*. London: Victor Gollancz, 1999.

Gittings, Robert and Jo Manton. *The Second Mrs Hardy*. London: Heinemann, 1979.

Good, Joe. *Enchanted by Dreams: The Journal of a Revolutionary*. Edited by Maurice Good. Dingle: Kerry, 1996.

Gould, Warwick. 'Yeats and his Books'. In *Essays in Honour of Eamonn Cantwell: Yeats Annual No. 20: A Special Number*. Cambridge: Open Book Publishers, 2016. Available online: http://books.openedition.org/obp/3448 (accessed 12 March 2019).

Goulding, Douglas. *South Lodge: Reminiscences of Violet Hunt, Ford Madox Ford and The English Review Circle*. London: Constable, 1943.

Green, David. *People of the Rookery: A Pauper Community in Victorian London, Occasional paper 26, Kings College Department of Geography*. London: King's College London, 1986.

Gruetzner Robins, Anna. 'Sickert "Painter-in-Ordinary" to the Music-Hall'. In *Sickert, Paintings*, edited by Wendy Baron and Richard Shone, 13–24. New Haven: Yale University Press, 1992.

Hall, Reginald Richard. *Irish Music and Dance in London, 1890–1970: A Socio-Cultural History*. PhD Thesis. University of Sussex, 1994.

Hanley, Evelyn A. 'Dora Sigerson Shorter: Late Victorian Romantic'. *Victorian Poetry* 3, no. 4 (Autumn 1965): 223–34.

Hardy, Thomas. *Winter Words in Various Moods and Metres*. London: Macmillan and Co., 1928.

Harper, George Mills and Karl Beckson. 'Victor Plarr on "The Rhymers' Club": An Unpublished Lecture'. *English Literature in Transition, 1880-1920* 45, no. 4 (2002): 379–85.

Hart, Peter. *Mick: The Real Michael Collins*. London: Macmillan, 2005.

Harvey, David. *The Enigma of Capital: And the Crises of Capitalism*. London: Profile, 2010.

Heinrick, Hugh. *A Survey of the Irish in England*, 1872. Edited by Alan O'Day. London: Hambledon Press, 1990.

Helland, Janice. *British and Irish Home Arts and Industries 1880–1914: Marketing Craft, Making Fashion*. Dublin: Irish Academic Press, 2007.

Herr, Cheryl. *Joyce's Anatomy of Culture*. Urbana: University of Illinois Press, 1986.

Herr, Cheryl. *For the Land They Loved: Irish Political Melodramas, 1890–1925*. New York: Syracuse University Press, 1991.

Herron, Tom, ed. *Irish Writing London: Volume 1: Revival to the Second World War*. London: Bloomsbury, 2013.

Hollingshead, John. *Ragged London in 1861*. London: Smith, Elder and Co., 1861.

Hutchinson, John. 'Diaspora Dilemmas and Shifting Allegiances: the Irish in London between Nationalism, Catholicism and Labourism (1900–22)'. *Studies in Ethnicity and Nationalism* 10, no. 1 (2010): 107–25.

Hutchinson, John and Alan O'Day. 'The Gaelic Revival in London, 1900–1922: Limits of Ethnic Identity'. In *The Irish in Victorian Britain: The Local Dimension*, edited by Roger Swift and Sheridan Gilley, 254–76. Dublin: Four Courts Press, 1999.

Hutton, Clare. 'Francis Fahy's "Ireland in London – Reminiscences" (1921)'. In *Yeats's Collaborations: Yeats Annual, 15: A Special Number*, edited by Wayne K. Chapman and Warwick Gould, 233–80. Basingstoke: Palgrave Macmillan, 2002.

Hutton, Clare. 'Joyce and the Institutions of Revivalism'. *Irish University Review, Special Issue: New Perspectives on the Irish Literary Revival* 33, no. 1 (Spring/Summer 2003): 117–32.

Hyde, Douglas. 'Dora Sigerson Shorter'. *Studies: An Irish Quarterly Review* 7, no. 25 (March 1918): 139–44.

Hyde, Douglas. *Language, Lore, and Lyrics*. Edited by Breandán Ó Conaire. Dublin: Irish Academic Press, 1986.

Jerome, Jerome K. *Stageland: Curious Manners and Customs of Its Inhabitants*. London: Chatto and Windus, 1890.

Joyce, James. *Dubliners: Text, Criticism and Notes*. Edited by Robert Scholes and A. Walton Litz. London: Penguin, 1996.

Joyce, James. *Ulysses*. 1922. London: Bodley Head, 2008.

Kandola, Sondeep. '(Re)Hibernicising Wilde? A Genetic Analysis of *The Picture of Dorian Gray*'. *Irish Studies Review* 24, no. 4 (2016): 351–69.

Kelly, John. *A W. B. Yeats Chronology*. Basingstoke: Palgrave, 2003.

Kelly, M. J. *The Fenian Ideal and Irish Nationalism, 1882–1916*. Woodbridge: Boydell Press, 2006.

Kenna, Shane. 'The Philosophy of the Bomb: Dynamite and the Fear in Late Victorian Britain'. *Postgraduate History Journal: A Collection of Essays Presented at the TCD-UCD Postgraduate History Conference* 1 (2009): 89–100. Available online: https://issuu.com/gearoid.orourke/docs/phcj_2009 (accessed: 6 November 2018).

Kift, Dagmar. *The Victorian Music Hall: Culture, Class and Conflict*. Cambridge: Cambridge University Press, 1996.

Killeen, Jarlath. 'The Greening of Oscar Wilde: Situating Ireland in the Wilde Wars'. *Irish Studies Review* 23, no. 4 (2015): 424–50.

Kirkland, Richard. 'Dr. Corry's National Diorama of Ireland and Irish Performance in Nineteenth-century Urban Popular Culture'. *New Hibernia Review/Iris Éireannach Nua* 19, no. 4 (December 2015): 14–31.

Knight, Charles. *London: Volume III*. London: Charles Knight & Co., 1842.

Koven, Seth. *Slumming: Sexual and Social Politics in Victorian London*. Princeton: Princeton University Press, 2004.

Koven, Seth. *The Match Girl and the Heiress*. Princeton: Princeton University Press, 2014.

Langton, James. 'The Volunteers Irish Citizen Army IRA Cumann Na mBan Photo File Part 3'. Available online: https://irishvolunteers.org/the-volunteers-irish-citizen-army-ira-cumman-na-mban-photo-file-part-3/ (accessed 5 November 2019).

Laqueur, Walter, ed. *Voices of Terror: Manifestos, Writings and Manuals of Al Qaeda, Hamas, and Other Terrorists from around the World and throughout the Ages*. New York: Reed Press, 2004.

Lawlor, Bridget F. 'Dora Sigerson Shorter. An Appreciation'. *The Irish Monthly* 48, no. 560 (February 1920): 100–6.

Le Roy, George. *Music Hall Stars of the Nineties*. London: British Technical and General Press, 1952.

Lees, Lynn Hollen. *Exiles of Erin: Irish Migrants in Victorian London*. Manchester: Manchester University Press, 1979.

Lenin, V. I. *Collected Works, XVII*. Moscow: Progress, 1952.

Lydon, James. *The Making of Ireland: From Ancient Times to the Present*. London: Routledge, 1998.

MacAtasney, Gerard. *Seán MacDiarmada: The Mind of the Revolution*. Manorhamilton: Drumlin Publications, 2004.

MacDonagh, Donagh. 'The Reputation of James Joyce: From Notoriety to Fame'. *University Review* 3, no. 2 (Summer 1963): 12–20.

Mackay, James. *Michael Collins: A Life*. Edinburgh: Mainstream, 1996.

MacQueen-Pope, Walter. *The Melodies Linger On: The Story of Music Hall*. London: W. H. Allen, 1950.

Maguire, Michael P. *A Community at War: The Irish in Britain and the War of Independence*. PhD Thesis. University of Surrey, 1983.

Mahar, Margaret. 'Hardy's Poetry of Renunciation'. *ELH* 45, no. 2 (Summer 1978): 303–24.

Maloney, Paul. '"Flying down the Saltmarket": The Irish on the Glasgow Music Hall Stage'. *Nineteenth Century Theatre and Film* 36, no. 1 (2009): 11–36.

Marx, Karl. 'Twenty-Six: The Secret of Primitive Accumulation'. *Capital: Volume One*. Available online: http://www.marxists.org/archive/marx/works/1867-c1/ch26.htm (accessed 8 July 2018).

Marx, Karl and Friedrich Engels. *Selected Correspondence*. Moscow: Progress Publishers, 1975.

Masefield, John. *So Long to Learn: Chapters of an Autobiography*. London: William Heinemann, 1952.

Masefield, John. 'My First Meeting with Yeats'. In *W. B. Yeats: Interviews and Recollections*, edited by E. H. Mikhail, 44–7. London: Macmillan, 1977.

Mayhew, Henry. *London Labour and the London Poor: Volume 4*. 1861. London: Dover Publications, 1968.

Mayhew, Henry and John Binny. *The Criminal Prisons of London and Scenes of Prison Life with Numerous Illustrations from Photographs*. 1862. Cambridge: Cambridge University Press, 2011.

McDowell, R. B. *Alice Stopford Green: A Passionate Historian*. Dublin: Allen Figgis, 1967.

McGuire, James and James Quinn, eds. *Dictionary of Irish Biography*. Cambridge: Cambridge University Press, 2009.

McKenna, Joseph. *The Irish-American Dynamite Campaign: A History, 1881–1896*. North Carolina: McFarland and Co., 2012.

Mhic Sheáin, Brighid. *Glimpses of Erin: Alice Milligan: Poet, Protestant, Patriot*. Belfast: Fortnight Educational Trust Supplement (free with Fortnight 326), 1994.

Miller, Thomas. *Picturesque Sketches of London Past and Present*. London: Office of the National Illustrated Library, 1852.

Mitchell, Angus. 'Too Dark Altogether'. *Dublin Review of Books* (July 2018). Available online: http://www.drb.ie/essays/too-dark-altogether (accessed 7 May 2019).

Mitchell, Angus. 'The Stopfords of Blackwater House: Alice Stopford Green's Family Circle'. *Ríocht na Midhe* 30 (2019): 176–212.

Moore, George. *Confessions of a Young Man*. 1886. London: Heinemann, 1929.

Moulton, Mo. *Ireland and the Irish in Interwar England*. Cambridge: Cambridge University Press, 2014.

Murray, Tony. 'Winifred M. Patton and the Irish Revival in London'. *Irish Studies Review* 22, no. 1 (February 2014): 22–33.

Nelson, J. M. 'From Rory and Paddy to Boucicault's Myles, Shaun and Conn: The Irishman on the London Stage, 1830-60'. *Eire-Ireland* 13 (1978): 79–105.

Nic Dháibhéid, Caoimhe. *Seán MacBride: A Republican Life, 1904–1946*. Liverpool: Liverpool University Press, 2011.

Nolan, Janet. 'Education and Women's Mobility in Ireland and Irish America, 1880–1920: A Preliminary Look'. *New Hibernia Review/Iris Éireannach Nua* 2, no. 3 (Autumn 1998): 78–88.

Noonan, Gerard. *The IRA in Britain, 1919–1923: 'In the Heart of Enemy Lines'*. Liverpool: Liverpool University Press, 2014.

O'Brien, Deirdre. 'Dora Sigerson Shorter'. *The Irish Monthly* 56, no. 662 (August 1928): 403–8.

Ó Broin, Leon. *Revolutionary Underground: The Story of the Irish Republican Brotherhood 1858–1924*. London: Gill and Macmillan, 1976.

O'Byrne, Cathal. *The Grey Feet of the Wind*. Dublin: Talbot Press, 1917.

Ó Conaire, Pádraic. *Exile [Deoraíocht]*. 1910. Translated by Gearailt Mac Eoin. Indreabhán: Cló Iar-Chonnachta, 1994.

O'Connell, Helen. *Ireland and the Fiction of Improvement*. Oxford: Oxford University Press, 2006.

O'Connor, Frank. *The Big Fellow: A Life of Michael Collins*. London: Thomas Nelson and Sons, 1937.

O'Conor, Manus, ed. *Old Time Songs and Ballads of Ireland*. New York: Popular Publishing Company, 1901.

Ó'Donghaile, Deaglán. *Blasted Literature: Victorian Political Fiction and the Shock of Modernism*. Edinburgh, Edinburgh University Press, 2011.

O'Growney, Eugene. *Simple Lessons in Irish: Giving the Pronunciation of Each Word*. Dublin: Gaelic League, 1901.

O'Hegarty, P. S. *The Victory of Sinn Féin: How It Won It, and How It Used It*. Dublin: Talbot Press Ltd., 1924.

O'Keeffe, J. G. and Art O'Brien. *A Handbook of Irish Dances: With an Essay on Their Origin and History*. Dublin: O'Donoghue, 1902.

O'Leary, Paul. 'Mass Commodity Culture and Identity: The "Morning Chronicle" and Irish Migrants in a Nineteenth-Century Welsh Industrial Town'. *Urban History* 35, no. 2 (August 2008): 237–54.

O'Leary, Philip. *The Prose Literature of the Gaelic Revival, 1881–1921: Ideology and Innovation*. Pennsylvania: Penn State University Press, 1994.

O'Riordan, Michael. 'Marx: The Irish Connection'. *The Crane Bag* 7, no. 1 (1983): 164–6.

O Súilleabháin, Donnchadh. *Conradh na Gaeilge i Londain, 1894–1917*. Baile Átha Cliath: Conradh na Gaeilge, 1989.

O'Sullivan, Niamh. *Gorry Gallery Catalogue, An Exhibition of 18th–20th Century Irish Paintings*. Dublin: Gorry Gallery, 2008.

Ó Tuathaigh, M. A. G. 'The Irish in Nineteenth-Century Britain: Problems of Integration'. *Transactions of the Royal Historical Society* 31 (1981): 149–73.

Paterson, Adrian. '"On the Pavements Grey": The Suburban Paradises of W. B. Yeats and William Morris'. In *Irish Writing London: Volume 1: Revival to the Second World War*, edited by Tom Herron, 34–53. London: Bloomsbury, 2013.

Pearl, Cyril. *Three Lives of Charles Gavan Duffy*. Sydney: New South Wales University Press, 1979.

Pearse, P. H. *Letters of P. H. Pearse*. Edited by Séamus Ó Buachalla with a foreword by F. S. L. Lyons. Gerrards Cross: Colin Smythe, 1980.

Pierce, David. *Yeats's Worlds: Ireland, England and the Poetic Imagination*. New Haven: Yale University Press, 1995.

Raw, Louise. *Striking a Light: The Bryant and May Matchwomen and Their Place in Labour History*. London: Continuum, 2011.

Rhys, Ernest. 'Yeats and The Rhymers Club'. In *W. B. Yeats: Interviews and Recollections*, edited by E. H. Mikhail, 41. London: Macmillan, 1977.

Riggs, Pádraigín. 'Pádraic Ó Conaire's London – A Real or an Imaginary Place?'. In *Irish Writing London: Revival to the Second World War*, Vol. 1. edited by Tom Herron, 84–97. London: Bloomsbury, 2013.

Roberts, Arthur. *Fifty Years of Spoof*. London: Bodley Head, 1927.

Rolleston, T. W. *Sea Spray: Verses and Translations*. Dublin: Maunsel, 1909.

Rooney, Brendan. 'The Irish Exhibition at Olympia, 1888'. *Irish Architectural and Decorative Studies* 1 (1998): 100–19.

Rowley, Richard. The *City of Refuge and Other Poems*. Dublin: Maunsel, 1917.

Russell, Dave. *Popular Music in England*. Manchester: Manchester University Press, 1987.

Ryan, Mark F. *Fenian Memories*. Dublin: Gill and Son, 1945.

Ryan, W. P. *The Irish Literary Revival: Its History, Pioneers and Possibilities*. London: Ward and Downey, 1894.

Saddlemyer, Ann. *Becoming George: The Life of Mrs W. B. Yeats*. Oxford: Oxford University Press, 2004.

Schneer, Jonathan. *London 1900: The Imperial Metropolis*. London: Yale University Press, 1999.

Schuchard, Ronald. 'The *Countess Cathleen* and the Revival of the Bardic Arts'. *South Carolina Review* 32, no. 1 (1999): 24–37.

Scott, Harold. *The Early Doors: Origins of Music Hall*. London: Nicholson and Watson, 1946.

Sebald, W. G. *Austerlitz*. London: Penguin, 2011.

Shaw, George Bernard. *The Matter with Ireland*. London: Rupert Hart Davies, 1962.

Sheehy, Ian. *Irish Journalists and Litterateurs in Late Victorian London c.1870–1910*. D.Phil. thesis, Hertford College, University of Oxford, 2003.

Sheppard, Francis. *London 1808–1870: The Infernal Wen*. London: Secker and Warburg, 1971.

Short, K. R. M. *The Dynamite War: Irish-American Bombers in Victorian Britain*. Dublin: Gill and Macmillan, 1979.

Shorter, Clement, ed. *In Memoriam Dora Sigerson 1918–23*. London: privately published, 1923.

Shorter, Clement. *CKS: An Autobiography. A Fragment by Himself*. Edited by J.M. Bulloch. London: privately published, 1927.

Sigerson Shorter, Dora. *The Sad Years*. London: Constable and Company, 1918.

Sigerson Shorter, Dora. *Sixteen Dead Men, and Other Poems of Easter Week*. New York: Mitchell Kennerley, 1919.

Sigerson Shorter, Dora. *A Dull Day in London and Other Sketches with an Introductory Note by Thomas Hardy*. London: Eveleigh Nash, 1920.

Sims, George. *How the Poor Live*. 1889. New York: Garland, 1984.

Smyth, Gerry. *Music in Irish Cultural History*. Dublin: Irish Academic Press, 2009.

St. Pierre, Paul Matthew. 'Music Hall Mimesis in *Those Were the Days* (1934), *Champagne Charlie* (1944), and *The Entertainer* (1960)'. *Quarterly Review of Film and Video* 18, no. 4 (2001): 437–49.

Standlee, Whitney. 'A World of Difference: London and Ireland in the Works of Katharine Tynan'. In *Irish Writing London: Volume 1: Revival to the Second World War*, edited by Tom Herron, 70–83. London: Bloomsbury, 2013.

Stokes, John. *In the Nineties*. London: Harvester Wheatsheaf, 1989.

Storey, Mark. *Poetry and Ireland since 1800: A Source Book*. London: Routledge, 1988.

Sturgis, Matthew. *Walter Sickert: A Life*. London: HarperCollins, 2005.

Swensen, Steven P. *Mapping Poverty in Agar Town: Economic Conditions Prior to the Development of St. Pancras Station in 1866*. London: London School of Economics Working Papers on the Nature of Evidence, 2006.

Swift, Roger. 'Heroes or Villains?: The Irish, Crime, and Disorder in Victorian England'. *Albion: A Quarterly Journal Concerned with British Studies* 29, no. 3 (Autumn, 1997): 399–421.

Swift, Roger, ed. *Irish Migrants in Britain, 1815–1914*. Cork: Cork University Press, 2002.

Swift, Roger, and Sheridan Gilley, eds. *The Irish in Britain 1815–1939*. London: Pinter Publishers, 1989.

Swift, Roger, and Sheridan Gilley, eds. *The Irish in the Victorian City*. London: Croom Helm, 1985.

Talbot, Hayden. *Michael Collins' Own Story*. London: Hutchinson & Co., 1923.

Taylor Fitzsimon, Betsey, and James H. Murphy, eds. *The Irish Revival Reappraised (Nineteenth-Century Ireland)*. Dublin: Four Courts Press, 2004.

'The London Irish'. *Blackwood's Edinburgh Magazine* 170 (July 1901): 124–34.

Thomas, William Moy. 'A Suburban Connemara'. *Household Words* (8 March 1851): 562–5.

Thornbury, Walter. *Old and New London: Volume 3*. London: Cassell, Petter and Galpin, 1878.

Thornton, R. K. R. 'Dates for the Rhymers' Club'. *English Literature in Transition, 1880–1920* 14, no. 1 (1971): 49–53.

Timbs, John. *Curiosities of London*. London: Virtue & Co., 1867.

Tynan, Katharine. *The Wind in the Trees: A Book of Country Verse*. London: Grant Richards, 1898.

Tynan, Katharine. *Innocencies: A Book of Verse*. Dublin: Maunsell, 1905.

Tynan, Katharine. *Twenty-Five Years: Reminiscences*. London: Smith, Elder and Co., 1913.

Tynan, Katharine. *The Years of the Shadow*. London: Constable and Co., 1919.

Tynan, Katharine. *Memories*. London: Eveleigh Nash and Grayson, 1924.

Tynan, Katharine. *Collected Poems*. London: Macmillan, 1930.

Tynan, Katharine. *Selected Letters of Katharine Tynan: Poet and Novelist*. Edited by Damian Atkinson. Newcastle: Cambridge Scholars Press, 2016.

Tynan, Patrick. *The Irish National Invincibles and Their Times*. London: Chatham and Co., 1896.

Vadillo, Parejo. 'New Woman Poets and the Culture of the *Salon* at the *Fin de Siècle*'. *Women: A Cultural Review* 10, no. 1 (1999): 22–34.

Van de Kamp, Peter. 'Whose Revival? Yeats and the Southwark Irish Literary Club'. In *Tumult of Images, Essays on W. B. Yeats and Politics*, edited by Peter Van de Kamp and Peter Liebregts, 154–81. Amsterdam: Rodopi, 1995.

Varian, Ralph. *The Harp of Erin: A Book of Ballad Poetry and Native Song*. Dublin: M. Glashan and Gill, 1869.

Walford, Edward. *Old and New London: A Narrative of Its History, Its People, and Its Places, Volume III*. London: Cassell, Petter and Galpin, 1897.

Ward, Margaret. *Unmanageable Revolutionaries: Women and Irish Nationalism*. London: Pluto Press, 1983.

Weaver, J. R. H., ed. *Dictionary of National Biography: 1922–1930*. Oxford: Oxford University Press, 1937.

Weygandt, Cornelius. 'The Irish Literary Revival'. *The Sewanee Review* 12, no. 4 (October 1904): 420–31.

Whelehan, Niall. 'Skirmishing, *The Irish World*, and Empire, 1876–86'. *Éire-Ireland* 42, no. 1–2 (2007): 180–200.

Whelehan, Niall. *The Dynamiters: Irish Nationalism and Political Violence in the Wider World, 1867–1900*. Cambridge: Cambridge University Press, 2012.

White, Jerry. *London in the Nineteenth Century: 'A Human Awful Wonder of God'*. London: Random House, 2016.

Wilde, Oscar. *The Importance of Being Earnest*. 1898. London: New Mermaids, 2004.

Williams, Raymond. *Culture and Society: 1780–1950*. New York: Anchor Books, 1960.

Willson Disher, M. *Winkles and Champagne: Comedies and Tragedies of the Music Hall*. London: B. T. Batsford, 1938.

Wyse Power Jennie. 'The Political Influence of Women in Modern Ireland'. In *The Voice of Ireland: A Survey of the Race and Nation from all Angles*, edited by W. G. FitzGerald, 158–161. Dublin: John Heywood, 1923.

Yeates, Pádraig. *Lockout: Dublin 1913*. Dublin: Gill and Macmillan, 2000.

Yeats, W. B. *John Sherman and Dhoya*. London: T. Fisher Unwin, 1892.

Yeats, W. B. *Responsibilities and Other Poems*. London: Macmillan, 1916.

Yeats, W. B. *The Trembling of the Veil*. London: T. Werner Laurie, 1922.

Yeats, W. B. *Autobiographies*. London: Macmillan, 1956.

Yeats, W. B. *William Butler Yeats's John Sherman and Dhoya*. Edited by Richard J. Finneran. Detroit: Wayne State University Press, 1969.

Yeats, W. B. *Letters to the New Island*. 1934. Cambridge Massachusetts: Harvard University Press, 1970.

Yeats, W. B. *The Collected Letters of W. B Yeats: Volume I: 1865–1895*. Edited by John Kelly and Eric Domville. Oxford: Oxford University Press, 1986.

Yeats, W. B. *The Collected Poems of W. B. Yeats*. London: Macmillan, 1989.

Yeats, W. B. *The Collected Works of W. B. Yeats, Volume X: Later Articles and Reviews*. Edited by Colton Johnson. New York: Scribner, 2000.

Yeats, W. B. *The Collected Works of W. B. Yeats, Volume VIII: The Irish Dramatic Movement*. Edited by Mary FitzGerald and Richard J. Finneran. New York: Scribner, 2003.

Yeats, W. B. *The Collected Works of W. B. Yeats, Volume IX: Early Art: Uncollected Articles*. Edited by Richard J. Finneran and George Mills Harper, John Frayne and Madeleine Marchaterre. New York: Scribner, 2004.

Index

Ingram Content Group UK Ltd.
Milton Keynes UK
UKHW020753030423
419517UK00005B/658